SHARED TRAUMAS, SILENT LOSS, PUBLIC AND PRIVATE MOURNING

SHARED TRAUMAS, SILENT LOSS, PUBLIC AND PRIVATE MOURNING

Edited by
Lene Auestad

KARNAC

First published in 2017 by
Karnac Books Ltd
118 Finchley Road
London NW3 5HT

British Library Cataloguing in Publication Data

A C.I.P. for this book is available from the British Library

ISBN-13: 978-1-78049-161-5

Typeset by V Publishing Solutions Pvt Ltd., Chennai, India

Printed in Great Britain by TJ International Ltd, Padstow, Cornwall

www.karnacbooks.com

To the memory of my mother, Anne-Marie Auestad
12 January 1931–22 May 2002

CONTENTS

ACKNOWLEDGEMENTS

After confrontations with contemporary manifestations of violence and othering had led to symposia on social exclusion and representation, neo-nationalism and xenophobia, the question of what shared mourning and working through the past might mean became prominent. This book is composed out of reflections stemming from these issues. I would like to thank the contributors to this volume for their patient efforts in elaborating and clarifying their thoughts, and Rod Tweedy and others at Karnac for careful comments and for steering this book towards publication.

Shared dialogues require a space; I am grateful to the Swedish Psychoanalytic Society for their generosity in opening their doors to the conference on which most of this book is based, and to the British Psychoanalytical Society for welcoming a later conference which continued to explore shared traumas and mourning.

The conference series Psychoanalysis and Politics is now more than seven years old. I am most grateful to everyone who has contributed, with their passionate engagement, to keeping the series alive as a space for thinking through political traumas and personal ruptures, remaining respectful of differences. I look forward to continuing our conversations.

For Chapter Two I thank Anthony Gormley and the White Cube for permission to reproduce Place of Remembrance, 2000, Steel—six chairs, permanent installation, Oslo, Norway. Photograph by Signe M. Andersen © the artist. I thank Rachel Whiteread and the Gagosian Gallery for permission for Holocaust Memorial, 2000. © Rachel Whiteread, photograph by Werner Kaligovsky.

For Chapter Three I thank Argos Films for permission to quote from Sans Soleil, by Chris Marker © 1983, Argos Films.

For Chapter Eight I thank the Taipei Women's Rescue Foundation (TWRF) for permission to use the photographs.

For Chapter Nine I thank the Penguin Group for permission to quote from Death and the Maiden by Ariel Dorfman, © 1992 by Ariel Dorfman. Used by permission of Viking Penguin, a division of Penguin Group, USA, LLC and the Wylie Agency, Penguin, UK.

ABOUT THE EDITORS AND CONTRIBUTORS

•

Lene Auestad (PhD in Philosophy from the University of Oslo) writes and lectures internationally on ethics, critical theory, and psychoanalysis. She was born in Oslo and lives in London. Her latest book, *Respect, Plurality, and Prejudice: A Psychoanalytical and Philosophical Enquiry into the Dynamics of Social Exclusion and Discrimination*, was published by Karnac in 2015. In 2010 she founded the international and interdisciplinary conference series Psychoanalysis and Politics, which continues to this day, and on which this book is based.

Jonathan Davidoff is holds a PhD from University College London and is an honorary psychotherapist trained at the Tavistock and Portman NHS trust. He was one of two coordinators of Psychoanalysis and Politics and has been involved in various other academic research groups. His background is in psychology and philosophy. His research interests are in the crossroads of psychoanalysis and the humanities as well as psychology and the digital space.

Nayla Debs has a master's degree in clinical psychology from St-Joseph University (Beirut) and a master's in cognitive neurosciences from Paris-Descartes University; she is completing her PhD in psychoanalytic studies at Paris-Diderot University. Her research touches on issues related to historical and political violence, cultural memory, and psychic processes. She also addressed themes in relation to gender studies and physical disability as well as somatic illnesses. She currently works as a clinical psychologist in Pitié-Salpêtrière Hospital in Paris.

Jane Frances Ph.D. works as a psychotherapist in private practice, in education policy for Changing Faces, and in medical education at Queen Mary College, University of London. Her main research areas are the role of the unconscious, both personal and social, in generating and perpetuating stigma, the social consequences of trauma, and the role of the arts in both personal and societal health and wellbeing.

Jean-François Jacques has an MA and is a PhD candidate at Anglia Ruskin University (Cambridge, UK). Jean-Francois is a dramatherapist and clinical supervisor in private practice and in a community adult mental health service in the NHS, a community theatre director, and a researcher. He is an invited lecturer on the MA programme in dramatherapy at Anglia Ruskin University where he is also undertaking a PhD on the co-creation of meaning in autobiographical performance in dramatherapy. He is published in the field of dramatherapy and has presented at a number of conferences in the UK and abroad. He has a special interest in the interplay between therapy, theatre, and politics.

Steffen Krüger (PhD) is a postdoctoral researcher and lecturer at the Department of Media and Communication, University of Oslo, Norway. He is interested in developing critical, psychosocial approaches to media texts and discourses. In his current research project, "Online Interaction Forms", financed by the Norwegian Research Council, he analyses forms of online interaction, applying Lorenzer's method of "scenic understanding" to a variety of online platforms—discussion forums and social networking sites. Krüger is contributing editor of the journal *American Imago—Psychoanalysis and the Human Sciences*.

Edna Mor was born in Jerusalem, Israel and holds an MA in clinical psychology from The Hebrew University of Jerusalem. She is a supervisor in psycho-diagnostics and psychotherapy at the Israel Psychological Association, and a training analyst in the Israeli and International Psychoanalytical Association. Edna has clinical experience with psychiatric patients and with first and second generation Holocaust survivors. She has a private practice as a clinical psychologist and psychoanalyst, and as a training analyst with adult patients.

Margarita Palacios PhD is the postgraduate research director at the Department of Psychosocial Studies, and senior lecturer in social theory, at Birkbeck College, University of London. She is the author of *Fantasy and Political Violence: The Meaning of Anti-Communism in Chile* (VS Verlag für Sozialwissenschaften, Wiesbaden, Germany; 2009) and *Radical Sociality: On Disobedience, Violence in Belonging* (Palgrave, London; 2013). Her current work concentrates on the study of transformation of meaning of ex-detention and extermination sites in post-conflict societies and the relation between aesthetics, cultural activism, and critique.

Jenyu Peng is a psychoanalyst practising in Taipei and at the *Espace Analytique* in Paris, and an assistant research fellow at the Institute of Ethnology, Academia Sinica, Taiwan. She is an associate member of the *Centre de Recherches Psychanalyse, Médicine et Société* (CRPMS) at the Paris Diderot University. She is the author of *À l'épreuve de l'inceste* (Presses Universitaires de France, 2009).

Hannah Zeavin is a PhD candidate in the Department of Media Culture and Communication at NYU. Her dissertation, *Distant Feelings: Mediated Therapy 1890–2015*, is a transnational history of efforts to expand the definition of psychodynamic therapy, and access to it, through communication technologies throughout the twentieth century. She has served as the assistant editor of *Public Culture* and is the co-founder of *Second Story* in New York City.

INTRODUCTION

Lene Auestad

This book aims to question the junctions of the private and the public when it comes to trauma, loss, and the work of mourning, notions that, it is argued, challenge our very notions of the individual and the shared. It asks, to paraphrase Adorno: What do we mean by "working through the past"? How is a shared work of mourning to be understood? With what legitimacy do we consider a particular social or cultural practice to be "mourning"? Rather than aiming to present a diagnosis of the political present, this volume instead takes one step back to pose the question of what mourning might mean and what its social dimension consists in.

Silent losses and communicability

Mourning can be thought of as a private endeavour, so familiar it seems hardly pathological, writes Freud. During mourning, the ego withdraws from the world. It re-visits the different aspects of the lost object, approaches it from a series of different angles. When reality testing has shown that the object no longer exists, it demands that one's attachments to the object be withdrawn. This is only done bit by bit, slowly and painfully, as "Each single one of the memories and expectations in which the libido is bound to the object is brought up and hyper-cathected, and detachment of the libido is accomplished in respect of it" (Freud, 1917e, p. 245). Darian Leader (2008) compares this work to the process leading up to Cubist artworks resulting from the combination and reshuffling of the conventional image of a person. Thus there is an aspect of mourning that confronts us with fragmentation, of the object mourned and of the experience of mourning. The chapters in this book question, in various ways, the act, experience, and results of mourning in terms of their possible or impossible completions. In a letter to Ernest Jones, Freud questions the source of the pain involved in the work of mourning, and his answer conveys how one struggles against the acknowledgement of the loss:

> One has to bring recognition of the reality principle to every single point of the libido, and this, in fact, is in agreement with your formulation: against one's own will. […] one then has the choice of dying oneself or acknowledging the death of the loved one, which again comes very close to your expression that one kills this person. (Freud-Jones 1993, pp. 652–653)

Mourning only happens under great protest. I can remember seeing my mother in the street, after she had died—and after my father had died, expecting it to be him at the other end of the phone line when the phone rang. A mad moment of wild hope, of immense joy, collapses a second later, with the thought that you will never see them again, never talk to them again. But this "never" is far too brutal to be handled, too cruel to be contemplated, and so you throw it aside, and continue as if searching for the lost person, renewing the hope that the next time they might turn up. This search and this questioning continue in dreams.

> It very commonly happens that in dreams of this kind the dead person is treated to begin with as though he were alive, that he then suddenly turns out to be dead and that in a subsequent part of the dream he is alive once more. […] It eventually occurred to me that this alternation between death and life is intended to represent indifference on the part of the dreamer. […] This indifference is, of course, not real but merely desired; it is intended to help the dreamer to repudiate his very intense and often contradictory emotional attitudes. (Freud, 1900a, p. 431)

While dreaming is a form of internal communication, a dialogue, or a battle, with unconscious parts of oneself, in question here is communication with others, and its social and political conditions. Leader suggests that mourning, however private, requires other people; a loss requires recognition, a sense that it has been witnessed and made real:

> Freud saw mourning as an individual task, yet every documented human society gives a central place to public mourning rituals. Loss would be inscribed within the community through a system of rites, customs and codes, ranging from changes in dress and eating habits to highly stylized memorial ceremonies. These involved not just the bereaved individual and their immediate family, but the much larger social group. (Leader, 2008, pp. 7–8)

In reflecting on Freud's, Abraham's, and Klein's ideas of mourning, he remarks on the peculiar absence in these psychoanalytic accounts of a social dimension; they appear to dispense completely with the role of other people. Mourning is portrayed as an intensely private process, where individuals are left alone with their own grief:

> In his important 1965 survey Death, Grief and Mourning, the anthropologist Geoffrey Gorer drew attention to this omission, pointing out that every documented human society has mourning rituals which involve public displays. Besides funeral rituals, even dress codes could reveal that someone had been bereaved, whom they had lost and how long it had been since the loss. [...] These outward signs would help to inscribe the mourner within a shared, public space. (ibid., p. 72)

The author comments on the age-old practice, now abandoned in this part of the world, of hiring professional mourners for funerals:

> As the professional mourners lamented and bewailed the passing of the dead, the mourners could access their own private grief. The public, ostentatious display of others was necessary for them to enter their own grief. [...] Without this artificial distance, the mourner remains in the same space as the dead, rather than being able to situate their loss within a different, more symbolic space. (ibid., p. 77)

The very fact of the artificiality of the professional mourners' grief, is the point, lent a distance to their display of affect, which distinguished it from the sorrow of those closer to the mourner and to the one who had died. Thus this public framework is one that allows for the articulation of private grief, for the expression of one's private mourning. Gorer had argued that the mass slaughter of the First World War brought about profound changes, leading to the decline of public mourning rituals in the West. The number of deaths, and the number of people who had lost their loved ones, was more extreme and concentrated than in earlier warfare; thus the scale of the losses made the work of mourning seem insurmountable: "What sense would it make for a community to mourn each dead soldier when the corpses were hardly even countable?" (Leader, 2008, p. 72) In many African societies the AIDS epidemic has led to a more recent similar decline in mourning rituals, the number of dead making traditional practices impossible to maintain. Perhaps, reflects Leader, the I is built up not just through our experience of losses but through our registration of them—the losses need to be represented. This opens up the question of the meaning of such representation.

Public mourning

Mourning can be conceived as a social effort that binds communities together. Conversely, if we think of how Freud reminds us of our tendency to recoil from any activity that causes pain, how there is "a revolt in our minds against mourning", we can also conceive of a refusal to mourn as a tie between communities. The Federal Republic of Germany, wrote Alexander and Margarete Mitscherlich (1975), rather than succumbing to mass melancholia, avoided self-devaluation as a group by breaking all affective bridges to the immediate past:

> Only a patient whose symptoms cause him suffering greater than the gain he gets from repression is willing to relax, step by step, the interior censorship preventing the return to consciousness of what has been denied and forgotten.[...] But here we are asking that this therapy be carried out by a society which, at least materially, is on the whole better off than ever before. Therefore, it feels no incentive to expose its interpretation of the recent past to the inconvenient questioning of others. (ibid., p. 15)

Their formulation is reminiscent of Elliot Jacques' (1955) hypothesis that one of the primary elements that bind people into institutionalised association is the motivation to defend against depressive and paranoid anxieties. In the same tradition, Menzies Lyth (1990) described how a social defence system might not only fail to alleviate but itself increase anxiety. What was insufficiently analysed was how inequalities of power structured this situation (Auestad, 2011). The aspect of asymmetry with regard to who may speak, appear, and become objects of shared mourning, has been further highlighted in Judith Butler's reflections on the public sphere as "constituted in part by what cannot be said and what cannot be shown" (2004, p. XVIII). In that context she referred specifically to the conflation of critiques of Israeli policies with antisemitism. Acknowledging a debt to the work of the Mitscherlichs, Butler stated in an interview:

> After 9/11, I was shocked by the fact that there was public mourning for many of the people who died in the attacks on the World Trade Center, less public mourning for those who died in the attack on the Pentagon, no public mourning for the illegal workers of the WTC, and, for a very long time, no public acknowledgment of the gay and lesbian families and relationships that had been destroyed by the loss of one of the partners in the bombings. Then we went to war very quickly, Bush having decided that the time for grieving is over. I think he said that after ten days that the time for grieving is over and now is time for action. At which point we started killing populations abroad with no clear rationale. And the populations we targeted for violence were ones that never appeared to us in pictures. We never got little obituaries for them. We never heard anything about what lives had been destroyed. And we still don't.
> (Aloni & Butler, 2010)

Drawing on Sandor Ferenczi's writings on trauma, Michael Balint argued in *Trauma and Object Relationship* (1969) that the structure of trauma has three phases. In the first phase, the child is dependent on the adult and is in a primarily trustful relationship. In the second phase, the adult, either once and suddenly, or repeatedly, does something highly exiting, frightening, or painful. The trauma is only completed in the third phase, when the adult acts towards the child as if nothing distressing or painful had happened, thus depriving the event that took place of its reality. Since what happened has not been acknowledged, not recognised, it continues to exert an influence in the present. It is this situation Adorno addressed in *The Meaning of Working through the Past*:

> The question "What does working through the past mean?" [...] follows from a formulation, a modish slogan that has become highly suspect during the last years. In this usage "working through the past" does not mean seriously working upon the past, that is, through a lucid consciousness breaking its power to fascinate. On the contrary, its intention is to close the books on the past, and, if possible, even remove it from memory. (Adorno, 1998, p. 89)

This political and ethical evasion is closely connected to an epistemic one: "surely one must assume that there is a relation between the attitude of 'not having known anything about it' and an impassive and apprehensive indifference" (ibid., p. 89). The lack of recognition goes hand in hand with a wish, a will, and even a demand to forget what was done. In this way, the violence done in the past continues to be performed in the present. When perpetrators of wartime atrocities enjoy impunity after the war, Elisabeth Rohr reflects, traumatisations will amplify. "Tolerating impunity on a political level supports the impression that victims are guilty themselves, and therefore responsible for their own suffering." (2012, p. 176) Jenyu Peng's chapter in this book further emphasises the importance of the public recognition of historical reality to the victims' reconstruction and to reparation. In the context of the aftermath of genocide, Stanley Cohen (2001, pp. 126–131) describes three variants of denial: literal innocence ("the atrocity never happened"), not knowing ("I did not know about it"), and forgetting ("it was so long ago, I have forgotten whether or to what extent I did anything"). At stake here is not only protection against individual guilt. By silencing testimonies of its assaults, a majority may keep the idea of the goodness of their nation or social unit intact. As Sara Ahmed puts it in a different context: "The organization becomes the subject of feeling, as the one who is easily bruised or hurt." (2012, p. 147) Thus the ones who identify a violence performed are represented as being the problem—to a social unit that aims to forget, those who remember are seen as thorns in the flesh of the social fabric.

"In psychoanalysis lies freedom, or at least the potential for freedom" (2011, p. 164), writes Jonathan Sklar in pointing towards the need for reflection on the traumas of European history in analytic thought and practice. The author compares the reconstructed city of Warsaw, recreated so as to have covered up all signs of its near total destruction, to a delusion "applied like a patch over the place where originally a rent had appeared in the ego's relation to the external world" (p. 166). The collective work of mourning may contribute to the construction of narratives, and to the writing of history. In this sense, memorials, works of art, monuments, public ceremonies, or other discursive practices, as long as they are not sentimentalised, exemplify scars or seams on social tissues. It is worth questioning both how something or someone is represented, and who is represented/who is rendered invisible or silenced.

Loss, when conflated with absence, is often called upon to operate in power discourses. The full unity and homogeneity of the body politic is often posited as lost, disrupted, or polluted by others (LaCapra, 2001). However, one may argue that this putative unity in fact never existed, it is an absence. It points to the fundamental socio-political problem that Jean-Luc Nancy (1991) describes as being in common, without common being. Thus, the conflation of absence and loss can become an alibi for nationalistic discourses, foundational philosophies, and fundamentalist ideologies that posit past utopias and paradises lost. This conflation leads to unmournability, for it touches on the sphere of ontological absence, and can provide testimony of melancholic mechanisms operating behind otherwise convincing cultural, social, political, or individual agendas. Such cultural attempts and failures at "working through" are the concern of the contributors to this volume, who question the descriptive and normative features of completed and uncompleted mourning.

Time and afterwardsness[1]

The mind incorporates distinct dimensions other than linear temporality.[2] Individuals as well as societies revise past events at a later date and return to past events in order to understand the present. In the paper on screen memories, Freud described two different movements: the screen memory is "pushed forward" when the earlier memory is used as a screen for a later event, and it is "retrogressive" when a later memory functions as a screen for an earlier event (1899a, p. 320). Experiences are only understood in retrospect, and we often reach for a past event to reflect on a more recent occurrence. "Just as it took World War II to 'remember' the lessons of World War I, so it took the experience of Vietnam to 'remember' the lessons of World War II, including the psychiatric lessons of the Holocaust." (Leys, 2000, p. 15) We could think of this situation as one where one event covers up or conceals the other, an earlier one covering for a later one or a later one for an earlier one; or as making use of one event in order to understand the other, as the mourning of one loss revives earlier losses. As in Winnicott's (1974) formulation, the catastrophic political scenario which functions as a negative regulative idea, what must not happen is what has already happened. The specific "X" in varieties of the political slogan "Never again X!" is a historical traumatic event, that which must not be repeated. The notion of afterwardsness (après-coup) makes clear how earlier memory-traces are reorganised in the light of the present—the past and the present interact so as to bring forth a new meaning, one which could arise only later (Freud, 1918). This happens specifically to what it has been impossible in the first instance to incorporate fully into a meaningful context. The traumatic event is the epitome of such unassimilated experience.

In one of the most memorable descriptions in the history of psychoanalysis, Karl Abraham recounts how he took his father inside him after the latter's death, an experience which led him to question Freud's (1917e) distinction between mourning and melancholia:

> Towards the end of the previous year my father had died. During the period of mourning which I went through certain things occurred which I was not at the time able to recognize as the consequence of a process of introjection. The most striking event was that my hair rapidly turned very grey and then went black again in a few month's time. [...] For I had seen my father for the last time a few months before his death, when I was home from the war on a short leave. I had found him very much aged and not at all strong, and I had especially noticed that his hair and his beard were almost white [...] My recollection of my last visit to him was closely associated with this impression. (Abraham, 1988, pp. 437–438)

Following on from the exchange between Freud and Abraham, and from Ferenczi's work on introjection, Nicholas Abraham and Maria Torok have described fantasmatic incorporation, where the object is settled in the I to compensate for the failed introjection (1994, p. 113). When denied acknowledgement and introjection,

> we are reduced to a radical denial of the loss, to pretending that we had absolutely nothing to lose. [...] Inexpressible mourning erects a secret tomb inside the subject. [...] Sometimes in the dead of the night [...] the ghost of the crypt comes back to haunt the cemetery guard, giving him strange and incomprehensible signals [...] or subjecting him to unexpected sensations. (Abraham & Torok, 1994, p. 130)

Such phantoms haunt future generations and influence political motives and social movements to come.

This links with Haydée Faimberg's (2005) work, an author who has explored how, in "the telescoping of generations", which always involves three generations, one carries alienated identifications with intrusive parents linked to their history and death.

A neglect of historical consciousness is characteristic of Western society today, a lack of reflection on relations between past happenings, past events, and the present. The past is rarely brought up in conversations, reflective retrospection is very rarely on the agenda. New technologies have increased our access to information enormously, and contemporary society places a high value on being up to date and incorporating more and more new information at the cost of memory. Furthermore, it is a sign of status to signal to other people that one is very busy, that one has no time to spare. Eva Hoffman reflects on the impacts such attitudes have on human relationships:

> Coming to know another person calls for a certain affective energy and sustained attention; for the willingness to travel into the inwardness of another person, to probe behind appearances, to let empathy follow its own unpredictable temporal pathways. Intimacy can rarely fit into sound-bite intervals, and it rarely happens on schedule. (Hoffman, 2009, p. 176)

Similarly, mourning requires sustained attention and a willingness to let one's mind travel beyond its usual horizon. It is a massively inefficient process, one that has no regard for external success. In today's busy and instrumentalised society, focused on instant gratification or definable goals, there is little space for remembrance, retrospection, and mourning. A lack of time to reflect and a lack of access to critical alternative perspectives of past events may have paved the way for today's fundamentalisms, where idealised, mythical narrations replace realistic and nuanced historiography. In so far as the past has not been worked through, the violence it initiated carries on, unreflectively, in the present.

About the chapters

This book was conceived on the basis of a Psychoanalysis and Politics[3] conference with the same title, held in the rooms of the Swedish Psychoanalytic Society in Stockholm in March 2012. We were following a thread of thought that had begun with problems of social exclusion and the politics of representation and continued engaging with contemporary neo-nationalism and xenophobia, reflections which have resulted in two previous books published by Karnac (Auestad, 2012, 2014). In retrospect, it can be seen that we were also working through a traumatic racist attack on the conference series by the organisation it first belonged to, stemming from an accusation that "these people are not Nordic, neither genetically nor intellectually", and supported by many. These events led to the setting up of Psychoanalysis and Politics as an independent organisation, which has held conferences internationally since then. The Stockholm conference was the first out of several symposia with the same title that continued to explore shared traumas and social manifestations of (non-)mourning.

The opening chapter, by Hannah Zeavin, "War games: mourning loss through play", focuses on the re-enactment of wartime trauma by veterans through war play—child's play that resurfaces in soldiers after they have returned home from combat. The author argues that public American memorialisation works to strip trauma and loss of its historical and lived referents. Public memorials codify the erasure of trauma, both of the soldier and those he fought. Therefore, those who lived through such trauma find it a necessity to interrogate sites of commemoration in order to redress their history in private. In discussing Kim Jone's performance pieces Rat Piece and War Maps, outsider artist Michael D. Cousino's Vietnam War dioramas, and Mark Hogankamp's miniature wartime village of Marwencol, she explores how this specific form of re-enactment constitutes a gesture of political resistance to the public culture memorialising such events.

Lene Auestad's chapter, "Public memory and figures of fragmentation", questions some public memorials of the Holocaust in relation to trauma, especially in its aspects of physical suffering, and to the possibility or impossibility of mourning. It begins by reflecting on the potential functions of art in this context, and relates this to the phenomenology of trauma, mainly as described by Ferenczi. Three sculptures or installations are discussed in relation to their communication to the spectator as an embodied, physical being: Anthony Gormley's chairs in Oslo, Peter Eisenman's memorial in Berlin and Rachel Whiteread's memorial in Vienna. These sculptures, it is argued, are not mimetic in the sense of depicting something recognisable. Rather, the spectator is the one who is put in the position of doing the mimesis, as the monuments evoke some of the sensations—physical and mental—related to trauma. These sculptures, it is argued, turn the spectator into an object in relation to them, constituting a relation to something that does not relate back, as if speaking to someone who neither listens nor answers.

The main objective of Emil Fackenheim's 1982 work *To Mend the World* is to lay the foundations of a post-Holocaust Jewish thought. Jonathan Davidoff's chapter, "To mend the world—trauma, mourning, and containment", engages with this work's confrontation with the possibility of collapse of Jewish, Christian and secular philosophies that results from the reality of Auschwitz and what was lost therein. It outlines the impact of what was irremediably lost in the Holocaust and what can be repaired and clung to that may serve as the means to survive the abyss left behind. He concludes by interrogating the scope of Fackenheim's work as a philosophical act of individual and shared mourning.

Edna Mor's chapter, "Holocaust survivor mothers and their daughters— the intergenerational mourning process as a journey in search of the mother", investigates processes of intergenerational transmission. Mothers who were young girls during the Holocaust and were separated from their parents for a long period of time or forever continued to live and develop, but the place which had contained their emotional and physical relations with their parent remained a vacuum. This vacuum formed in the psyche of the mother left its imprint on her children. The mothers' and daughters' therapists were interviewed separately, enabling the author to independently look at these relations from the mothers' and the daughters' points of view. When the survivor mother makes room for her daughter in her painful past, it is argued, a bridge of intimacy is constructed that brings the vacuum inside them and between them to life with emotions and memories. Such healing has ramifications for future generations.

In "Unable to mourn again? Media(ted) reactions to German neo-Nazi terrorism", Steffen Krüger reads the 2011 media discourse on right-wing terrorism in Germany in the context of media and communication as well as psychoanalytic theory. In what popular German media had crudely termed the "Doner Murders", eight people of Turkish and one of Greek origin were killed between 2000 and 2006. A trio calling themselves "National-Socialist Underground" were found to be behind at least two nail-bomb attacks on immigrant areas in Cologne, in addition to the killing of a police officer in 2007 (a second survived heavily wounded)—Europe's biggest unsolved series of murders so far. Drawing on Alexander and Margarete Mitscherlich's classic, the chapter raises the question of whether Germany's media-political culture has still not gained the ability to mourn—to mourn its victims, as well as itself, in order to integrate Germany's past as a continuous presence into its reasoning and actions.

Margarita Palacios' chapter, "Politicising trauma—a post-colonial and psychoanalytic conceptual intervention", argues in favour both of radicalising a social constructionist perspective (violence is always associated with processes of displacement of meaning) and of embracing paradoxically at the same time a notion of a "non-relational" space (or non-symbolisable space) of the experience of the death drive. Trauma (in the case of political violence), she argues, relates to the impossible knot of becoming in "the hands of the enjoying other" a purposeless thing (a "what" as opposed to a "who") that can be cut and burned, penetrated and disposed, and at the same time—always and inevitably—never becoming *just that*. Trauma points to the experience of inhabiting the mute death drive as an object of enjoyment of the other, and consequently, to the existential struggle of neither giving up to the demand of the other (of entering in a logic of an intersubjective sadomasochistic arrangement), nor giving up meaning and symbolic life altogether. The author argues that the existential counterpart of trauma is not found in the positions either of the understanding witness or in the silent witness, but only in the figure of the anxious witness—as only this witness can account for the affect (i.e., anxiety) that has triggered the acting out of the violent event in the first place.

How is mourning carried out and what forms of grieving does it prescribe when the trace of the lost object remains alive and when the attachment to what is lost is not dissolved despite the recognition of the loss? Nayla Debs' chapter, "Ongoing mourning as a way to go beyond endless grief: considerations on the Lebanese experience", considers this question in the context of the Lebanese society, where collective and individual lives have been marked by a series of losses caused by repetitive wars and the abrupt changes they have installed. By addressing different experiences of grief, the chapter sheds light on multiple forms of working through, thus questioning a normative reading of the Freudian model that establishes a clear distinction between mourning and melancholia. Drawing on Freud, Laplanche, Derrida, and Butler, the author points to the importance of unfinished mourning as the condition of its success, a condition that preserves the otherness of the trace and prevents its loss (the loss of the loss), allowing the formation of an "unencumbered" memory open to the future through ongoing mourning.

In "When the 'comfort women' speak: traumatic memory, recognition, and healing", Jenyu Peng examines the trauma of the sex slaves of the Japanese Imperial Army during the Pacific War, some of whom, after half a century of silence, started to reveal their suffering in the 1990s. With the help of feminists and human rights activists, they have attempted numerous lawsuits to urge the Japanese government to pronounce an official apology, in vain. As Ferenczi indicated in the case of childhood sexual assaults, the denial of the adult/abuser effectuates the after-effect of traumatisation (*Nachträglichkeit*). The fact that the Japanese right-wing majority fails to face the post-war responsibility aggravates the grief for the victims, and extinguishes their slight hope for reparation. The research on psychotrauma related to human violence shows that the recognition of historical reality is crucial in victims' reconstruction. Based on a fieldwork of clinical anthropology with Taiwanese former "comfort women", this chapter describes the healing settings offered by an international network of NGOs, and discusses the nature and function of psychoanalytical settings for victims of violence.

In "Trauma, mourning, and memory in three plays by Ariel Dorfman", Jean-François Jacques examines individual and collective responses to trauma resulting from political violence through three plays by the Chilean playwright and author Ariel Dorfman, "The Resistance Trilogy" (comprising "Death and the Maiden", "Reader", and "Widows"). These plays are set against the backdrop of the Chilean dictatorship of the 1970s and 1980s. In "Death and the Maiden", Dorfman depicts three characters that each personifies a different response to the resurgence of the demons of the traumatic past: retribution, denial, and forgiveness. In "Reader", the truth about the past is prevented from emerging because of a curtain of censorship that deprives access to personal and collective memory. In "Widows", the wish of women to mourn the bodies of their husbands washed ashore is confronted by an intense desire for truth and justice. By making use of the thoughts of the American psycho-analyst Doris Brothers, Daniel Siegel, and Judith Herman, the author discusses the questions raised by Dorfman's plays about the conditions for individuals and society to mourn their past and restore trust in the future.

What was the difference between the people who gave Clement Atlee's Labour government the electoral landslide to build a welfare state and a million new homes, and the people who chose Margaret Thatcher's Conservatives from 1979–1997, with their programme of radical privatisation? This question is raised by Jane Frances in the final chapter, "Victory and defeat: from Beveridge to Thatcher without tears". After 1918 Britain's military dead were grimly honoured with the con-struction of explicitly non-triumphalist memorials built in prominent sites in every city, town, and village across Britain. The 1939–1945 war saw each new and terrible development turned, for reasons of popular as well as military morale, into something positive: Dunkirk, the Blitz, the Home Front. Upon victory came newsreels of liberated concentra-tion camps, but not new war memorials: the names of the British mili-tary dead were added to the lists of names on the already existing Great War memorials. The author argues that, unlike the 1979 electorate, the 1945 electorate, who voted overwhelmingly Labour immediately after the 1939–1945 war, would have included many people born before the Great War of 1914–1918. The article focuses on the impact of these two world wars on British society, and draws upon attachment research to argue that a terrible mismatch between private loss and public mourn-ing shaped a generation, leading to reduced social concern. The analysis contends that the political and social "will of the people" is at least partly shaped by people's experiences of war, trauma, and loss, the failure of public and private mourning, and the transmission of the emotional consequences of these experiences to subsequent generations.

Notes

1. I follow Jean Laplanche in translating *Nachträglichkeit* as "afterwards-ness", which is closer to the original and captures the two directions involved (see Caruth & Laplanche, 2001).
2. Rosine Perelberg (2008) lists seven dimensions of time in Freud's work: development, regression, fixation, repetition compulsion, the return of the repressed, the timelessness of the unconscious, and après-coup, referring to the latter concept as providing a "general illumination" in his framework.
3. Psychoanalysis and Politics is an international and interdisciplinary conference series, founded in 2010. The series aims to address how crucial contemporary political issues may be fruitfully analysed through psychoanalytic theory and vice versa—how political phenomena may reflect back on psychoanalytic thinking. Perspectives from different psychoanalytic schools are most welcome. We emphasise room for discussion among the presenters and participants, thus the symposium series creates a space where representatives of different perspectives come together, participating in a community of thought (www.psa-pol.org).

References

Abraham, K. (1988). A short study of the development of the libido, viewed in the light of mental disorders. In: *Selected Papers of Karl Abraham*. London: Maresfield Library.

Abraham, N., & Torok, M. (1994). *The Shell and the Kernel*. Chicago, IL: University of Chicago Press.

Adorno, T. W. (1998). The meaning of working through the past. In: *Critical Models. Interventions and Catchwords*. New York: Columbia University Press.

Ahmed, S. (2012). *On Being Included. Racism and Diversity in Institutional Life*. London: Duke University Press.

Aloni, U., & Butler, J. (2010). Judith Butler: As a Jew, I was taught it was ethically imperative to speak up. In: *Haaretz*, 24 February. http:// www.haaretz.com/news/judith-butler-as-a-jew-i-was-taught-it-was-ethically-imperative-to-speak-up-1.266243 [last accessed 17 July 2016].

Auestad, L. (2011). Splitting, attachment and instrumental rationality. A re-view of Menzies Lyth's social criticism. *Psychoanalysis, Culture & Society, 16*(4): 394–410.

Auestad, L. (2012) (Ed.). *Psychoanalysis and Politics: Exclusion and the Politics of Representation*. London: Karnac.

Auestad, L. (2014). *Nationalism and the Body Politic: Psychoanalysis and the Rise of Ethnocentrism and Xenophobia*. London: Karnac.

Balint, M. (1969). Trauma and object relationship. *International Journal of Psychoanalysis, 50*: 429–435.

Butler, J. (2004). *Precarious Life. The Powers of Mourning and Violence*. London: Verso.

Caruth, C., & Laplanche, J. (2001). An interview with Jean Laplanche. *Postmodern Culture, 11*(2). http://pmc.iath.virginia.edu/text-only/issue.101/11.2caruth.txt [last accessed 17 July 2016].

Cohen, S. (2001). *States of Denial. Knowing about Atrocities and Suffering*. Cambridge: Polity.

Faimberg, H. (2005). *The Telescoping of Generations. Listening to the Narcissistic Links between Generations*. London: Routledge.

Freud, S. (1899a). Screen Memories. *S. E., 3*: 301. London: Hogarth.

Freud, S. (1900a). *The Interpretation of Dreams. S. E., 4–5*. London: Hogarth.

Freud, S. (1917e). Mourning and Melancholia. *S. E., 14*: 239. London: Hogarth.

Freud, S. (1918). From the History of an Infantile Neurosis. *S. E., 17*: 3. London: Hogarth.

Freud, S., Jones, E., & Paskauskas, R. A. (Eds.) (1993). *The Complete Correspondence of Sigmund Freud and Ernest Jones 1908–1939*. Cambridge: Harvard University Press.

Hoffman, E. (2009). *Time*. London: Profile.

Jacques, E. (1955). Social systems as a defence against persecutory and depressive anxiety. In: M. Klein, P. Heimann, & R. E. Money-Kyrle (Eds.), *New Directions in Psycho-Analysis* (pp. 478–498). London: Maresfield.

LaCapra, D. (2001). *Writing History, Writing Trauma*. Baltimore, MD: Johns Hopkins University Press.

Leader, D. (2008). *The New Black*. London: Hamish Hamilton.

Leys, R. (2000). *Trauma: A Genealogy*. London: University of Chicago Press.

Menzies Lyth, I. (1990). Social systems as a defense against anxiety: an empirical study of the nursing service of a general hospital. In: E. Trist & H. Murray (Eds.), *The Social Engagement of Social Science Vol. 1: The Socio-Psychological Perspective* (pp. 439–462). London: Free Association Books.

Mitscherlich, A., & Mitscherlich, M. (1975). *The Inability to Mourn: Principles of Collective Behavior*. New York: Grove Press.

Nancy, J. L. (1991). *The Inoperative Community*. Minneapolis, MN: University of Minnesota Press.

Perelberg, R. J. (2008). *Time, Space and Phantasy*. London: Routledge.

Rohr, E. (2012). Traces of trauma in post-conflict Guatemala: theoretical reflections on the effects of trauma on social organisation. In: L. Auestad (Ed.), *Psychoanalysis and Politics: Exclusion and the Politics of Representation* (pp. 173–195). London: Karnac.

Sklar, J. (2011). *Landscapes of the Dark. History, Trauma, Psychoanalysis.* London: Karnac.

Winnicott, D. W. (1974). Fear of breakdown. *International Review of Psychoanalysis, 1*: 103–107.

CHAPTER ONE

War games—mourning loss through play

Hannah Zeavin

In *Beyond the Pleasure Principle*, Freud discusses a child observed at home who repeatedly throws a toy away from his crib then reels it back in. Each time, the child is distressed at the toy's departure and joyful at its return. Freud interprets this gesture as a mimicking of the comings and goings of the boy's mother (Freud, 1920g). Later in this work, Freud describes the boy smashing his toy into the ground in rejection. The boy states that the toy, "has been sent to the front", much like his father had in going to fight in World War I (Freud, 1920g). In essence, the child acts out the situations that occur in his life through play. The child does to an object what objects, or events, have done to him—simultaneously mastering and repeating the events in question. This kind of play is not therapy. Instead, play-acting is a space in which a child recognises, manipulates, and comes to terms with his own life and its overwhelming moments.

Freud asks of himself and his reader, "How then, does his repetition of this distressing experience as a game fit in with the pleasure principle?" (Freud, 1920g). Freud understands the child's repetition of throwing and fetching his toy to be the child attempting to master and overcome the traumatic sensation evoked by his mother leaving and returning. The child, through rehearsing that loss with material objects, through play, comes to be able to protect himself from psychic harm. Freud continues:

> At the outset he was in a passive situation, he was overpowered by the experience; but, by repeating it, unpleasurable though it was, as a game, he took on an active part. These efforts might be put down to an instinct for mastery that was acting independently of whether the memory was in itself pleasurable or not. (Freud, 1920g, p. 15)

Another question might be, is this re-enactment of a trauma, through the loci of the toy, unique to childhood?

Play can and does operate as a tool for re-enactment and mastery of trauma beyond childhood. In the artworks of Kim Jones, Sasha Chavchavadze, and Mark Hogancamp play is used as re-enactment in order to first conjure and then control a past experience. These artists revisit childhood play itself and a central traumatic experience. Though these three artists refer to and make use of play as a substantial container and element in their works, this play in art goes beyond that of children working through. In these artworks and their respective artist statements, play is conceptualised as art, such that the psychic work also becomes a commentary on the traumatic incident and on the creation and use of a repetitive artistic practice. In making and performing art, these artists are able to simultaneously make artworks focused on remembrance, but also are able to make interventions on the process of remembering and performing. This includes references to therapy and ideas surrounding healing from trauma.

Returning to play-acting assists these artists in understanding and working through their specific traumatic experiences. However, the objective of these artworks is not to simply recreate tenets of an experience through familiar modes of childhood play. Instead, the mastery afforded through play recapitulates and rearranges the affect of these memories, their sensibilities, and their configurations. This shift takes place in time. Instead of the trauma being one of the past, the artworks recover the experience and re-enact it. This brings the trauma into the present moment. The only reference to a past is the mode of re-enactment, or the inclusion of childhood play in the artwork.

Freud discusses repetition and remembrance in terms of the relationship between analyst and analysand. Freud states that the patient "is obliged to *repeat* the repressed material as a contemporary experience instead of *remembering* it as something belonging to the past" (Freud, 1920g, p. 18). Hogancamp, Jones, and Chavchavadze each bear this out in their work. Their art removes trauma from the past, and puts it out in front of the artist and the spectator. The artwork is an encapsulated, repeating, ongoing experience of production and consumption. But because the methods for doing so inherently rely on a nostalgic medium—childhood play—the artist operates in two temporalities at once.

Mark Hogancamp created a miniature village set in Belgium during World War II called Marwencol. Marwencol is inhabited by figurines, such as Barbie and Ken dolls or GI Joes. Each has its own personalities, mythologies, and histories. Within this village, Hogancamp acts out the fantasies of his past, as well as the issues he faces in the present. Much like Freud theorises, Hogancamp does not remember, but rather acts things out: Hogancamp suffered from a massive brain trauma after being attacked in a bar for cross-dressing. He does not remember his life before the fight (Malmberg, 2010). In a sense, Hogancamp acts out his life in his village. He then documents these scenes with colour photos.

Kim Jones was a Vietnam War veteran who was stationed in the demilitarised zone (DMZ) for the United States Army from 1966 to 1969. Upon returning to America, Jones invented an alter ego named Mudman. Jones worked as a performance artist and gained notoriety after a 1976 performance of "Rat Piece" in which the artist immolated a cage of live rats. Jones said of this work that he was re-enacting a game that he and his fellow soldiers played in Vietnam when they were bored and stuck in trenches (Maine, 2006). The State of California sued Jones for animal cruelty, despite the fact that he was re-enacting a behaviour learned during his service in the United States military (Knight, 2007). Jones then began producing a series of acrylic paintings on his and his grandfathers' army fatigues. Called War Maps, these meticulous paintings chart the logistics for battles. Jones states that this type of work pre-dates his time in Vietnam. Instead he states that the works were initially based on a game he played in childhood. This game focused on positioning enemies, in which the armies were indicated by different shape. He then would draw maps of the wars and battles between these armies.

Chavchavadze's artworks, which take on many forms, are composed exclusively from matches. Her fixation on the match stems from the desire to understand the history and life of her father, who was gone much of her childhood working as a CIA operative in East Germany. Her father had played a war game as a child in which he set up opposing teams of matches—one "army" would have blue strikers, and another "army" would have green or red strikers. One team would flick lit matches or throw stones at the opposing army until it was decimated. Chavchavadze then played this game with her father when she was a child. Through this repetition, it became an allegory of that present moment: her father was a match, part of an army, and part of a war. Much like Freud's case study, Chavchavadze rehearsed her father at the front through play. She is the curator of the "Museum of Matches" in Brooklyn, New York.

Though these three traumas—Mark Hogancamp's experience of brain trauma and the inability to remember his own life, Kim Jones' experience of extreme violence in the Vietnam War, and Chavchavadze's absent father in the midst of the Cold War—are difficult to articulate and to recuperate, they are nonetheless recreated in play. Each one belongs to an individual, but is situated in public or collective traumas: violence against those perceived as queer, the Vietnam War era, and the Cold War. The artworks encapsulating these private traumas, however, are made public through their display and consumption. Returning to *Beyond the Pleasure Principle*, Freud writes:

> In play, children repeat everything that has made a great impression on them in real life, and in doing so they abstract the strength of the impression and, as one might put it, make themselves master of the situation ... It can also be observed that the unpleasurable nature of an experience does not always unsuit it for play. If the doctor looks down a child's throat or carries out some small operation on him, we may be quite sure that these frightening experiences will be the subject of the next game; but we must not in that connection overlook the fact that there is a yield of pleasure from another source. As the child passes over from the passivity of the experience to the activity of the game, he hands on the disagreeable experience to one of his playmates and in this way revenges himself on a substitute. (Freud, 1920g, pp. 16–17)

For Hogancamp, Jones, and Chavchavadze, the role of playmate in Freud's construction is the spectator. Each of their works invites an audience or playmate into the art and into the play. In doing so, the artists allow for the possibility of passing on the trauma and of demonstrating what it was like. The artists do not choose their form of play based on their specific traumas. Instead they return to their familiar play routines from childhood. Each of the three artists has made a career out of performing and creating the same type of play again and again. Kim Jones retells the story of his service in Vietnam through familiar war maps; Mark Hogancamp retells his ideas about his own life through the figurines he owned as a child; Chavchavadze returns to the game that her father played first in his youth and later with Chavchavadze during her childhood.

Freud remarks that, "the patient does not *remember* anything of what he has forgotten and repressed, he *acts* it out" (Freud, 1914g, p. 154). For Mark Hogancamp this is literally true, but it is not through the repression mechanism that he has forgotten his entire life story. In acting out a fantasy of what his life has been like, he is constantly performing and recuperating the trauma of that loss within the boundaries of his one-sixth-scale diorama village.

Marwencol has functioned as the centre of Hogancamp's life since he was in a coma, and then in the hospital for over a month. When he was discharged, he still had no recollection of who he was, aside from recognising his mother. He was, however, able to formulate and retain new memories. Hogancamp began therapeutic treatment, both psychical and psychic, but was unable to continue due to financial limitations. He then turned towards making a model village in his backyard, collecting materials, painting figurines, and building structures. Hogancamp would then, sometimes using his diaries, act out scenes from his past or his present. Yet all of these scenes are enveloped in the premise of Marwencol, a village trapped in the 1940s in Belgium. The Nazis are ever discovering and invading Marwencol. Hogancamp, in the world of the village, is an American soldier and, with the assistance of his friends, repeatedly slaughters these invaders. Though the "bad guys" are Nazis and the "good guys" are American soldiers, symbolically, the Nazis take on the role of Hogancamp's attackers. Aided with his diaries from before the attack, Hogancamp edits and reiterates some of the experiences that he previously had recorded. Upon finding out that he was formerly an alcoholic, Hogancamp decides instead to become addicted to coffee, both within the confines of his town and in his real life.

Hogancamp's miniatures look almost exactly like the people they are modelled on. According to the documentary about Hogancamp's recovery and entry into the art world, part of the pleasure Hogancamp derives from his play is the sense of control that he gets not only over his "life" but his friends' and acquaintances' lives inside the village (Malmberg, 2010). Each figurine is tailor-made in Hogancamp's workshop to mirror and exaggerate the features of his real-life subjects. Susan Stuart writes in her book *On Longing: Narratives of the Miniature, the Gigantic, the Souvenir, the Collection* that, "the body of lived experience is subject to change, transformation, and most importantly, death. The idealized body implicitly denies the possibility of death—it attempts to present a realm of transcendence and immortality … This is the body-made-object …" (Stuart, 1993).

Hogancamp attempts to codify his desire to remember his life by filling the void of his memory, reconfiguring it through the re-enactments within Marwencol. By making miniature versions of the key players in his life, Hogancamp is able to assure himself control, or mastery. He is also able to ensure continuity. His figurines will always be there, unless Hogancamp decides to take one out of the story and out of his life. The control that Hogancamp exhibits over his characters mimics childhood play scenes in which bad guys and good guys are created and acted out by children. The good guys occupy an extreme, infallible masculinity. They are grafted onto an American icon, and become a heroic, idealised body. The bad guys fall at the opposing end of the spectrum. Hogancamp complicates these character tropes by cleaving his past, and a historical past, onto them. Hogancamp represents himself within Marwencol as well. He portrays himself within the contained scenes as a strong Army man, a slayer of Nazis, and a man with various girlfriends who has a close relationship with his mother. Only one of these traits, his relationship with his mother, is borne out in real life.

Hogancamp does not simply build and act out the goings-on of Marwencol. He also records, through photographs, each of his scenes, and his characters' developments. Because of the indexical record he maintains, these figurines will not perish. Instead, they maintain any given person who is being represented even after any possible loss or rejection of that person. The photographs of Marwencol replace Hogancamp's diaries as the record of his life. Hogancamp first reconstructs and re-enacts his life, pre-accident. Then, he records it as a self-protective gesture: he photographs his Marwencol life so that he can never be robbed of it again.

Because Marwencol is the focus of Hogancamp's life, functioning as his play, his work, and his therapy, the scenes and plot lines that take place there unfold in almost-real time. Hogancamp's understanding of his life as it was before his injury, his life post-brain trauma, his fantasies, and a general historical plot of World War II combine in Marwencol. Though the scenes are documented, they are not constructed for documentation. Instead, Hogancamp's psyche becomes located and played out therein. The miniature, Susan Stewart argues, is an object that contains. Marwencol runs parallel to Hogancamp's life because it is his life. Marwencol folds in on itself. Hogancamp, after some time, constructed a miniature Marwencol inside Marwencol so that his alter ego could play as he plays. Mark Hogancamp's figurine can often be found, or is placed, in front of this miniature village. There, the alter ego again plays with reduced and to scale, miniature figurines. The alter ego takes photographs of scenes he plays out in solidarity with his real-world counterpart (Malmberg, 2010). In a sense, Hogancamp's work needs only Hogancamp to participate as a spectator. Marwencol serves as a document of a recreated and manipulated life narrative, absent after the brain trauma.

Kim Jones's War Map paintings simultaneously foreground his childhood play and military service in Vietnam. Using his own military fatigues as a canvas, Jones diagrams battles between opposing armies. The intricate markings are not the result of a single process or single painting. Instead, Jones often revisits his paintings over a period of years, even decades. These works are, much like Marwencol, unfolding in real time and across time. Jones, by his own admission, and demonstrated by his work, has carried the horror of war with him his entire life. Both his grandfathers and his father were soldiers. One of his grandfathers was brutally murdered—a scene which Jones has also re-enacted in his work. In that piece, Jones destroys a series of objects, covers himself in his own faeces, hugs an audience member, and then leaves the performance space. In this performance, as well as in Rat Piece, the object is to demonstrate the trauma, and then pass it on. Sometimes the substitute is a cage of rats, sometimes an unsuspecting audience member. Jones' work focuses on acting, reconfiguring, and repeating a series of traumas related to war and violence that have reverberated within his life and his family's history since his childhood.

War Maps, drawn over decades, re-enact a childhood rehearsal for war. Jones traces this genre of his work to an early age, when he began pitting armies against one another on paper. His gaming, like the gaming of so many children of his and previous generations, was a preparation for what later occurred in real combat. In play, as Freud delineates, the idea is to master and understand experiences and trauma *after* the scene has occurred, not before (Freud, 1920g). It is impossible to prepare a child for war through this kind of play, in which casualties are sketched, and landscapes can be redrawn when the battles are over.

The tenor of Jones' work shifts when his war gaming stops being a rehearsal and becomes a re-enactment. The works are often gigantic and totalising in scale. Studies for his War Maps are shown as art works in and of themselves; whereas the physical parameters of the War Maps that Jones paints on his fatigues are controlled by the size of his own shirt—one study, done in graphite, is 1,500 square feet in size. Jones creates these studies in an erasable medium, so that he can re-draw sections of the maps. Each modification to a War Map just slightly alters the positions of the armies, and therefore depicts the progression of war. Despite all the logistics present within these drawings, and attempts to avoid battle, the maps always end with war. These studies are repetitive. Positions of various armies change as Jones manipulates them because the works are continuous and ongoing.

War Maps makes use of and references relics of Jones' self and his service in the war. These fatigues serve as material witnesses to Jones' corporeal experiences in Vietnam. They are military-issued, and were worn in the field. When carried into a post-war era, in a setting in which their work is to assist in a re-creation, these objects point to the experiential reality of the war. The fatigues do not enact their original function. They do, however, serve as the container of Jones' War Maps. The fatigues become a double witness, first having born witness to Jones, his body, and actions in the Vietnam War, and second having been used as a witness to the evolution of each individual war map. These objects have been, in their material history, an extension of the state, the military, and the soldier. These extensions are incorporated into each of Jones' War Maps, transferring, recuperating, and re-enacting their original effects.

These fatigues function as souvenirs of Jones' formative experiences in Vietnam. Susan Stuart writes about the souvenir that it,

> involves the displacement of attention into the past. The souvenir
> is not simply an object appearing out of context, an object from the
> past incongruously surviving in the present; rather its function is to

> envelop the present within the past ... Yet the magic of the souvenir is a kind of failed magic ... The place of origin must remain unavailable in order for desire to be generated. (Stuart, 1993, p. 151)

Vietnam and the war is a temporality that, despite feeling deeply present, is unattainable for Jones. Because of this "failed magic", his desire to re-enact the war, to put it in front, to be able to access it, is totalising and engulfing. By surrounding the representational artworks with mimetic and real objects from the war, Jones is able to, as Stuart writes, "envelop the present" works of art within the past. The inaccessibility of Vietnam, the regimens of the army, and the sites of horror set up an absence, constantly present in the work. Along with this desire to be there, the works are fatalistic, and drive towards the same ending: war. It does not matter which of the various War Maps one looks at, or which garment contains them. They differentiate themselves only by the minute particulars of each battle scene, not in whether or not war is waged.

Sasha Chavchavadze works predominately on the intersection of Cold War and her personal familial memory. Her father was absent during the Cold War and Chavchavadze's childhood. Chavchavadze seeks to recuperate her father and those years of her life. Chavchavadze turned to matches upon reading a section from Vladimir Nabokov's novel *Speak, Memory* that references a match game similar to one that the artist had played with her father as a child. She was then inspired to begin rehearsing and reconfiguring this game. The match game itself is at once a part of her father's childhood play, a symbolic re-enactment of the war her father had participated in, and the precariousness of his life therein.

Chavchavadze's response to remembering the match game was to produce works that re-enact it. She incorporates sculpture, text, painting, and film. Chavchavadze says of her own work:

> Since I am not an historian, I searched for visual forms for insight into my father's life and career. I began to draw matches, then to glue wooden match sticks perpendicularly to paper in grids and patterns. Sometimes I rolled the paper, forcing the matches to conform to the surface, creating three-dimensional forms that resembled architectural models or topographical maps. I often visualised "matchwork" as I awoke, the project ballooning. The meditative

process felt like planting seedlings. Tiny units of energy that can save a life or kill, matches evoke both the nurturing and the destructive sides of human nature. (Chavchavadze, 2014)

Chavchavadze describes a compulsion to repeat and act out as a way to access her father's life, as well as his career. The match is described as functioning as a miniature container holding both life and death. The artist wrote her father asking him to describe the match game. Her father replied:

> The match game was invented by me in 1940. In those days there were kitchen matches that could be lit by almost anything and different companies had different colored match heads. The matches represented individual soldiers and had insignia of rank. The game was played outdoors and the matches were stuck upright in the sand or dirt representing trenches or foxholes. If it was my turn I fired a BB gun at the enemy's matches, one shot for each match I had on the front. There was also artillery represented by rocks being lobbed at the enemy. Matches that were knocked down were wounded and given a stripe. If a match was lit it was dead. I have never described this in writing. (Chavchavadze, 2014)

Chavchavadze, her project ballooning, then took it upon herself to put the match game into writing, creating the Book of Matches. She also modelled table-top war games on her fathers' precise descriptions. She then created the Museum of Matches in Brooklyn, New York. These various forms demonstrate her exclusive attention to repeating this childhood scene. Like the child reiterating the scene of his mother's comings and goings, Chavchavadze works to master the match game. This repetition is further confused in terms of temporal ownership: the game was first played by her father as a boy, and then by her father with the artist as a young child. Like Jones, Chavchavadze's father began preparing for war in childhood. Though the Cold War in East Germany did not often make use of literal trenches and foxholes, it was a war of strategy, of secrecy, and of horrible, corporeal pain. As in Jones' works, Chavchavadze's father playing the match game before and after the Cold War represents two different kinds of play. The former is a rehearsal and the latter is a re-enactment. Chavchavadze herself only played the game in conjunction with her father after the war. In those scenes, she participated in a repetition and reconfiguration of her father's time in East Germany.

The match game encapsulates three different temporalities, allowing it to act out and repeat two childhoods, making them one and the same, or parallel, in each of Chavchavadze's works. She, of course, has no first-hand memory of her father's childhood. In her "match work" Chavchavadze is able to re-imagine her father's life, as well as hers, situating this re-imagining around a game for two people. The reimagining goes against an idea of recognising the absence and loss of her father: it prevents her from actually contending with it. Instead, she rehearses the opposite of loss: a moment of togetherness. Chavchavadze's works occupy a melancholic position (Freud, 1917e). She cannot both love her father and hate him for his secret disappearances. She cannot stop idealising him, or their moments of play in her childhood.

The moments in which Chavchavadze played the match game are, perhaps, the only moments in which she can remember the presence of her father. It may be that this scene functions as a screen memory that has blocked out other, more significant moments of togetherness (Freud, 1899a). Chavchavadze seeks to master her own history, to repeat it, to strengthen it, to gain an understanding of an absence through this single moment. Chavchavadze's pieces suggest a monumental effort to recover a lost object. Chavchavadze is fixated on the match, across all of the formal boundaries that she works within, taking it as her symbolic object. It seems that if only Chavchavadze can re-enact the match game in every permutation, as a table-top war game, as the basis of a book, at the opening for the Cold War Museum, she can recover her lost object. For Chavchavadze, her object is not lost—she refuses to understand the loss of her father. Instead, she produces works that seek to pin down the absence of her father like a specimen behind glass.

These re-enactments, by Hogancamp, Jones, and Chavchavadze, are a form of self-commemoration. These are artworks that repeat and reconfigure personal traumas, and those occurring in families. The works memorialise trauma in ways that come close to making the impossible possible: putting the artist or spectator back inside the moments in which trauma is occurring. This desire, to be contained within the moment of trauma, is wrought though artistic gestures which work to recuperate violence by recreating the scenes in which it occurs. This desire stems from an inability to recognise the trauma as belonging to the past. Were the artist to relegate the trauma to the past, he or she would have to recognise the loss of loved objects associated with that trauma. In order for Hogancamp to live in the world and relinquish Marwencol, he would have to understand psychically that he has lost his memory. For Jones to stop producing War Maps, he would have to recognise that the war is over and not ongoing. Chavchavadze has idealised her father, such that she compulsively acts out her childhood memory of the match game in order to attain him, and prevent herself from recognising his absence.

These works make use of miniature configurations of traumatic scenes in order to allow the artists to master them, to be in full possession of their own memory and history. This, of course, is an impossibility. No one is ever in possession of one's own memory and history—the mind is constantly reconfiguring and repressing the past.

These art works raise questions about what it means to return to the site of trauma, loss, and absence literally and psychically. These artists prioritise containment, but also artistic sensibilities that allow for a feeling of "being there" with oneself, in a past moment reconfigured to occur in the present. These containers (a village, fatigues, a match) are both symbolic and indexical referents to the scene of trauma, pushing the past into the present. This evocation, or conjuring, of the past, is a melancholic gesture. The artworks inflict pain on the artist, turning the self against the self. In their compulsiveness, the works turn the artist away from the outside social world.

It is a self-destructive gesture, in an attempt to affirm one's memory and history, to repeat, re-enact, reiterate, and reinvent trauma. In that the works codify and contain these traumas, the pieces produced are identity shaping. They articulate memories that were they not *acted* out, might not be complete or remembered at all. Despite the three artists focusing exclusively on their trauma, the artworks do not function as a therapy. Instead, they allow the compulsive repetition to go on, unchecked and uninterpreted. Because the works are destructive and ongoing, the pieces are often made at the price of recognising the lost object for what it actually is: lost. These artists bring the products of their internalised trauma to the public gallery. In doing so, they begin the process of moving away from a melancholic psychic position, and invite spectators to view their work and personal histories, to be a playmate. This gestures at both working-through and an affirmation of the power of the self to comment on and reinvent memory. Yet, these artists have huge resistance to a complete recognition of their lost objects in this public forum. They make use of the spectator as a witness to the repetitive art practice, and in order to revisit their traumas in a performative context. Despite showing their works to an audience, the same artists return to the same symbolic site in order to produce their next show and their new works.

References

Chavchavadze, S. (2014). *Museum of Matches*. http://museumofmatches. com/the-match-game [last accessed 25 July 2016].

Freud, S. (1899a). Screen Memories. *S. E.*, *3*: 301–322. London: Hogarth.

Freud, S. (1914g). Remembering, Repeating and Working-Through (Further Recommendations on the Technique of Psycho-Analysis, II). *S. E.*, *12*: 147. London: Hogarth.

Freud, S. (1917e). Mourning and Melancholia. *S. E.*, *14*: 239. London: Hogarth.

Freud, S. (1920g). Beyond the Pleasure Principle. *S. E.*, *18*: 7–24. London: Hogarth.

Knight, C. (2007). What rose up out of the Mudman. *Los Angeles Times*, 30 March.

Maine, S. (2006). Kim Jones with Stephen Maine. The Brooklyn Rail. www. brooklynrail.org/2006/11/art/kim-jones [last accessed 25 July 2016].

Malmberg, S. (2010). Marwencol. Open Face and Different by Design Studios.

Stuart, S. (1993). On Longing: Narratives of the Miniature, the Gigantic, the Souvenir, the Collection. Durham, NC: Duke University Press.

CHAPTER TWO

Public memory and figures of fragmentation

Lene Auestad

This chapter constitutes an attempt to think about public memorials in relation to trauma and to the possibility or impossibility of mourning. More specifically I would like to address some sculptures or installations as three-dimensional artworks to think about their communication to the spectator as an embodied, physical being.

Neither Klein's conception of art as "reparation" nor Winnicott's ideas on art as "play" seem to quite fit what I aim to describe. Although Winnicott emphasises that "play" may be a serious, explorational activity, there is a tension between his stress on the precondition of not having to ask what is inside and what is outside, subjective and objective, and creation as a response to trauma, where there would be a pressing need to get a firmer hold on a reality that is felt to be withering, too fragile. Furthermore, his mention of the "confidence related to the dependability of the [...] environmental elements" (1971, p. 135) describes precisely what would be lacking in the case of trauma. "It is obvious that the desire to make reparation, to make good the injury psychologically done to her mother and also to restore herself," writes Klein about the artist Ruth Kjär, "was at the bottom of the compelling urge to paint" (1929, p. 218). Where before there was an empty space on the wall, as well as inside Ruth herself, it is described how, with Ruth's

15

restoration of her mother in the shape of a forceful portrait, the blank space had been filled (pp. 216–217). The description leaves open the question of how to think of cases where reparation is not possible—and where redemption is not a solution to aim for.

To Freud, the experience of an artwork is associated with the pleasure principle and with wish-fulfilment. We enjoy it, he states, because it liberates the tension in our minds; it enables us "to enjoy our own day-dreams without self-reproach or shame" (1908e, p. 153). To continue the parallel with dreams, in his late writings, Ferenczi put forth the thesis that wish-fulfilling transformation is not, as Freud suggested, the sole function of the dream. The recurrence of the day's residues, he argued, serves a function in itself; the tendency to repeat traumatic incidents has "in itself a useful function [...] it endeavours to bring about a better [...] solution than was possible at the time of the original shock" (1994, p. 238). What is assumed is first that so-called day's residues in dreams, episodes referring to real-life incidents, are repetition symptoms of traumata. Second, it is assumed that this repetition performs a central function; that of bringing about a (full or partial) recovery from the impact of traumatic experiences. In Ferenczi's words:

> [I]nstead of 'the dream is a wish-fulfilment' a more complete definition of the dream function would be: every dream, even an unpleasurable one, is an attempt at a better mastery and settling of traumatic experiences, [...] which is made easier in most dreams because of the diminution of the critical faculty and the predominance of the pleasure principle. (Ferenczi, 1994, p. 238)

It is claimed that a dream represents an attempt at better mastery; in other words, it is a claim to the effect that it serves an epistemic function. Thus the last part of the statement, that this is made easier by the predominance of the pleasure principle, appears as somewhat puzzling on the background of Freud's (1911b) distinction between the pleasure principle and the reality principle. If a mental process governed by the pleasure principle represents an evasion of reality, one would hardly think that this process could contribute to a settling of traumatic experiences. In *Beyond the Pleasure Principle* Freud asserts that dreams in traumatic neuroses exemplify a function that is earlier than and independent of the pleasure principle: "These dreams are endeavouring to master the stimulus retrospectively, by developing the anxiety whose omission was the cause of the traumatic neurosis" (1920g, p. 32). In my view, Ferenczi's emphasis differs from Freud's on this point in that his concern is less about repetition compulsion as a symptom of the death drive, than about the epistemic function of this repetition. This tendency is clearer in the next passage in the text, where the thesis is further elaborated as follows:

> I would like the return of the day's and life's residues in the dream not to be considered as mechanical products of the repetition instinct but to presume that behind it is the functioning of a tendency (which should be called psychological) towards a new and better settlement, and the wish-fulfilment is the means which enables the dream to achieve this aim more or less successfully. (Ferenczi, 1994, p. 239)

In this formulation the function of wish-fulfilment is described as a means rather than as an independent aim; the future situation of a new and better settlement has entered into the foreground. What follows is a description where separate levels of dreaming are indicated. A patient he had seen for many years recounted two or several dreams from each night, the first, experienced in the hours of the deepest sleep, was devoid of psychic content but left behind vague recollections of both physical and mental pain. A second period of dreaming resulted in memories of very vivid images—distortions and attenuations of the events of the first dream. The same occurrences, it seemed, were experienced in different ways in different layers of unconsciousness:

> Gradually it became clear that the patient could and must repeat the traumatic events of her life, purely emotionally and without any ideational contents, only in a deep unconscious, almost comatose sleep; in the subsequent less deep sleep, however, she could bear only wish-fulfilling attenuations. (Ferenczi, 1994, p. 239)

It would appear, then, that different kinds of dreaming are ascribed to different layers of the unconscious; in periods of deeper sleep traumatic occurrences are relived, whereas in periods of lighter sleep, the element of wish-fulfilment is more prominent. The patient described woke up after the first, painful dreams; presumably the overwhelming experience was interrupted, and in the second period of sleep the dream-images were variations of the first theme, only now they were distorted so as to be less painful or unpleasurable. "The first dream," Ferenczi sums up, "is purely repetition; the second an attempt at settling it somehow by oneself [...] Under the condition of an optimistic counterfeit the trauma may be admitted to consciousness" (1994, pp. 240–241). The distortion which takes place under the influence of the pleasure principle, then, serves the function of allowing for a partial admittance of the trauma to perception—as much as is bearable. Thus the various transformations of the shifting dreams can be seen as being closer to or more remote from the incidents depicted or symbolised. This description of the relative value of the transformative rendering of the event made possible by the pleasure principle does not yet explain the function of the repetition itself. To understand the purpose of this repetition one must take account of the description of the effects of traumatic shock on perception. An unexpected shock, writes Ferenczi, acts like an anaesthetic, by inhibiting mental activity of any kind, provoking a state of passivity completely devoid of resistance (ibid., p. 239). It results, though this sounds paradoxical, in a state where impressions are received, though they cannot be said to be perceived: "no memory traces of such impressions remain, even in the unconscious" (1994, p. 240), thus in the repetition of the trauma in the dream material, the traumatic incident is not being perceived (or glimpsed) for the second time but for the first time. When the original event took place, it was in some sense recorded, though it was not experienced. Something was impressed upon the one who was there at the time of the occurrence, but not on the "I", so that it left behind a trace somewhere, though what happened remained alien. This seemingly logically confused description can be seen to presuppose the notion of splitting. If not even unconscious memory traces of the event remain, the part of the person that recorded the event must have been split off and made alien, thus being phenomenologically regarded "somewhere else" and not accessible to perception in a normal waking state.

Might we think of the monument in this sense as making something visible not for the second time but for the first time, even though its subject matter relates to the past? The nuances between the more or less wish-fulfilling elaborations on the original traumatic event, resulting in more or less bearable, but also more or less distorted, products are illuminating in relation to artistic attempts to approach the theme of trauma.

In Bion's (1962) description of "nameless dread" the emphasis is on the verbal- and thought-configuration; that which cannot be spoken about, that which cannot be thought. By contrast, Winnicott's contribution makes reference both to the bodily and to the mental aspects of these processes. In the articles Ego Integration in Child Development (1962) and Fear of Breakdown (1963), he presents lists of what he calls primitive agonies, stating that anxiety is not a strong enough word in this context. The following is put together out of the two papers:

1. A return to an unintegrated state, or going to pieces.
2. Falling for ever.
3. Failure of indwelling in the body, or having no relation to the body.
4. Loss of sense of real.
5. Loss of capacity to relate to objects, or failure of communication, or complete isolation.

He goes on to describe how a fear of breakdown is a fear of something that has already happened, but that has not been experienced (Winnicott, 1962, p. 58; 1963, pp. 89–91).

One reason why a trauma was never experienced is what we may call its too-much-ness, the overwhelming nature of the event. Freud defines as "traumatic", excitations "which are powerful enough to break through the protective shield", flooding the mental apparatus with "large amounts of stimulus" (1920g, p. 29). This is one cause of its apparent unreality; another is how its reality is denied by the third party, as described by Balint (1969) (see also Auestad, 2012, 2015). Thus the isolation, failure of communication, or communication being denied, is linked with the loss of reality. Third, there is the fact that a previously safe, trustful relationship has been destroyed. In Ferenczi's words:

> Shock always comes upon one unprepared. It must needs be preceded by a feeling of security, in which, because of the subsequent

events, one feels deceived; one trusted in the external world too much before; after, too little or not at all. One had to have overestimated one's own powers and to have lived under the delusion that such things could not happen, not to me. (1994, pp. 253–254)

He remarks on how a shock is linked with a loss of shape: "The word *Erschütterung* is derived from *schütten*, i.e. to become 'unfest, unsolid', to lose one's own form and to adopt easily and without resistance, an imposed form—'like a sack of flour'."

Furthermore, if an organism is not to some extent held together by its surroundings, it fragments. "At an unfavourable change in their environment the mechanism falls to pieces" (1994, p. 220). Splitting has both a mental and a bodily side to it; a purely physical, unconscious suffering, pure affect that is remote from consciousness, or "a body progressively divested of its soul, whose disintegration is [either] not perceived at all or [merely] watched from the outside" (1988, p. 9). Attentive to the phenomenology of splitting, Ferenczi argues that fragmentation may be advantageous:

> by creating a more extended surface towards that external world, [enabling] an increased discharge of affects; [Second,] from the physiological angle: the giving up of concentration, of unified perception, at least puts an end to the simultaneous suffering of multiple pain. [...] the unbearable unification of all pain qualities and quantities does not take place; [and] the absence of higher integration, [enables] greater adaptability. (p. 230)

Esther Bick described an early "frantic search for an object—a light, a voice, a smell, or other sensual object—which can hold the attention and thereby be experienced, momentarily at least, as holding the parts of the personality together" (1968, p. 484). "This containing object," she wrote, "is experienced concretely as a skin" (p. 484). Its absence leads to attempt at self-containment by the creation of a defensive structure, a "second skin". Brown (2005) has drawn a parallel to Bion's theories on how the ego seeks to cobble together a semblance of cohesion from its fragments, or beta elements, through the formation of a rigid traumatic organisation (the beta screen). In both cases, cohesiveness is reinstated, but at the cost of the capacity for imagination and symbol formation, thus reinforcing a tendency towards repetitive enactments. A massive trauma that overwhelms the I's alpha function, leads to the formation of a rigidly organised beta screen that gives the psyche a sense of structure in the face of that which cannot be managed.

In relation to the work of the artist Susan Hiller, which constitutes a visual list, a sequence rather than a story, Leader (2008, pp. 32–33) comments on how "Every attempt to give the Holocaust a narrative frame risks turning it into a story of heroism and valour or of death and defeat [...] because human narratives follow certain set patterns." And this is precisely what makes representation as a single story inappropriate. Thus Claude Lanzmann's film Shoah presents such a listing, a series of interviews, perhaps, he remarks, the only option available. In the same way as a fully formed narrative provides a sense of closure, a presentation of a whole, undamaged object would do the same.

I would like to think about some configurations, some monuments, that speak to the spectator as a physical, spatial being about trauma as something that is physically sensed. Where one could often think of an artwork as an object, as something like a quasi-person with whom one may engage in a dialogue, the sculptures or installations that follow could perhaps be thought of as non-objects, or rather, as conveying, making visible, an absence or non-responsiveness. One might state that rather than communicating, they communicate a non-communicativeness, or that to the extent that the spectator interacts with them, it is the paradoxical interaction with a non-interactive other.

As a contrast to what is to follow is represented by Frank Meisler's statue commemorating the Kindertransport at London Liverpool Street, a large train station in East London. One would often arrive at London Liverpool Street if one travels by train, and this is where many of these refugee children arrived in 1938 and 1939 from Germany, Austria, Czechoslovakia and Poland; about 10,000 in total, to be met by foster families. Although a small number were reunited with their families after the war, the majority found that their families had been killed, and stayed on in Britain. This is a traditional, figurative statue, and depicting a relatively hopeful moment. It shows London as a place of arrival, and the children, with their suitcases, are looking around, somewhat curiously, wondering what to expect. And these children were ones that survived.

By contrast, the statues of chairs by Anthony Gormley in Oslo mark Oslo as a place of departure. These are chairs, and yet they are not chairs, since they are chairs on which one cannot sit. They lack seats, so if one tried to sit on them one would fall, and this is precisely the feeling they address—the feeling of falling, of not being held, which is also historically accurate. The chairs are placed by the quay next to Akershus fortress, facing the sea. This is the place from which the ship Donau left on 26 November 1942, and from Gothenland on 25 February the following year, for Auschwitz. Out of the 767 Norwegian Jews who were deported in total, hardly anyone, that is no more than 30, all adult men, returned. The place in which these sculptures stand is a bit of no-man's land, a lawn between the stone wall of the fortress and the open sea to which they point. Thus the statues of these empty chairs convey the accurate sensation of being dropped, of "falling endlessly" because no one is there to catch one.

The Holocaust Memorial in Berlin by Peter Eisenman, unveiled in 2005, consists of a large site, a square, covered with 2,711 concrete slabs arranged in a grid pattern on a sloping field. The slabs vary in height from 0.2 to 4.8 metres. This memorial is massive, 19,000 square metres, and being inside it produces a sense of confusion, of spatial disorientation, of a loss of a position in space. Visitors can follow a labyrinth of pathways between the stone slabs, which partially gives rise to a sense of being trapped, abandoned, between them. At times, as you can see in the second picture, there is a complete lack of overview; you cannot look out and see where you are. Thus this piece seems to address the purely physical sense of disorientation that can be felt in a state of shock, along with the shattering experience of failed attempts at reality testing in states of mourning; alternating between: "Is the loved one really dead or not?" "Oh, good, she is not dead after all," and "Oh, yes, she is."

The idea of such a memorial was conceived of just before the fall of the Berlin wall, through a citizens' initiative in East Berlin, spearheaded by journalist and publicist Lea Rosh and historian Eberhard Jaeckel. Later, the politician Norbert Lammert argued that "the government's move to Berlin after reunification needed to begin with such a demonstrative sign" (Fuerstenau, 2010). An information centre was later added

beneath the terrain, where visitors can learn about the victims of the Shoah. The monument is set in the middle of the capital, in the historic heart of Berlin only a few hundred metres from the site of Hitler's bunker. Much of it has been erected over surviving underground tunnels used by Joseph Goebbels. "I had the idea of silence," said Eisenman about his monument. "What was taken away from people was their ability to speak. I wanted a memorial that spoke without speaking" (Harding, 2005).

How can one give absence a presence and a form without violating the memory of loss? Or, to refer to the earlier descriptions of reparation as filling the empty space, to what extent do memorials appear to fill in and even compensate the void left behind by the murders? Rachel Whiteread's Holocaust memorial in Vienna presents a cast of the empty space between the book-leaves and the wall in a full-size library. "It was clear to me from the outset," said the artist, "that my proposal had to be simple, monumental, poetic and non-literal. I am a sculptor. Not a person of words but of images and forms", and she added that

the sculpture "functions both as a private and a public space" (Young, 2004, p. 167). It is a public memorial, measuring ten metres in one direction, seven in another, and almost four metres high. Its outer surface is the rough negative space next to the edges of book leaves. A closed double-wing door, cast inside out and inaccessible, faces the square. The site is the Judenplatz in Vienna, where a synagogue was burned down in a pogrom in 1421, followed by hundreds of murders. The shopkeepers nearby wanted the archaeological excavations, seen through a window from above, to represent the more recent murders of Austrian Jews as well. A petition against Whiteread's memorial, referring to the lost parking and potential for lost revenue, gathered 2,000 signatures. Today, the only memorial to the medieval massacre, next to an image of Jesus being baptised, is an inscription in Latin that reads: "The flame of hate arose in 1421, raged through the entire city, and punished the terrible crimes of the Hebrew dogs" (p. 169). Since Austria had been occupied by Germany, its Nazi past had found little place in its historical self-image. It looked like the memorial would never be built, though a compromise was finally found, by moving the monument one metre so as to make room for the excavations. Fittingly addressing the discontent associated with the reintroduction of a long-suppressed Jewish memory into Austria's civic landscape, Robert Storr wrote: "Whiteread's work is the solid shape of an intangible absence—of a gap in a nation's identity, and a hollow at a city's heart" (Young, 2004, p. 169). Rachel Whiteread's memorial presents a void made visible. It calls forth an object that is remote, impenetrable, one that does not respond to the spectator, but seems to withdraw, inert and mute, looming large, though remaining not there, a non-object.

After the First World War new antirealist and fragmentary artistic forms appeared, relating to the recent experiences of terror. Darian Leader comments on how, in the process of mourning as described by Freud, our memories and hopes about a lost loved one are brought up again in all the different ways they are registered; we run through them time and time again, arranging and rearranging them. Similarly, in a cubist image, "the model becomes equivalent to a series of fragments seen from different points" (2008, p. 29), different angles and aspects of a human being are reassembled as a collection of different perspectives. In these art works we are presented with a fragmented, shattered object. But in the three sculptures or monuments I have referred to in this chapter, Gormley's, Eisenman's and Whiteread's, we seem not quite to be presented with an object at all. Rather, it is as if you, as the spectator, become the object in relation to them, as an embodied, physical being. With all these three sculptures, you relate to them physically as a spectator, while you relate to something that does not relate to you, that seems rather to withdraw from you, or at times to close you in—these pieces do not respond to you; they confound your attempts at making sense. They are not mimetic in the sense of depicting something recognisable. Rather, the spectator is the one who is put in the position of doing the *mimesis*, as the monuments evoke in you some of the sensations—physical and mental—described in the opening of this chapter.

Adorno meditates on how the separation between subject and object, when fixed without mediation, becomes ideology, and the mind arrogates to itself the status of absolute independence, announcing its claim to domination: "Once radically separated from the object, subject reduces the object to itself; subject swallows object, forgetting how much it is object itself." (1998b, p. 246) Thus the subject's enforced claim to sovereignty does violence to one's own being as an object and also to the other, whose difference is eliminated. The epistemic violence of reducing the other to the same, to being identical with what has already been encountered, precedes the physical brutality of destruction. In other words, in prejudice, stereotyping, reification, objectification, the other is rendered as mere sameness, a mental appropriation that parallels its annihilation, hence: "Genocide is the absolute integration" (1996, p. 362). Such identity thinking can take the form of idealism, absolutising the subject or, conversely, a seemingly anti-subjectivist, scientifically objective positivism or reductivism (1998b, p. 252). Instead, a non-destructive relationship between subject and object would lie in a state of differentiation without domination, a dialogue between the two. When the subject, passively and without anxiety entrusts itself to its own experience, it can realise that it is the agent, not the constituent, of object, separate, and yet dependent: "In the places where subjective reason senses subjective contingency, the primacy of the object shimmers through: that in the object which is not a subjective addition" (1998b, p. 254).

To relate these reflections to the themes of trauma and mourning, in a modish slogan, states Adorno, "working through the past" is given the contrary meaning of closing the books on the past, or even remove it from memory (1998a, p. 89). Thus the innocent sounding dictum is appropriated for the purpose of killing those murdered a second time, through the destruction of memory, by de-realising the past into a figment of the imagination. "One wants to break free of the past: rightly, because nothing at all can live in its shadow, and because there will be no end to the terror as long as guilt and violence are repaid with guilt and violence; wrongly, because the past that one would like to evade is still very much alive" (p. 89).

The question of mourning as finished or unfinished has been discussed by Judith Butler, who comments on how Freud's conceptualisation of the process in *Mourning and Melancholia* was altered in *The Ego and the Id* with the notion of identification as a way of preserving the object, indicating that the attachment is never-ending (1997, pp. 133–134). In the earlier essay Freud had supposed that the lost object had been set up again inside the ego, so as to replace the tie to the object with an identification.

At that time, however, "we did not appreciate the full significance of this process and did not know how common and how typical it is. Since then we have come to understand that this kind of substitution has a great share in determining the form taken by the ego and that it makes an essential contribution toward building up what is called its 'character'". He concludes this discussion by speculating that "it may be that this identification is the sole condition under which the id can give up its objects [...] it makes it possible to suppose that the character of the ego is a precipitate of abandoned object-cathexes and that it contains the history of those object-choices." What Freud here calls the "character of the ego" appears to be the sedimentation of objects loved and lost, the archaeological remainder, as it were, of unresolved grief (Butler, 1997, p. 133).

In this latter version the emphasis has changed from a resolution of grief through a dismantling of emotional ties and a making of new ones to new objects to incorporation as a form of preserving the object— a paradoxical resolution of letting go and not letting go. In a letter to Binswanger, Freud wrote in 1929:

> We will never find a substitute. No matter what may fill the gap, even if it be filled completely, it nevertheless remains something else. And actually, this is how it should be, it is the only way of perpetuating that love which we do not want to relinquish. (Leader, 2008, p. 98)

In relation to the memorials we have been discussing, "It may be that the finished monument," Young suggests, "completes memory itself, puts a cap on memory-work and draws a bottom line"—a reading of "working-through" that constitutes forgetting, so that: "the surest engagement with Holocaust memory in Germany might actually lie in its perpetual irresolution, that only an unfinished memorial process can guarantee the life of memory" (1993, p. 92). These monuments are increasingly seen by new generations, who were not here when the Holocaust happened, but who carry with them ghosts from generations past.

The cubist art works of Braque and Picasso may be thought of as representing fragmentation as the result of trauma, thus pointing backwards to a shattering event, or as Leader suggests, the ongoing work of mourning as a reshuffling or rearranging, where the model "becomes equivalent to a series of fragments seen from different points, a process that seems to embody Freud's notion of a person being mourned through our piecemeal collection of our representations of them" (2008, p. 29). The monuments we have been discussing convey the unfinished in a different sense, as they are unfinished without the spectator's revisiting of them, or rather participating in them—cast in a position of being addressed by an overwhelming, confusing absence, one is made to sense being dropped, being trapped, being lost, and of non-responsiveness; of speaking to someone who neither listens nor answers. "Perennial suffering has as much right to expression as a tortured man has to scream" (Adorno, 1996, p. 362)—and it is as sensorial beings, as creatures that are objects as well as subjects, as potentially vulnerable and experiencing beings, that we may take the risk and allow ourselves to hear them.

References

Adorno, T. W. (1996). Negative Dialectics. London: Routledge.

Adorno, T. W. (1998a). The meaning of working through the past. In: Critical Models. Interventions and Catchwords (pp. 89–103). New York: Columbia University Press.

Adorno, T. W. (1998b). On subject and object. In: Critical Models. Interventions and Catchwords (pp. 245–258). New York: Columbia University Press.

Auestad, L. (2012). Subjectivity and absence: prejudice as a psycho-social theme. In: L. Auestad (Ed.), Psychoanalysis and Politics: Exclusion and the Politics of Representation. London: Karnac.

Auestad, L. (2015). Respect, Plurality, and Prejudice. A Psychoanalytical and Philosophical Enquiry into the Dynamics of Social Exclusion and Discrimination. London: Karnac.

Balint, M. (1969). Trauma and object-relationship. International Journal of Psychoanalysis, 50: 429–435.

Bick, E. (1968). The experience of the skin in early object-relations. International Journal of Psychoanalysis, 49: 484–486.

Bion, W. R. (1962). A theory of thinking. In: Second Thoughts (pp. 110–119). London: Karnac.

Brown, L. J. (2005). The cognitive effects of trauma: reversal of alpha function and the formation of a beta screen. Psychoanalytic Quarterly, 74(2).

Butler, J. (1997). The Psychic Life of Power. Theories in Subjection. Stanford, CA: Stanford University Press.

Ferenczi, S. (1988). The Clinical Diary of Sándor Ferenczi. J. Dupont (Ed.). Cambridge, MA: Harvard University Press.

Ferenczi, S. (1994). Notes and fragments. In: Final Contributions to the Problems and Methods of Psycho-Analysis (pp. 216–297). London: Karnac.

Freud, S. (1908e). Creative Writers and Day-Dreaming. S. E., 9: 143. London: Hogarth.

Freud, S. (1911b). Formulations on the Two Principles of Mental Functioning. S. E., 12: 215. London: Hogarth.

Freud, S. (1920g). Beyond the Pleasure Principle. S. E., 18: 7. London: Hogarth.

Fuerstenau, M. (2010). Five years on, Berlin Holocaust Memorial is a landmark of remembrance. In: Deutsche Welle 10 May. http://www.dw.com/en/five-years-on-berlin-holocaust-memorial-is-a-landmark-of-remembrance/a-5559425-1.

Harding, L. (2005). 60 years on, Berlin honours Hitler's victims. In: The Guardian 11 May. http://www.theguardian.com/world/2005/may/11/secondworldwar.germany.

Klein, M. (1929). Infantile anxiety-situations reflected in a work of art and in the creative impulse. In: Love, Guilt and Reparation. New York: Seymour Lawrence.

Leader, D. (2008). The New Black. London: Hamish Hamilton.

Winnicott, D. W. (1962). Ego integration in child development. In: The Maturational Processes and the Facilitating Environment. New York: International Universities Press, 1965.

Winnicott, D. W. (1963). Fear of breakdown. In: Psycho-Analytic Explorations. London: Karnac, 1989.

Winnicott, D. W. (1971). Playing and Reality. London: Routledge.

Young, J. E. (1993). The Texture of Memory. Holocaust Memorials and Meaning. New Haven, CT: Yale University Press.

Young, J. E. (2000). At Memory's Edge. After-Images of the Holocaust in Contemporary Art and Architecture. New Haven, CT: Yale University Press.

Young, J. E. (2004). Rachel Whiteread Judenplatz Memorial in Vienna. Memory and absence. In: C. Townsend (Ed.), The Art of Rachel Whiteread. London: Thames & Hudson.

CHAPTER THREE

To mend the world—trauma, mourning, and containment

Jonathan Davidoff

He wrote me that in the suburbs of Tokyo there is a temple consecrated to cats. I wish I could convey to you the simplicity—the lack of affectation—of this couple who had come to place an inscribed wooden slat in the cat cemetery so their cat Tora would be protected. No she wasn't dead, only ran away. But on the day of her death no one would know how to pray for her, how to intercede with death so that he would call her by her right name. So they had to come there, both of them, under the rain, to perform the rite that would repair the web of time where it had been broken.

—*Marker*, 1983

The main objective of Emil Fackenheim's 1982 work *To Mend the World* is to lay the foundations of a post-Holocaust Jewish thought. This work's urgency is to confront the possibility of collapse of Jewish, Christian, and secular philosophies that results from the reality of Auschwitz and what was lost therein (Morgan et al; 2008). Fackenheim takes seriously Adorno's claim of the metaphysical capacity being arrested in Auschwitz and takes it to its last consequences.

On his part, Freud describes mourning as a process whereby "each single one of the memories and expectations in which the libido is bound to the lost object is brought up and hyper-cathected, and detachment of the libido is accomplished in respect of it" (Freud, 1917e, p. 245). Therefore Fackenheim's enterprise may be understood as an instance of such a work as it revisits the history and historicity of the Holocaust. It outlines the impact of what was irremediably lost in the Holocaust—almost to the point of total collapse—and what can be repaired and clung to that may serve as the means to survive the abyss left by the titanic loss.

In order to reflect on the scope of Fackenheim's thought as a work of mourning, I will follow Fackenheim's steps by exploring his preliminary considerations regarding the pre-Holocaust state of things in Jewish thought. Then, I will explore Fackenheim's confrontation of the Holocaust proper, comprising the logic of destruction of Auschwitz as well as the instances, which according to Fackenheim, prevent thought from collapsing totally, namely the acts of resistance to the logic of destruction of Auschwitz understood as acts of *tikkun olam*.

I conclude by interrogating the scope of Fackenheim's work in terms of a philosophical act of mourning understood as an act of reparation of the container. Furthermore, I explore the hitherto unacknowledged essential role that hope plays in working through trauma and in the acts of *tikkun olam*.

Fackenheim's systematic activity of thought

From the outset, it is clear that Fackenheim believes that the Holocaust had strong enough implications so as to think of a post-Holocaust state of things in Jewish thought, and therefore in Christian and Western secular philosophies as well. In an earlier stage of his thought, Fackenheim's objective was to create a philosophical system based on Jewish philosophical principles, but he abandoned that endeavour due to his later agreement with Martin Buber's (1965) ideas on the Jewish take on revelation. A philosophical system, such as Hegel's *The Phenomenology of Spirit* (1807), is possible when it is thought that all things can be explained, which in Jewish theological terms amounts to a complete revelation. However, Fackenheim follows Buber in that Jewish revelation is necessarily open-ended, incomplete, and, therefore, bound to a work of interpretation that would come to an end at revelation's completion. It follows that an all-encompassing Jewish philosophical system is impossible under these circumstances. What Fackenheim believes possible is, however, a systematic activity of thought.

In this sense, *To Mend the World* interrogates the conditions of possibility for Jewish religion and philosophy being systematically thought in the late twentieth-century particularly after the Holocaust. The main question is, can the Holocaust be thought of systematically without thought collapsing in the attempt of doing so? Fackenheim asserts that there is a gulf between the pre- and post-Holocaust states of things. Jewish, Christian, and secular philosophies, according to Fackenheim, are threatened with collapse by the realities with which the Holocaust confronts them.

Fackenheim begins by describing the state of things in Jewish thought before the Holocaust. Therefore, he explores the philosophies of two modern Jewish thinkers, namely Baruch Spinoza and Franz Rosenzweig. Simultaneously, he introduces some of Hegel's philosophy as a necessary link between these two Jewish thinkers. Fackenheim criticises many aspects of Spinoza's philosophy, in particular those that result from Spinoza's assertion that Jews ought to become "men-in-general, inhabitants of the liberal state" (Fackenheim, 1982, p. 57) and the inevitable rejection of Jewish revelation that this implies.

Fackenheim's take on Rosenzweig has a very different tone, and his exploration of Rosenzweig's main philosophical work, *The Star of Redemption*, leads him to affirm that Rosenzweig's post-Hegelianism is visible in that *The Star of Redemption* is the dialectical opposite of *The Phenomenology of Spirit*. I cannot go into detail about Fackenheim's careful description, explanation, and contrast of the ideas of these authors; I will only point out three main aspects of it.

First, Fackenheim finds the configurations of Rosenzweig's tripartite structure of elements (God, Man, World) central to contrast the Star of Redemption with Spinoza's and Hegel's thought. These elements "are not arbitrary postulates [...] they are the positive result of the demonstrated failure of more than two millennia of Western metaphysics to reduce all things, respectively, to 'God', 'World' and 'Man'" (Fackenheim, 1982, p. 65). Each of these elements, explains Fackenheim, is posited by Rosenzweig as a "Not-Yet, i.e. ontologically occult powers which are not, but as it were, *strive* to be. And to this ontological status, corresponds, epistemologically, a 'knowledge' that remains ignorance until the striving-to-be has *revealed itself as being*" (Fackenheim, 1982, p. 68).

Second, Fackenheim distinguishes his work from the "old thinking" embodied mainly in the old rabbinic philosophical tradition and places it along Rosenzweig's "new thinking" (1999). The old thinking, to some extent, causes Spinoza's antagonism to Jewish religion. Rosenzweig's new thinking, as opposed to the old thinking, on the one hand does not rely on old recognised authorities, which makes it un-fanatical. And on the other hand, each of the elements of the tripartite configuration (Man, God and World) keeps its singular place instead of "Man and God being dissipated into World (ancient period), Man and World into God (medieval period), and God and World into Man (modern period)" (Fackenheim, 1982, p. 64).

And third, the particular dialectics between Judaism and Christianity that Rosenzweig describes in *The Star of Redemption* as a relation of mutual necessity and a sort of complementariness, contrasts with Spinoza's claims of Jews having to become men-in-general, that is, Jews undistinguishable from Christians. This comparison between Spinoza's and Rosenzweig's thought is what Fackenheim feels to be the necessary step to bring about a pre-Holocaust state of things of Jewish thought.

Almost at once, when discussing the preliminary details of the Holocaust, Fackenheim introduces some of Martin Heidegger's (1962) thought. He calls Heidegger's affiliation to the Nazi party, however brief and disputed, an academic scandal. Furthermore, Fackenheim condemns ruthlessly Heidegger's bystanding of the victimisation of his hitherto friend and professor, Edmund Husserl, and his subsequent failure to account philosophically for the Holocaust. Notwithstanding, Fackenheim finds Heidegger's philosophy essential to understand the gulf that the Holocaust opened in Jewish, Christian and secular thought.

In *The Star of Redemption* (2005) Rosenzweig depicts the Jewish relation to history as "a vigil for redemption", hence the cyclical and unaffected cannons of Jewish calendar and festivals. However, to Rosenzweig's mind, thought needs to undergo "school with life". This is an influence coming from a well-known Hegelian principle: the owl of Minerva will spread its wings at dusk, that is, knowledge is possible only *a posteriori*. Therefore, thought can never be detached from events, neither can it precede or prescribe them. So, Jews seem to hold a vigil for redemption that places them "outside of history" on the one hand, but on the other, thought cannot detach itself from history and can only come about a posteriori. Thus Rosenzweig sets forth this complex relation between Jewish religion and time, both outside and inside history. Nevertheless, he does seem to think that in Jewish history, only redemption could be a true event. Rosenzweig wrote this before the Holocaust, and therefore Fackenheim sharply rejects this idea by asserting that it cannot be ignored that, in the Holocaust, Jews were dragged back into history (Fackenheim, 1982).

Heidegger's ideas on history and historicity, which are not too dissimilar from Rosenzweig's account of the relation between Judaism and time, play an important role on the way Fackenheim believes a systematic activity of thought ought to be carried out for it to be *authentic*. According to Heidegger, in a stern and implacable fashion, history and historicity cannot be detached from one another without falling into inauthenticity. In other words, history, an idea of time "seen from the outside" as it were, cannot be detached from historicity, that is, the dimension of existence, that is, of Dasein's being-toward-death. To do so, would mean avoiding the confrontation of the anxiety proper of existence, and above all, the finitude that death is for Dasein.

Furthermore, Fackenheim's reading of Heidegger's notion of transcendence is central to his account. Fackenheim explains that being-towards-death, or the finitude of Dasein, is one of the sources of anxiety, which can be either avoided by recourse to inauthenticity or confronted. Confronting anxiety implies confronting finitude, that is, being-towards-death. Fackenheim believes this is the way to transcendence, which can, however, be avoided by falling into inauthenticity. When it comes to history and historicity, the same can be said: thought can flight into history-in-general as an avoidance of historicity, that is, the finite dimension of temporality. The condition of possibility of transcendence, however, lays precisely in the authentic existence, in facing finitude and death. Therefore, an authentic transcendence of time means both to remain *immersed in* time as well as to *rise above it*. In Rosenzweig's words, this would amount to remain outside of history, but undergoing school with life as well. The contrast of Rosenzweig's and Heidegger's ideas of temporality, historicity and transcendence, serve to lay the ground on which, according to Fackenheim, the Holocaust must be confronted.

Auschwitz: impossible systematic and authentic activity of thought

Fackenheim asserts that to feel that the Holocaust has in any way been transcended means to do without its historicity, and therefore, to lapse into inauthentic thought. According to Fackenheim, to test if the putative gulf of the Holocaust can be traversed by thought, first and foremost, the historicity of Auschwitz needs to be confronted by thought. It is this enterprise that, Fackenheim fears, arrests thought and makes it collapse. How can the historicity of Auschwitz be confronted by thought if, following Adorno, the metaphysical capacity of thought is arrested in Auschwitz? Thought sees itself overwhelmed by Auschwitz and its natural tendency is to recoil from thinking about it. However, the alternative is for Jewish, Christian, and secular thought to collapse into senselessness, for on what basis topics like evil, good, human dignity, victimhood, criminality, justice, ethics and morals could be thought thence? Fackenheim explains that:

> *After* Auschwitz, [human dignity] can no longer be believed, for
> [...] humanity was destroyed in [the victim and the perpetrator]—
> the good will of both was destroyed as well, and with it the right
> to the dignity of the human being as such. After this, the value of
> humanity has therefore become questionable, and this radically
> and forever: the destruction of humanity remains possible, for in
> Auschwitz it was actual. Elie Wiesel [1968] has therefore rightly
> said that the Holocaust destroyed not only human beings but also
> the idea of humanity. (Fackenheim, 1982, p. 65)

Fackenheim reflects briefly in the preliminary considerations section on the language that, he believes, is necessary to use when speaking of the Holocaust. I believe this is something important to highlight. He explains that "the *facts themselves* are outrageous; it is they that must speak through our language. And this is possible only if one's feelings are subject to a disciplined restraint. The language necessary, then, is one of sober, restrained but at the same time, unyielding outrage" (Fackenheim, 1982, p. 28).

Fackenheim's reflection on Auschwitz is careful, detailed and considers the many possible arguments and counter-arguments of each step and each assertion about it. I will explore only the skeleton of it, and focus on the main pillars of his ideas.

First, Fackenheim asserts that the extermination of non-Aryans, in particular Jews and Gypsies, was the corollary and true core of the Third Reich. The proof of this, according to Fackenheim, is that when Nazis were losing the battle in the eastern front, more trains were nevertheless sent to Auschwitz so as to accelerate the extermination of the

Jewish population. Thus Auschwitz, observes Fackenheim, was the Third Reich's priority.

Fackenheim believes Auschwitz to be a world in its own right and with its own logic; rightly called "planet Auschwitz" by some survivors. The logic of the Auschwitz world was "a logic of destruction", and this makes it a precedent-less *novum* in history. It is a well-known fact that the whole purpose of Auschwitz was to exterminate non-Aryans. The sin of the victims was being, and therefore nothing could prevent their death. Fackenheim paraphrases Primo Levi and explains that as soon as the victims arrived to the camps:

> they [were] overcome before they [could] adapt themselves; they [were] beaten by time, they [did] not begin to learn German, to disentangle the infernal knot of laws and prohibitions until their body [was] already in decay, and nothing [could] save them from selection or from death by exhaustion. (Fackenheim, 1982, p. 99)

Thus, there were from the outset contradicting and absurd rules to which the prisoners who were not murdered instantly were forced to comply. For example, the arch in the entrance of Auschwitz read: "work sets free"; prisoners had to be perfectly shaved while having no razors; perfectly clean while having no soap or running water; it was forbidden to defecate during work, and so forth. Dysentery was a common illness in the camps, and not being able to defecate led prisoners to what became known as "excremental assault". Of course, the punishment for disobedience of these contradicting rules was death. These rules drove common sense to insanity and were not randomly set, but were purposely designed so as to lead prisoners to feel contempt and disgust for themselves and their fellows (Fackenheim, 1982). Fackenheim quotes Pelagia Lewinska (1968), a noble Polish Christian woman who was sent to Auschwitz, and who, to Fackenheim's mind, grasped perfectly Auschwitz's logic of destruction:

> At the outset the living places, the ditches, the mud, the piles of excrement behind the blocks, had appalled me with their horrible filth ... And then I saw the light! I saw that it was not a question of disorder or lack of organisation but that, on the contrary, a very thoroughly considered conscious idea was in the back of the camp's existence. They had condemned us to die in our own filth, to

drown in mud, in our own excrement. They wished to abase us, to destroy our human dignity, to efface every vestige of humanity ... to fill us with horror and contempt toward ourselves and our fellows. (Fackenheim, 1982, p. 25)

Fackenheim tried to grasp the innermost essence of Auschwitz, and explores "medical" experiments performed on victims, or the idea of babies drowned in buckets or thrown to the flames of the crematoriums without being gassed first. But this seemed insufficient to account for the absolute novelty and uniqueness of Auschwitz's logic of destruction. According to Fackenheim, "the most original, most characteristic product of the entire Nazi Reich were the *Muselmänner*, the downed ... and anonymous mass ... of non-men who march and labour in silence, the divine spark dead within them ..." (Fackenheim, 1982, p. 25). The so-called *Muselmann* is the most characteristic prisoner of Auschwitz: the senseless, wandering man whose skin-and-bones image haunts thought and understanding. Primo Levi wrote about the *Muselmänner*: "one hesitates to call them living; one hesitates to call their death death" (Levi, 1989, p. 82). It is the *Muselmann*, the core and epitome of Nazism: the man who has been robbed of transcendence, for his death and the consciousness of it has been taken away from him; and whose divine spark and dignity, have also been extinguished; in short, a man who is a no-man. The *Muselmann* could not repent, rebel, or become a martyr for he has been purposely deprived of choice and consciousness. It is in this sense that humanity was, in fact, destroyed in Auschwitz. It is here where the metaphysical capacity of thought collapses.

In Fackenheim words, when trying to confront the historicity of Auschwitz "we reach an impasse with the question of whether perhaps no thought can be where the Holocaust is; whether perhaps all thought is 'paralysed' vis-à-vis that event; and whether perhaps paralysis at this catastrophic point calls into question significant post-Holocaust thought everywhere" (Fackenheim, 1982, p. 249).

But Fackenheim interrogates this even further, because he believes that the limit of philosophical intelligibility is not the limit of all thought. He explains: "the circular thought movement that fails produces a result in its very failure, for it grasps, to the extent possible, *a whole*" (Fackenheim, 1982, p. 238). Hegel's philosophy is the best example of this, and in Hegel's view, once this whole is grasped it is comprehended, transcended and the meaning of it is perceived from a higher standpoint by putting it in perspective. But the whole of the Holocaust is a whole of horror that we cannot comprehend, but only comprehend its incomprehensibility; "we cannot transcend it but only be struck by the brutal truth that it cannot be transcended" (Fackenheim, 1982, p. 238).

Resistance as a novum

In this sense, it becomes clear that the gulf that the Holocaust opened by means of destroying humanity cannot be fully breached and overcome. But Fackenheim furthers:

> One asks: why did so many become Muselmänner? One ought to ask: How did even one *not* become a Muselmann? The logic of destruction was irresistible: then how was it, nevertheless, resisted? […] The demands of the bowels overcame them; yet some washed in water that made them no cleaner, or attempted to shave, to comb their hair. Why did they do it? How could they do it? (Fackenheim, 1982, p. 217)

Fackenheim finds acts of resistance to the logic of destruction the only possible way for thought to traverse the gulf, and therefore they are ultimate. Fackenheim posits resistance during the Holocaust as a *novum* in history. It was a way of holding fast to human dignity and therefore it was a way of being authentically. For Fackenheim's thought, in the here and now, resistance is an ontological category that was *ontic*, there and then.

Fackenheim explores different acts of resistance: the uprisings of the Warsaw ghetto and Sobibor extermination camp; the explosion of Treblinka's crematoriums by the prisoners, the Jewish and Christian partisans, and so forth. He explores each case and considers whether each of these can be thought of as resistance in this sense. But, there is a kind of act of resistance in particular that Fackenheim finds worthy of attention: old Hassidic rabbis who traded bread in exchange for phylacteries in Buchenwald concentration camp; a group of women who fasted on Yom Kippur (the Day of Atonement) while being prisoners in Auschwitz; or a group of Hassidic Jews who, before being killed outside Lublin by the SS officer Glowoznik, danced ecstatically while praying for redemption. These acts are of significant importance and now we turn to them.

In 1943 in Germany, there was a group of German students called the White Rose, led by philosophy professor Kurt Huber, which distributed anti-Nazi propaganda. They knew that their actions were futile, that they were going to be caught, judged, and put to death. Indeed, in the final statement of his trial, Huber claimed that they were acting in responsibility for all Germany; that their act was not illegal but rather an attempt to restore legality, and he quoted Fichte:

> And act thou shalt as though
> The destiny of all things German
> Depended on you and your lonely acting,
> And the responsibility were yours. (Fackenheim, 1982)

According to Fackenheim, Huber and the White Rose did, in fact, restore legality in Germany, *ontically* then and there, and *ontologically* here and now. From Huber's quote of Fichte, we infer that Huber acted with full consciousness of his and the White Rose's actions. Indeed, he knew that all things depended on his actions and the responsibility was his. Fackenheim observes that "the Idea of Man can be—has been—destroyed, for humanity can be—has been—destroyed. But because of humanity itself has been mended—*in* some men and women *by* some men and women—the Idea of Man can be mended" (Fackenheim, 1982, p. 276).

These acts—in different measures, senses, and fashions—restored partially what was broken, namely humanity, human dignity, the divine spark of Man or the Idea of Man. It is paramount to keep in mind that this restoration is partial, the gulf can never be fully breached, and that something unthinkable became actual then and forever. Can philosophy ever go back to being what it was? Fackenheim believes that this question will be answered by the action of recovery and reinterpretation of the old in the light of the new.

Resistance *as* tikkun olam

Fackenheim explains that Huber's actions were given strength by the Idea of Man, and in turn, they gave strength to that Idea itself—this is dialectic worthy of exploration. This same dialectic exists between the owl of Minerva that flies at dusk and the cock that announces sunrise; that is, thought that precedes and determines events, and thought that comes after events and is determined by them. An idea that determines an action, and in turn, an action that determines an idea, is the dialectic of the Kabbalistic notion of "mending the world" or *tikkun olam*.

Kabbalah is the mystic discipline of Judaism. In it, symbols have a metaphysical reference and they are not figures of speech as they are in mainstream Judaic texts. Rabbi Leon Luria is one of the main Kabbalistic thinkers who developed the idea of *tikkun olam*. According to Luria, God created nothingness so that space could exist for something to be there. Therefore God squeezed himself into a point so that creation could be possible. This is called *tsimtsum* or contraction, and preceded the emanation of divine light from God who was in a state of absolute contraction. The light emanated was contained in a vessel. This vessel, however, could not contain the divine light and therefore creation amounted to the fragmentation of the vessel and the spilling of its contents. The fragments of the vessel, when in a state of brokenness and scatter, are, according to the Kabbalistic account, the source of evil, for they amount to fragments of chaotic uncontained divine energy (Scholem, 1965a, 1965b).

An act of *tikkun olam*, or mending the world, restores order where hitherto was chaos. It restores a fragment of the vessel and liberates a fragment of divine light that returns to its container. The belief is that enough acts of *tikkun olam* might fully repair the broken vessel, thus containing God again and precipitating redemption. This may sound like magical thinking to the secular mind; nevertheless, it can be read as a metaphysical account of what in psychoanalysis is meant with the notions of container, contained and reparation.

Supported by the figure of thought of the divine vessel, the acts of restoration of fragments of the vessel amount to containment for they entail a movement towards growth. In this case, containment amounts to the meeting of container and contained as well as the reparation of the very container whose state of brokenness is intrinsic to it. If we take the description of a world where broken, essentially evil fragments are to be reintegrated to a main vessel, container, or object, we can clearly recognise the uncanny similarity to the paranoid-schizoid world of split and uncontained elements described by psychoanalyst Melanie Klein (1946) and further outlined by her disciple Wilhelm Bion (Berke, 1996). Bion himself argued, "Tikkun is an age-old myth which was transformed by the genius of the revolutionary mystic Isaac Luria" (Lutzky, 1989, p. 500).

In the Kabbalistic account, the divine, the cosmic, and the historical are broken. Man shares this brokenness with the cosmic, and Fackenheim explains that "it is precisely if the rupture, or the threat of it, is total, that all powers must be summoned for a mending. If the threat is to man, there is need to invoke divine as well as human power" (Fackenheim, 1982, p. 253); and vice versa, that is, human power may aid the divine if a rupture is visited upon it. Fackenheim exemplifies this notion by quoting Gershom Scholem who believes that "the impulse below calls forth an impulse from above" (Scholem, 1965b, p. 270). Thus the dialectic *of tikkun olam* becomes visible, and thus retrospectively we understand that the Idea of Man aided Huber in his actions and his actions aided the Idea of Man, nay, his actions mended or repaired the idea of Man. Otherwise put, the divine spark of man motivated Huber's actions, and in turn, this very action restored the divine spark of man. Huber's trial, explains Fackenheim, was the most important trial in philosophy since Socrates' trial, and Huber's act of *tikkun olam*, like the other acts of resistance to Auschwitz, are therefore a *novum* in history.

Kabbalistic thinkers would assert that this *tikkun* perhaps redeemed fully those who died. But Fackenheim does not go that far. He explains, "we must accept from the start that at most only a fragmentary *tikkun* is possible. This is because we are situated in the post-Holocaust world and we must accept our situatedness. We must live with it." (Fackenheim, 1982, p. 256) Fackenheim, therefore, does not share the idea of *tikkun olam* of the Kabbalah *stricto sensu*. However, he chooses its ethical dimension to be what must cross the abyss of Auschwitz: "a philosophical *tikkun* (mending) is possible nowadays because a philosophical *tikkun* already took place in the Holocaust itself" (Fackenheim, 1982, p. 266). Thus he asserts that the *tikkun* is not only "possible", but also "necessary", and it is ethical in this sense. It is, in my view, Fackenheim's urgent answer to the question, how can we not resist it today, if it was indeed resisted there and then?

To mend the world as mourning

The loss in the Holocaust was such that it was almost absolute. Therefore, I believe that no mourning will ever do. In psychoanalytic terms, this might strike us as a melancholic statement, for it singles the Holocaust as an object in history that cannot be totally mourned. In other words, the Holocaust exceeds not only what can be thought systematically and authentically, but also what can be mourned. This is so because to mourn the Holocaust would imply to posit humanity or the Idea of Man as a "mournable object", that is, to place this object within the series of objects that can be lost. This is perhaps one of the few objects that, in Fackenheim's and my own viewpoint, cannot be lost. This viewpoint, however, can be disputed by many other philosophies that consider that we can do without, and in fact we actually do without the Idea of Man or of humanity. In this sense, the retreat of metaphysics in the twentieth century may hold an intimate dialectic with the Holocaust, and perhaps the Holocaust was possible insofar as the Idea of Man had been already abandoned, lost, or damaged prior to it.

In a normal process of mourning the object is finally decathected and the libidinal energy hitherto invested in it, is released to cathect other objects. But in the case of the Holocaust the nature of the almost total loss would have entailed the loss of hope in humanity and, perhaps, life in general. Paradoxically, if this work of mourning succeeded, we would fall in metaphysical despair for we would have to come to terms with the death of humanity. In psychoanalytic terms, this would mean coming to terms with having no good object left, no container, and no containment possible. This devastating reality and the impossibility to mourn it, indeed, lock us almost completely in a melancholic state. It leads us to affirm that the Holocaust can mostly be remembered, or re-introjected, as one of the darkest periods of history, wherein understanding and mourning will collapse ever anew. Perhaps Fackenheim's suggestion of using a language of outrage keeps the Holocaust at a distance that allows for the self not to collapse in it.

However, the attempt itself to authentically confront the Holocaust can be thought as a work of mourning that, albeit fragmentarily, provides a means for surviving the total collapse. First, to single out the object that cannot be mourned confines the collapse, in this case, to the Idea of Man. The Idea of World and God are kept untouched enough so as to be able to assert that "an impulse below may call forth an impulse from above" (Scholem, 1965b, p. 270). This assertion can be disputed, as the questions of the presence of God and the caring of the World during the Holocaust is engraved particularly in the survivors' memory, or presumably in the thoughts of the countless who committed suicide or despaired. Furthermore, perhaps a damage visited upon one element of this triad entails damaging the others. However, one could hold on to the partial un-touchedness of God and World, as destroying these two, according to Fackenheim, was not necessarily the primary goal of the Third Reich. These two elements of the triad, to some extent, give to the acts of mending the Idea of Man a source of power and thrust. In the example of Kurt Huber's trial, World was understood as Germany, and mending Germany was perhaps as important as to mend legality and human dignity.

The acts of resistance are the true kernel of Fackenheim's contribution as they are the only and ultimate way of preventing the total collapse. We have learned that resistance as an ontological category and the acts of resistance there and then understood as *tikkun olam*, call for acts of resistance in the here and now and allow to cross the gulf of the Holocaust. In this sense, the loss is not total, but partial, as there is a continuum in what otherwise would be an unbreachable abyss. The recognition of the possible mending and its limits makes of Fackenheim's work an effective act of mourning, for, in this sense, the self survives the loss. But given that surviving the total collapse means resisting the Holocaust as an ethical imperative, the only way of surviving it, today, is by keep resisting it. That is why Fackenheim adds a 614th commandment to the canonical Jewish law: "you will not grant Hitler any posthumous victories", that is, you ought to resist Auschwitz's logic of destruction forever (Fackenheim, 1982).

The notion of *tikkun olam* is a bridge between an individual symbolic act and its meddling in shared reality, hence its effectiveness. Fackenheim's work of mourning effectiveness, in this sense, comes from the act of reparation, albeit partial, of what was lost and damaged. The acts of resistance of Huber, the Hassidim in Buchenwald or the women in Auschwitz, individual as they were, affect us here and now. Fackenheim believes that this is so because they mended the Idea of Man then and there for us here and now. Therefore, these acts of resistance are good examples of the private—or individual—becoming shared; that is, individual acts of *tikkun olam* that mend The Idea of Man for all mankind.

The role of hope in tikkun *and trauma*

Notwithstanding, Fackenheim also emphasises that something was lost in Auschwitz, then and forever. In this sense, philosophy does not collapse totally, but it cannot breach the gulf totally by means of a systematic activity of thought either. Has then philosophy breached the gulf opened by Auschwitz or not? Has philosophy done so partially? Can one breach a gulf partially without actually drowning all the same? The fact that resistance cannot stop because the threat of collapse has not stopped is Fackenheim's answer to this. My answer to this, however, is that in order to cross the gulf that Auschwitz opened in history, philosophy and the activity of thought need to leap.

To my mind, in Fackenheim's work, the leap consists of shifting from systematically thinking the logic of destruction of Auschwitz to systematically thinking the acts of resistance to it. This is visible in his negatively formulated question: How can we not resist Auschwitz here and now given that they resisted it then and there? A shift into the negative, a formulation of this question in the "no" is an act of resistance because it interdicts the alternative.

Whilst this may appear obvious, the question is why is this shift even worthy of making given that the Idea of Man, that which should be the very motivation to shift, is broken? In other words, the question is how and why to invoke what is broken? Where does the invocation force come from if it ought to come precisely from what is broken? I believe that the brokenness of the ideas of Man, God and World results in absolute solitude and despair. These are finely depicted in the book of Psalms (Tehillim) Chapter 121. The first line reads: "I raise my eyes to the hills, where will my aid come from?" The rest of the chapter assures the reader in different ways that aid will come from God the lengthy reassurance contrasts with the shortness of the moment of solitude; so much language deployed to contain such an experience.

The Auschwitz moment of solitude may last for a second, a lifetime or haunt philosophy forever. Rosenzweig's historical situatedness (prior to Auschwitz) makes his description of the three "not-yet" elements (God, Man and World) insufficient to account for the kind of absence of these Ideas prior to this particular kind of rupture. This brokenness is a novelty in history; the resulting solitude is so in no less measure. In order to mend this brokenness, the individual can only act *as if* the Idea of Man did precede and motivate the act of mending it; thereby the Idea of Man precedes the act a posteriori.

The *as-if* quality of these acts of mending must be understood with the outmost precision, for it does not mean "pretending" the Idea is not broken or that the act is not one of mending. They necessitate, in fact, the truest of convictions and the total consciousness of their brokenness. However, if the idea is broken, it must seem weak, unimportant, illogical, worthless of fighting for, and so forth (First, 1997). Therefore, they have to be acts of conviction motivated by very unconvincing ideas. Some may call them "acts of madness". Indeed, these acts defy logic, of dialectics and of common sense.

The acts of mending defy dialectics because there is a leap involved in them. The leap consists of acting as if the Idea preceded the act whilst knowing that this is impossible due to the brokenness of the Idea. But the individual leaps and acts nonetheless. I think this leap is under-pinned by what we understand as hope. To my mind this is what hope consists of: the expectancy of the impossible to come about, in this case, the reparation of the Idea of Man due to its impossible precession to the act of mending it. This impossibility and the entailing solitude and despair, however, are precisely the conditions of possibility of hope. Hope is therefore an inexplicable and awe provoking dialectical move-ment that defies dialectics altogether. It is an act that constitutes its antithetic predecessor a posteriori, except that this very movement is impossible without its predecessor. This makes it, to my mind, inexpli-cable (or "mad") because of the necessity to assume that the impossible can or has indeed happened.

Can we not say that clinically, a subject must also leap to work through trauma? In psychoanalysis there is a container that transcends the subject, that is, an object that exists beyond him. The object or con-tainer is vital for the subject: the container must call the contained. This is one of the implications of what in psychoanalysis is under-stood as primary maternal preoccupation (Winnicott, 1956) or reverie (Bion, 1963). But in the case of trauma, when the subject is in a state of despair (needing desperately the call of the object or container) and the container broken, how can containment come about? (Weather-ill, 1995; Ferro, 2006) How can a traumatised subject, whose internal or external objects have been shattered, nevertheless seek an object, repair it, and work through trauma? In order to work through trauma, the subject must repair a broken object or container, and in order to do so he needs the containment from the very object that is broken. Is there not a leap involved in this that is similar to the one described in the acts of *tikkun*?

There is a moment of mutual seeking, of object and subject, whereby they somehow meet, overcome their state of brokenness, repair each other, and precipitate containment and understanding. Is this not expli-cable, yet inexplicable?

Thus, there is a broken Man and a broken Idea that seek to mend each other, analogous to a traumatised subject and a shattered object that need and seek each other in order to work through. Both sides, albeit being perhaps the same thing, necessitate each other's calling, seeking, and aid. But this is not enough. An impossible leap that allows them to link and meet must be made. This is the only way to avoid the precipice that separates them and perpetuates the trauma or brokenness. Hope is, to my mind, the inexplicable and awe provoking leap that allows Fackenheim and every other subject who works through loss and trauma, to repair.

References

Berke, J. H. (1996). Psychoanalysis and Kabbalah. *Psychoanalytic Review, 83*(6): 849.

Bion, W. R. (1963). Elements of Psychoanalysis. In: *Seven Servants*. New York: Jason Aronson, 1977.

Buber, M. (1965). Between Man and Man. Boston, MA: Beacon.

Fackenheim, E. (1982). To Mend The World. Indianapolis, IN: Indiana University Press.

Ferro, A. (2006). Trauma, Reverie, and The Field. *Psychoanalytic Quarterly, 7*(4): 1045.

First, E. (1997). Irreparable objects—when there's nothing to mend: commentary on paper by Anne Alvarez. *Psychoanalytic Dialogues, 7*(6): 769.

Freud, S. (1917e). Mourning and Melancholia. *S. E., 14*: 239. London: Hogarth.

Hegel, G. W. F. (1807). The Phenomenology of Spirit. Oxford: Oxford University Press, 1977.

Heidegger, M. (1962). *Being and Time*. J. Macquarrie & E. Robinson (Trans.). New York: Harper & Row.

Klein, M. (1946). Some notes on schizoid mechanisms. International Journal of Psychoanalysis, 27: 99–110.

Levi, P. (1989). The Drowned and the Saved. R. Rosenthal (Trans.). New York: Vintage.

Lewinska, P. (1968). Twenty Months at Auschwitz. New York: Lyle Stuart.

Lutzky, H. (1989). Reparation and tikkun: a comparison of the Kleinian and Kabbalistic concepts. *International Review of Psycho-Analysis, 16*: 449–459.

Marker, C. (1983). *Sans Soleil*. Argos Films.

Morgan, M., & Pollock, B. (Eds.) (2008). The *philosopher* as *witness*. Fackenheim and *responses* to the Holocaust. Albany, NY: NY University Press.

Rosenzweig, F. (1999). *The New Thinking*. Alan Udoff & Barbara Galli (Trans.). Syracuse, NY: Syracuse University Press.

Rosenzweig, F. (2005). The Star of Redemption. Madison, WI: University of Wisconsin Press.

Scholem, G. (1965a). Major Trends in Jewish Mysticism. New York: Schoken.

Scholem, G. (1965b). On the Kabballah and its Symbolism. New York: Schoken.

Weatherill, R. (1995). Violence and privacy: what if the container fails? *Free Associations*, 5(2): 150.

Wiesel, E. (1968). Legends of Our Time. New York: Avon.

Winnicott, D. W. (1956). Primary maternal preoccupation. In: Collected Papers: Through Paediatrics to Psycho-Analysis (pp. 300–306). London: Tavistock, 1958.

CHAPTER FOUR

Holocaust survivor mothers and their daughters—the intergenerational mourning process as a journey in search of the mother

Edna Mor

"Trying to understand my mother is like picking up a book and starting in the middle," writes Schumer in her book *Motherland* (2000). The author, a journalist by profession, describes a journey with her mother to the small town in Germany where she was born. Her mother's parents sent her to the United States at the age of twelve, thereby saving her life. She did not speak about her past for fifty-four years.

During this visit, her mother for the first time openly wept for her parents, for other relatives who perished, for her lost home and her childhood. This was the first time that she accepted the fact that the loss was real and irreversible. She said to her daughter: "Until now they were still alive for me, they lived in me ... in my mind." During this trip the daughter discovered more and more details about her mother's past. For the first time she heard about her grandparents and they became flesh and blood people to her. Throughout the years the daughter felt that she had absorbed her mother's suffering, but these feelings were never put into words. To the daughter her mother always seemed distant and reserved, "as if she has developed a kind of fail-safe for her emotions". Relations between the mother and daughter became more emotional following this journey.

Several themes discussed in the professional literature about Holocaust survivors and the second generation are expressed in the story of this journey (Jucovy, 1992). Much has been written about the silence of Holocaust survivors (Adelman, 1995; Krell, 1979; Lichtman, 1984). Many of them felt that they had to devote all their energy to the struggle for survival and could not indulge in remembering and mourning. There was also a feeling that there was no one willing to listen. When they became parents they wanted to protect their children and spare them the knowledge of the horrors. In this framework I cannot go into the findings of studies carried out on this subject, but in my view, there is a difference between describing the terrible experiences of physical abuse, humiliation, isolation, and hunger and talking about the loss, about the moments of separation from significant figures and about the figures themselves. Who were these people who disappeared so suddenly and what was the connection with them? The manner of talking is also important: whether it is a true sharing of the experience or is motivated by something else. Others have described the difficulty survivors had in mourning their closest relations (Gampel, 1992; Klein, 1974; Shoshan, 1989; Davidson, 1992; Fresco, 1984; Pines, 1992). In many cases the mourning was deferred for many years or became chronic. Much has been written about the role of the children who were born to survivor parents to compensate their parents for the suffering they underwent, and to serve as a replacement for family members that perished (Wardi, 1990). The child who was chosen to be a "memorial candle" symbolically resurrects those who were lost, and in this way helps the parent deal with the traumas she suffered, and also, according to Bergmann and Jucovy (1982), to circumvent the mourning process.

Rosenthal (1998) talks about the fact that the mourning process does not end with one generation but continues from one generation to the next. In interviews with three generations of one family she shows how the children and grandchildren continue to work through the mourning that their mother couldn't complete. In recent years we have witnessed the fact that Holocaust survivors who were silent for many years are beginning to tell their stories. The second generation, which has meanwhile also matured, is more interested in hearing the stories and is even searching for information about the families that perished. In many cases, the children, with their survivor parents, journey in search of their roots, as described above, or help their parents document their stories. Wardi (1990) states that these journeys express a personal and even a national need to put an end to denial and repression of the traumatic past. To the same extent, it can also be said that they are an important and essential stage in the working through of mourning.

The idea for the present study grew out of the therapeutic work carried out in Amcha, an organisation offering psychotherapy to Holocaust survivors and the second generation. In several cases, both the survivor parent and the son or daughter are in therapy in the same clinic. My idea was to follow the mourning process and examine to what extent and in what way the parent was able to deal with the loss, and whether the task was passed on to the next generation. The nature of the parent's relationship with the son/daughter and how close they are to each other are questions that we thought relevant to the subject.

We found seven mother–daughter pairs, where both are in therapy at Amcha. The mothers' and daughters' therapists were interviewed separately.

Description of the sample and the main findings

The mothers' ages at the beginning of the therapy ranged from fifty-one to seventy-one, and the daughters' ages ranged from twenty-four to fifty-three.

Three of the mothers came from Poland, one from Hungary, one from Romania, one from Italy, one from Transylvania. Six of the daughters were born in Israel and one was born in Romania.

The mothers' ages during WWII range from birth to fourteen. Two were born during the war. Each of them has her own story. Some girls were hidden in convents, with or without their mother. Some families lived constantly on the run, and some families were evicted from their homes to the ghetto and from the ghetto to the concentration camp. Three of them lost both their parents. Two of them lost one parent and two did not lose anyone in their nuclear family. Consequently, we are referring to women who were children during the war. The oldest among them were still at an age of total dependence upon their parents. In addition to losing their parents, they also lost their family framework, their home, and their school.

After the war, the majority of these girls found themselves alone in the world. Most of them were in a hurry to establish a family of their own. They looked for mates. In four cases they found a survivor like themselves. In many cases they married a man many years their senior.

They frequently rushed to get married before examining whether the man suited them in other respects. They rushed to bring children into the world from the desire to establish a family as quickly as possible. Some of the women managed to study and acquire a profession and academic education. Three of them had no formal education and worked as caretakers.

I was particularly interested in the relationship of the Holocaust survivor mother and her daughter. In the present sample, three of the daughters were the first-born children and one was an only child, that is, her mother's first child. Among the other three, one was born after a son, one after a sister who was sickly from birth, and one after an older sister who is not in therapy.

Generally speaking, in most of the homes that we "entered", whether through the mother's or the daughter's story, the atmosphere was harsh and gloomy. Statements such as, "Our home was difficult, depressing, and joyless", or "It was a home in which no one ever laughed", were typical of the entire group.

In a large proportion of the homes the relations between the parents were extremely tense. In three of them there were severe arguments between the parents. In two of them there was distancing, and the husband was emotionally and/or physically absent. One case ended in divorce. Most of the quarrels were about money matters. The husband, who at first had seemed like a good provider, over time was revealed as not being one. The emotional bond was also disappointing. The husband came across as indifferent, distant, and inaccessible.

The expectations from the first daughter to be born were enormous. Many of these girls were named for their grandmother who had perished, that is, they were "memorial candles" (Wardi, 1990). The survivor mother wanted to raise her daughter under normal conditions in a regular home with two parents, a home containing food and clothing, a home that provides the conditions for development and education; everything that the survivor mother didn't have or which she had had and lost. Although the daughters in most cases received these conditions, in many of the homes relations with the mother were problematic, especially between her and the oldest daughter (Adelman, 1995; Brom, Kfir, & Dasberg, 2001).

I will try to examine the explanation for these problematic relations in greater depth. The material I have collected enables us to view them from two points of view, that of the mother and that of the daughter.

The general impression is that the relations between the mother and daughter were characterised by emotional distance, and frequently also physical distance. In two cases it was reported that the mother was not capable of naturally touching her daughter, and the daughter also developed a physical aversion to her mother. Most of the cases reported lack of intimacy and emotional withdrawal to the point of detachment. One mother testified: "I didn't find warmth towards my (firstborn) daughter within myself." Only one case reported emotional closeness. In two cases the daughters were sent to boarding institutions because the mothers couldn't care for them due to illness, or because she was the sole provider. When the daughter returned home, the relationship deteriorated. In other cases, the mother was very involved in the child's life and disappointed that her daughter began to be assertive and to choose directions that were contrary to the mother's wishes and expectations. These daughters were perceived by their mothers as overly independent, critical, and assertive.

A common complaint for many of the daughters was that their mothers expected them to fill the role of a parent towards them. In general the reference was not to physical care but to emotional support: "My mother expects me to take care of her", or "I am like my mother's mother." Some of the daughters felt that their mothers were too intrusive and expected them to realise their unfulfilled ambitions. Most of them reported feeling emotionally distant from their mothers and lonely. As I stated, in two of the cases the daughters spent most of their childhood in a boarding institution and felt neglected and unwanted.

I asked whether the mother had talked to her daughter about her past. In fact, in all but one case I was told that she hadn't. There are mothers who shared their daily worries with their daughters, perhaps overly so, such as with regard to their relations with the father, but did not share their story with them, except indirectly (for example in statements such as: "You don't throw out food. You don't know what it means to be hungry"). It was especially important for me to know whether the mothers had told their daughters about their relatives who perished, about their parents or siblings. In most cases they had not. There were two cases in which the daughters, having reached mature adulthood, helped their mothers to document their stories, and in both cases the problematic relations between mother and daughter much improved. Only one mother–daughter pair, both of whom reported that the mother had shared her life story with her daughter from the time she was a child, had close mother–daughter relations, and they have close emotional relations to this day. This home was also not a happy one, and the mother said that she was depressed.

I asked about the mother's dominant emotional state, and especially about the emotional expression of mourning. The general impression is that there were more expressions of anger than of sorrow, guilt, or anxiety. I received the impression that in many cases the feelings of having missed out on opportunities and of deprivation continued to distress the mothers. They wished their daughters a better life, but nevertheless there were manifestations of envy of their daughters for having a better lot in life. However, most of the mothers were proud of their daughters and their achievements.

Discussion

In his paper "The intuition of the negative in playing and reality" (Green, 1999), Green describes a patient who was in therapy with Winnicott and later came to him for therapy. The patient was a woman who at the age of eleven was evacuated to England during WWII. She completely forgot her childhood, but on the other hand refused to call the people who took care of her "Aunt" and "Uncle". She managed not to call them by any name, and according to Winnicott this was the negative of her memory of her parents. This is the absence of memory, the absence of contact, the absence of feeling alive. In the patient's words: "When I was there in the country to which I was evacuated, it was as though they had taken my heart, plucked it out and put it aside, but life went on." When she returned home three years later, her parents were alive but her contact with them, especially with her mother, had been lost, and with it the sense of continuity. In certain cases the objects' physical presence is not enough to correct the destructive effect of an overly long absence. Non-existence dominates the mind and erases previous representations of the object that existed prior to its absence. According to Green, in many cases this is an irreversible process, at least until the person receives psychotherapy.

Similar to Winnicott and Green's patient, the mothers in our sample were children during the Holocaust and were separated from their parents before adolescence, and certainly before they had reached emotional maturity. Wolfenstein (1966) asks how the mourning process, which ends with a final acceptance of the loss, becomes possible. Her conclusion, based on observation of adolescents who lost a parent, is that the mourning process becomes possible only after completion of the maturation process. Growing up is like an experimental mourning process in which a gradual separation from the first love object takes place, while it still exists physically. The process is accompanied by feelings of sadness and by memories of the childhood that will not return. Only after this process has taken place can the individual mourn later losses. Before the completion of the maturation process, a child that loses one of its parents searches for substitutes to fill the parental functions that were interrupted.

It seems to me that the girls who found themselves without parents after the war continued searching for parenting, first from their mate and then from their first-born daughter. We saw that in a large proportion of the families relations between the married partners were extremely tense. The women expected their partner to take care of them, not just financially but also emotionally. In many cases the partner had also lost his parents, and perhaps had similar expectations. The frustration and disappointment led to anger and quarrelling, and sometimes to separation.

The first child born to a survivor mother was extremely significant. Much has been written about the role of this child to serve as a memorial candle and to compensate its parents for their losses. It has also been stated that these children enabled their parents to evade mourning for their parents (Wardi, 1990; Bergmann & Jucovy, 1982; Barocas & Barocas, 1979).

Schumer (2000, pp. 60–61) writes:

> For my mother I am an avenue to restoration, restitution, resurrection. I am a replacement for her lost family. I embody the dreams and hopes, the love and emotion, that should have come from others in the family who were killed in the war, especially her mother. I bring meaning to her life and theirs. Sometimes I see my relationship with my mother in those small Russian Matrushka dolls that neatly fit inside each other. In my mother's life, a small Matrushka doll lost a larger doll—her mother—and for years, she stood alone. With the birth of her daughter, there were two Matrushka dolls again, but their relative sizes were reversed—the daughter held and protected the mother. I became her mother because she needed one more than I did. Still, I am the daughter too, the great hope.

We saw that most of the daughters in our sample had similar feelings: they had to take on the role of the mother because their mother needed it.

In his article "The dead mother" (Green, 1986), Green writes about mothers who are depressed because they have lost someone dear to them. The cause of the mother's depression is not known to the child, but the child experiences loss despite the fact that the mother is physically present. The mother figure, which was lively and loving, changes. The child tries in vain to restore the mother sunk in her grief, but when the child despairs, the child goes on to "unconscious identification with the dead mother. Its result is the constitution of a hole in the texture of object relations with the mother." At the same time, the mother continues to care for and love the child, but "her heart is not in it". In fact there is no real reparation, but mimicry, with the aim of continuing to possess the object (who one can no longer have) by becoming not like it but the object itself. The identification comes about unawares to the ego of the subject and against his will (1986, p. 151). Elsewhere, Schumer (2000) states: "I have absorbed a sense of what she has suffered, what she has lost, even what her mother endured and handed down. It is my emotional gene map" (Schumer, p. 55).

Modell (1999), in his response to Green's article, writes that in many cases the way to avoid the dead mother syndrome is through counter-identification, to become the opposite of the mother, thus retaining the sense of individuality. In these cases as well, the dead, sad, or detached core exists deep down. Nevertheless, in cases of primary identification, the daughter's individuality is completely lost and she merges with her mother as she perceives her, including her unconscious attitudes. Identification with the dead mother, who is unable to love, contributes to a parallel inability in the daughter to love others and herself.

It seems that some of the daughters in our sample identified with their depressed mother. One of them clearly stated, "I myself am a Holocaust survivor" even though she was born after the war. Another one spoke about her parents' past as though she had been there. In contrast, other daughters chose to distance themselves from their mother, developed in directions contrary to their mothers' expectations and expressed anger and rejection towards their mother, and unwillingness to know about her past.

We have seen that in four out of the seven pairs the mother didn't speak about her past with her daughter, and the daughter showed no interest in the Holocaust story of her mother and the family members who perished. In two of the seven pairs the mother shared her story with her daughter at a later stage, when the daughter had grown up. This sharing led to the documentation of the story at Yad Vashem. In one case the mother also began a belated mourning process: she went to Poland, gave lectures, and wrote a testimony. The daughter also dealt with the Holocaust through art: painting, and writing. The relations between the mother and the daughter improved. In the second case, the daughter helped her mother document her story. Both of them went for therapy and afterwards their relationship improved. In the third case the mother and daughter had a close relationship from the start. The mother shared her life story with her daughter, and dealt with her own mourning. The daughter was interested in the Holocaust, went to Poland, and knew the history of her mother and her family in detail. The mother and daughter had a warm and loving relationship.

Conclusion

The purpose of psychotherapy for the mother is to help her mourn her losses and to meet her daughter as a separate, independent figure, differentiated from past figures. The purpose of therapy for the daughter is to help her define her unique personal identity, and as such to detach herself from her mother and meet her anew. When the daughter becomes a real partner in the mother's feelings of mourning, their relationship can be rehabilitated. It is to be hoped that both the mother's and the daughter's psychotherapy will lead to the emotional closeness that they both need, and in addition will bring the intergenerational mourning process to a successful resolution.

References

Adelman, A. (1995). Traumatic memory and the inter-generational transmission of Holocaust narratives. Psychoanalytic Study of the Child, 50: 343–367.

Barocas, H. A., & Barocas, C. B. (1979). Wounds of the father, the next generation of Holocaust victims. International Review of Psychoanalysis, 6: 331–340.

Bergmann, M. S., & Jucovy, M. E. (Eds.) (1982). Generations Of The Holocaust. New York: Basic Books.

Brom, D., Kfir, R., & Dasberg, I. (2001). A controlled double-bind study on children of Holocaust survivors. Israel Journal of Psychiatry and Related Sciences, *38*: 47–57.

Davidson, Sh. (1992). Holding On To Humanity (Ch. 8). New York: New York University Press.

Fresco, N. (1984). Remembering the unknown. International Review of Psychoanalysis, *II*: 417–432.

Gampel, Y. (1992). Thoughts about the transmission of conscious and unconscious knowledge to the generation born after the Shoa. Journal of Social Work and Policy in Israel, 5–6.

Green, A. (1986). The dead mother. In: *On* Private Madness. London: Hogarth.

Green, A. (1999). The intuition of the negative in playing and reality. In: G. Kohon (Ed.), The Dead Mother: *The Work of André Green*. London: Routledge.

Jucovy, M. E. (1992). Psychoanalytic contributions to Holocaust studies. International Journal of Psychoanalysis, *73*: 267.

Klein, H. (1974). Delayed affects and after-effects of severe traumatization. Israel Annals of Psychiatry, *12*: 293–302.

Krell, R. (1979). Holocaust families, the survivors and their children. Comprehensive Psychiatry, *20*: 6.

Lichtman, H. (1984). Parental communication of Holocaust experiences and personality characteristics among second generation survivors. Journal of Clinical Psychology, *40*: 914–924.

Modell, A. H. (1999). The dead mother syndrome and the reconstruction of trauma. In: G. Kohon (Ed.), The Dead Mother (pp. 76–86). London: Routledge.

Pines, D. (1992). The impact of the Holocaust on the second generation. Journal of Social Work and Policy in Israel, 5–6.

Rosenthal, G. (Ed.) (1998). The Holocaust in Three Generations. London: Cassell.

Shoshan, T. (1989). Mourning and Longing from Generation to Generation. *American Journal of Psychotherapy* 43(2): 193–207.

Schumer, F. (2000). Motherland. New York: Penguin.

Wardi, D. (1990). Memorial Candles. Jerusalem: Keter Publishing House.

Wolfenstein, M. (1966). How is mourning possible? Psychoanalytic Study of the Child, *21*: 93–123.

CHAPTER FIVE

Unable to mourn again? Media(ted) reactions to German neo-Nazi terrorism

Steffen Krüger

T his chapter will appraise the 2011–2012 media debate on right-wing terrorism in Germany against the background of psychoanalytic, as well as media and communication, theory. Drawing on Alexander and Margarete Mitscherlich's classic *The Inability to Mourn* (1967), it will ask whether or not Germany's political media culture (cf., Pfetsch, 2007, who speaks of "political communication culture") has gained the ability to mourn—to mourn the victims of the terror attacks, as well as itself, in order to integrate Germany's past as a continuous presence into its reasoning and actions. The results of this appraisal give a mixed impression. I argue that in the—absolutely credible—attempt to take on an apt posture, the political media culture in Germany risked losing sight of the actual victims of Nazi terror, as well as of its own role in the events.

Introduction

On Friday, 4 November 2011, two men in their mid-thirties were found dead in a burned-out camper van close to the East German town of Eisenach. The men had shot themselves, and either they themselves or an accomplice had set fire to the van. Banknotes connected with two robberies in the Eisenach area, as well as the pistols of two police officers who were shot in 2007, were found in the van (As of today fifteen bank robberies are found to have been committed by the two men). Two days later, on Sunday, 6 November, a house in a residential area in Zwickau exploded; the two men, Uwe Böhnhardt and Uwe Mundlos, had lived there together with Beate Zschäpe, their close friend and alleged accomplice. On Tuesday, 8 November, Zschäpe, who in the meantime had been the subject of a nationwide search, handed herself in to the police. By then, the case had received considerable media attention because of the unexpected light it shed on the attack on the two police officers in 2007. Yet its decisive turn came when, on 12 November, the news weekly *Der Spiegel* reported on a fifteen-minute film that was found in the apartment.

The video amounts to a claim of responsibility; it implies that the trio was responsible not only for the killing of the police officer in 2007 (the second survived heavily wounded), but also for Europe's biggest unsolved series of murders so far. In what popular German media crudely termed the Doner Murders (a term designated "un-word" of 2011 by a commission of linguists, German scholars, and social and political scientists), eight people of Turkish and one of Greek origin were killed between 2000 and 2006—literally executed at their workplaces, small-sized businesses, with several shots to the head and chest in broad daylight. Additionally, the video credits the trio, which called itself National-Socialist Underground, with at least one nail-bomb attack on an immigrant area in Cologne.[1]

The day after this find, on 13 November 2011, politicians and the media began to fathom the scope and political dimension of the neo-Nazis' deeds. For the first time in Germany's post-war history, a minister of the interior, Hans Peter Friedrich, had to publicly attest to the existence of German right-wing terrorism, a phenomenon the existence of which had been denied in an uninterrupted string of annual reports by the Federal Office for the Protection of the Constitution (the highest office of the several German intelligence services on union level). But the suspicion went deeper: the notion that the three terrorists—apparently with the help of others in the right-radical scene (in the weeks and months after the events, there were five arrests on strong suspicion of support of a terrorist network)—could have committed so many vicious crimes without the German police and intelligence services even considering racist motives, led many news media to question whether these institutions had not been "blind in their right eye". (One example out of many: *3sat* [TV station], 30 November 2011, 22:25: "Auf dem rechten Auge blind? Das braune Geschwür: Zwickau." ["Blind in the right eye? The brown ulcer: Zwickau"]).

In the ensuing media debate, a dynamic unfolded that can be seen to equate to what psychoanalysis calls the "return of the repressed"— the sudden, symptomatic resurfacing of an unresolved, ongoing past. A first step in approaching the notion of "the return of the repressed" for the field of news media can be taken by looking at some simple numbers. A search for the term "Rechtsextremismus" ("right-wing extremism") in some of the major German newspapers for the period between 11 November 2011 and 11 January 2012 results in 250 finds.[2] By comparison, the same search within the time span two months before the findings of 11 November results in eight. Suddenly the theme that had hardly registered with the news media in a long time (and apparently neither with the intelligence services) became omnipresent and acute. And since the findings of 11 November 2011 refer to deeds committed in the past, the sudden resurgence is tied to a strong sense of *Nachträglichkeit* ("deferred action"; see Laplanche & Pontalis, 1972, p. 585, p. 632)—the urgent need to reassess and reinterpret vital, highly guarded parts of one's history and present existence. As Toralf Staud, journalist and right-wing extremism expert, quotes an earlier statement by state secretary of the interior, Ole Schröder: "There is no reason to assume that the state fails to identify victims of right-wing extremist violence." In the light of the findings of November 2011, Staud can add drily: "Today everything is different" (Staud, 2011, p. 8).

What was invoked in many of the articles and features immediately following the findings were glimpses of a déjà vu or fleeting encounters with a *Doppelganger* (cf., Freud, 1919h), in whom one is suddenly confronted with an autonomously acting vision of one's self—another self, displaying a potency and violent, ruthless energy previously unknown and unaccounted for in one's self-conception (Žižek in Fiennes 2006). "Germany's brown writing on the wall," writes *Spiegel Online* (Kuzmany, 2011a); a "daunting image," exclaims *Frankfurter Allgemeine Zeitung* with media-critical overtones (von Altenbockum, 2011, p. 1). "Now we get hold of a thread at which one dreads to tug because one senses that one will not like what's hanging at the other end," comments Nils Minkmar in *Frankfurter Allgemeine Sonntagszeitung* (Minkmar, 2011, p. 49), and Jacob Augstein sums up the situation in his *Spiegel Online* column as "the renewed flaring of the mark of Cain of the German Nazi-past" (Augstein, 2011). In a sentence, what became invoked in many of the immediate reactions of the news media was a shocking reencounter with Germany's history of violence—a history of which Alexander and Margarete Mitscherlich wrote in their classic study, *The Inability to Mourn* (1967), that it had been thoroughly and entirely repressed from the moment of Germany's capitulation in 1945.

I am going to assess and evaluate the media coverage of the events following in the wake of the initial statements of consternation. I want to conceive of this coverage as a mourning process facilitated and structured by the news media. How does it stand with the ability to mourn in a society now constituted and permanently re-actualised through its media environments? Would the knowledge freed by the findings be repressed, as the Mitscherlichs diagnosed after WWII, or would the coverage face up to the dangers itself implied in its reporting in a mature and reasoned manner? In order to answer these questions I have read widely in the online archives of the mainstream newspapers—the broadsheets and the *boulevard* (the German term for tabloid press). I have watched television news, the special features of political magazine formats, and late-night talk shows (all via online archives or with special permission of the production companies) that sought to make sense of the findings of November 2011. For a more systematic analysis, I have looked at four mainstream media sources over the course of approximately two months from 11 November 2011 to mid-January 2012. These are: the news weekly *Der Spiegel* and the tabloid daily *Bild*, together with their online platforms; as well as two television news programmes, *Tagesschau/Tagesthemen* on public service channel ARD and the online news archive of Germany's biggest private station *RTL* consisting of clips of all of the channel's news shows, as well as those of *ntv*, a twenty-four-hour news channel by the same owner.

Enacting trauma?

Before entering into this analysis, however, it is wise to take a step back and assess the complexity of the situation the application of psychoanalytic concepts to the study of this particular case of media discourse creates. After all, psychoanalytic thinking has deeply penetrated everyday life and language. In particular, the Mitscherlich study on the *Inability to Mourn* (1967) is well known in German intellectual circles as a milestone in critically applied psychoanalysis and has played an important role in (West-) Germany's efforts to come to terms with its Nazi past.[3] Therefore, it is hardly surprising that the notion of the "return of the repressed" was invoked in many of the news articles, television, and radio features, since this invocation must have appeared as the logical continuation of the post-war efforts at coming to terms with the German Nazi past. Therefore, in view of this feeling of inevitability held by many, a certain automatism, even clichédness, can be expected in the mediated reactions to this renewal of guilt. With Alfred Lorenzer (1986), one could say that in these cases the symbolic was reduced to a sign-like state at which it was disconnected from lived experience (Lorenzer, 1986, p. 53).

At the same time, however, I believe it would be wrong to extend the suspicion of a clichéd nature of the media coverage to all incidences of reporting and, on this basis, dismiss as inauthentic and hollow the notions of shock and indignation, of fear and sadness, to which many media outlets gave vent in the face of what had come to light. Therefore, the mediated reactions to the findings of German neo-Nazi terror will have to be reckoned with for their nature as acculturated, rehearsed, and at times clichéd positions taken due to the media's complex role between facilitating public political participation and selling the news to the biggest possible audience, as well as for their more immediate emotional content—or for what one could call the reactions' persisting "psychic energy" (cf., Herding & Stumpfhaus, 2004).

Mourning and the news

Framing the news reporting on German neo-Nazi terror as a mourning process thus has a twofold diagnostic merit. First, it takes seriously the notions of shock and trauma, which are frequently invoked by the media as something of a "news-value reflex". This means that, if a news article exclaims, say, "Republic in state of shock" (Weiland, 2011a), the focus on mourning serves as a reminder that one should not be too media-savvy and cynical to not expect this to be followed by a series of articles that thoroughly process and work through this "shock". Second, the framing of news reporting as mourning enables me to confront the media coverage with psychodynamic, relational concepts with which the impact of the often automatic interplay of socio-cultural routines—that is, the acting upon professional roles and self-images, political and public-relations strategies, institutional concerns, and so on—can be tested and made sense of. For the case at hand, the two main concepts are those of fetishism and melancholia.

Narrative fetishism

In his article "History beyond the Pleasure Principle" (1992), Eric L. Santner introduces the concept of "narrative fetishism". Parallel to Freud (1927e), who defines a fetish as a stand-in by virtue of which the recognition of a catastrophic lack is disavowed, Santner describes narrative fetishism as a means to undo a loss. "Both narrative fetishism and mourning are responses to loss, to a past that refuses to go away due to its traumatic impact," Santner writes, and further:

> The work of mourning is a process of elaborating and integrating the reality of loss or traumatic shock by remembering and repeating it in symbolically and dialogically mediated doses; it is a process of translating, troping, and figuring loss [...]. Narrative fetishism, by contrast, is the way an inability or refusal to mourn employs traumatic events; it is a strategy of undoing, in fantasy, the need for mourning by simulating a condition of intactness, typically by situating the site and origin of loss elsewhere. (Santner, 1992, p. 144)

This concept of narrative fetishism enables me to assess the potentially helpful and harmful effects of single news items, as well as more general structural characteristics of the coverage. And while Santner's article draws on the *Historikerstreit*, the historians' dispute in Germany in the 1980s, in order to explicate his concept further, the 2011–2012 German media coverage on right-wing terror is by no means devoid of examples either. The clearest case in point is the term "Doner murders", mentioned above, which was taken out of circulation shortly after the findings of November 2011 precisely because of its fetishist tendencies. As journalist Hatice Akyün points out, it made the murder series appear as "an internal affair amongst Turks" (Akyün, 2011). By thus locating the problem elsewhere it granted an ethnic-German audience supposedly unproblematic libidinous access to the subject.

In general it can be said that it was specifically the articles and clips that focused on the perpetrators and the criminological aspects of neo-Nazi terrorism that were most prone to narrative fetishism, with the tabloid paper *Bild* producing the majority of incidences. For example: "The Nazi bride passed for a hottie" (Völkerling, Reichelt, & Ley, 2011); "The sick hatred of the Nazi killers" Kiewel et al., 2011); and "Three hours later they are dead—the last photos of the killer-Nazis" (*Bild.de*, 2011a). In varying Santner's observation, one can say that this obsessive kind of poring over the perpetrators—the sexualisation of which is openly perceivable—makes the victims disappear from sight completely.

The missing victims

And indeed, if a central element was missing from the German media coverage of neo-Nazi terrorism it was the victims and their bereaved. A content analysis of the four main sources, *Der Spiegel*, *Bild*, *Tagesschau/Tagesthemen*, and *RTL*'s news archive, gives an indication of what the media did cover (see appendix at the end of this chapter for a list of topoi and their share in the overall coverage). First and foremost, the media focused heavily on the details of the terrorists' deeds, the whos and whats, wheres and whens, hows and whys, thus putting the perpetrators at the centre of attention. Furthermore, the media reported intensely on the political reactions to the findings and became densely populated with politicians and high-ranking officials from various government institutions. The German intelligence services and their failure to solve the murder series, as well as the right-wing party NPD (National Democratic Party of Germany) and its (alleged) relations with the terrorists, and German right-wing extremist culture in general—they all played major parts in the news media's reporting and commenting on the case. Yet the people that had become the actual victims of the so-called National Socialist Underground hardly figured in any of this. The highest percentage of news items focusing on themes directly related to the victims was seven per cent of the total coverage by *Tagesschau/Tagesthemen* on public service channel ARD; *Bild* made it to four per cent; *Spiegel* and *RTL* remained around two.[4]

In the face of these findings, one can say that the concrete incidents of narrative fetishism presented above correspond to the near absence of the victims from the overall reporting. The perpetrators and their deeds seemed to be as much obsessed about as the victims kept out of the narrative altogether. Facing this situation, one is reminded of the Mitscherlichs' assessment of a striking failure on part of the Germans after the war to empathise with the victims on either side (1967, p. 36). However, again one has to be cautious not to merely transplant an observation from forty years ago into the current situation, since not only has the socio-cultural set-up changed but also, in the case of the 2011 findings, the specific rules of media conduct have to be taken into consideration.

Systemically, the news proves to be interested in the "doers", rather than in those "done by". Both groups, perpetrators and victims, fall out of the normative societal frame; but since the act of investigative reporting bears an aggressive element in itself, it might appear as though the victims were spared the keen eye of the observer that was cast upon the perpetrators without such scruples. The least one could do now was to leave the victims their privacy, the argument might have run. However, such considerations are decisively weakened by the fact that the victims' absence was not total. They were featured with some frequency during the initial wave of reporting, and in this initial phase they were given the function of Cassandra figures who could finally tell a gasping audience that they had suspected a right-extremist background of the attacks from the start. For example: "The Police did not take our neo-Nazi suspicion seriously" (Schneider [quoting Gamze Kubasik] 2011); "Now the children of the victims accuse: 'Why did nobody think of Nazi-murders?'"(*Bild.de*, 2011b); and on *Tagesthemen*, 12 November 2011, Aiman A. Mazik, the head of the Central Commission of Muslims in Germany, stated: "That it [right-extremist terrorism] had existed already—we all knew."

An internal affair amongst Germans

This initial display of a secret knowledge might have been symptomatic of the victims' subsequent disappearance from most of the further reporting. After all, they had obtained this knowledge through their belonging to an ethnic minority group, whereas the process of working through which was subsequently set in motion by the political media culture aimed at a fundamental act of social hygiene on part of the ethnic German majority. Therefore, the very notion of the "return of the repressed", which had been circulated at the onset of the coverage, added to the whole of the ensuing reporting the unarticulated sense of an exclusively German family affair. It was the ethnic Germans who had been caught unawares by the findings of right-extremist terrorism.

Therefore, it was first and foremost the ethnic Germans who needed the sight on their right eyes checked, to be enlightened about the true ideological dimension of the terrorist attacks. And because the initial findings were understood as a problem that required a narrower definition of what it means to be German than the multicultural versions that many politicians were quick to promote in the aftermath of the findings, it seems that neither the news media nor the politicians knew what to do with the victims after their Cassandra function had been used up. They were neither given a clear place in this process nor asked to make a relevant contribution to it henceforth. At the same time, their being out of sight was self-critically observed by some media commentators, for example by Stefan Kuzmany on *Spiegel Online*, who wrote in view of the television documentary "Eight Turks, one Greek, and a policewoman" (Deiß, Müller, & Thüringer, 2011) which, as an exception to the rule, concentrated on the victims: "The ARD-documentary [...] does what so far apparently nobody has done: it looks closely. It cares about the victims" (Kuzmany, 2011b).

No one else but oneself—a move towards melancholia

Yet in view of the magnitude of the mourning process, as well as its ethnic frame, the political-media culture in Germany quickly began to lose sight of the concrete victims of the terrorist attacks and began to focus on itself. Once more the Mitscherlichs' observation started to ring true that the "feelings only suffice for the cathexis of one's own person, hardly for empathic feelings of any kind. If there is a pitiable object at all, it is mostly no one else but oneself" (1967, p. 37). In the case of the 2011 findings, however, the constellations that made this statement ring true had changed. At this point the relation between mourning and melancholia, which Freud introduced in his 1917 article, can be rendered productive for the present study. For unlike the post-war situation the Mitscherlichs (1967) described, the existence of the victims of the National Socialist Underground did not have to be repressed together with the deeds; this time, the victims were pushed aside and forgotten because of the very significance the deeds took on for the ethnic German majority. When Freud (1917e) observed of melancholia that one frequently "cannot see clearly what it is that has been lost, and [...] [t]his, indeed, might be so even if the patient is aware of the loss [...], but only in the sense that he knows whom he has lost but not what he has lost in him" (Freud, 1917e, p. 245), the disappearance of the actual victims from the reporting might be taken as a symptom of this confusion and ambivalence characteristic of melancholia.

In my view, this disappearance came about in three consecutive steps. First, political and media players (who, after the perpetrators, received the news reporting's main attention) demonstrated their absolute solidarity with the victims; second, due to the victims' absence—an absence that seemed agreed upon and fatally natural—these political and media players took the role of the victims' advocates; and, third, this advocacy in turn led to precarious and hasty identifications with the victims and ultimately the occupation of the place of the latter. This did not happen intentionally but seemed to be the result of an unfortunate dynamic—a dynamic that will become clearer when turning to some of the official responses by politicians. These responses were praised by many news commentators, and not unreasonably so. They might have been lacking in pathos and empathy, as some other commentators complained, but gradually the political elite in Berlin rose to the occasion. Chancellor Merkel reacted promptly in her party convention speech and articulated her sympathy with the victims; then-Federal President Wulff spoke words of condolence and invited the victims' families to his residence; the most sincere and adequate gesture was that of the presiding officer of the German parliament, Norbert Lammert, who apologised to the victims in the name of the country, followed by a minute's silence. These statements were made vital parts of the media's coverage.

Taking a closer look at these reactions, however, specifically at those of Angela Merkel and of her then-minister of foreign affairs, Guido Westerwelle, one can detect the seed of ambivalence that would grow and gradually begin to determine the further development of the mourning process. Not without hints of (auto-)aggression, Merkel spoke of the findings as a "disgrace for Germany" (Merkel, 2011); and in Westerwelle's comment (quoted in Weiland, 2011b), the—probably unacknowledged—shift towards self-interest is even less hidden: "Not only is this terrible for the victims, not only is this bad for the whole country, above all it is very, very bad for the reputation of our country in the world."

In these statements, it is ultimately an ego-ideal of national scope that has been dealt the heaviest blow; the concern for the victims and their families comes into the picture only afterwards. But since these victims are largely absent from the unfolding discourse, the politicians' advocacy is quickly hollowed out by national concerns; and consolation for the victims (as well as containment of their emotional states) is superimposed by attempts at consoling the public at large—a public that is automatically and unconsciously conceived of as mainstream ethnic German. Symptomatic of this sneaking superimposition of self-interest are statements, such as that of Sigmar Gabriel, head of the Social Democratic Party (SPD), who, during a media-geared visit to one of the terror sites, called the terrorist acts "attacks on the core of our society," stressing further that "this concerns each and every one in Germany" (Gabriel, 2011). And while, at bottom, this was surely a well-meant call for solidarity, its call for the "core of our society" to feel attacked proves to be populist and misleading.

Against the background of this gradual occupation of the victims' position by the core of a disgraced German society, the rest of the coverage receives its decisive drift. By virtue of their solidarity, every ethnic German audience member who felt shocked and indignant was given open access to the victims' side and was allowed to follow the search for the guilty and responsible at a safe distance both from the immediate anxiety and suffering of the real victims, as well as from serious and far-reaching implications of guilt. It cannot surprise one, then, that the rest of the coverage had a strong tendency towards splitting, with the perpetrators, their supporters, as well as those held responsible for the many accidents and mishaps in the search for the terrorists on one side and the rest of the disgraced—historically guilty, but currently unknowing—Germans on the other. When Wilhelm Heitmeyer, head of the Research Institute for Conflict and Violence in Bielefeld, stated in an interview with *Tagesthemen* that he thought the debate on Nazi terrorism was problematic, because it tended to separate the criminals from their social environment (Heitmeyer, 2011), this statement points to the tendency that is described here.

Therefore, in looking back at the various aspects of the German media's work of mourning, one can say that none of these aspects in isolation can account for a repeated inability to mourn, that is, for constructing a narrative that undid or circumvented the need to mourn. Rather, what I want to point to is the overall dynamic of the German news reporting on neo-Nazi terror that, paradoxically, gave the whole of the coverage a fetishist air precisely by swiftly invoking an unprocessed historical guilt and pointing to a repressed that had now returned. In so doing, the political media culture started a process not of mourning, but first and foremost of melancholia that repeated the Mitscherlichs' assessment of a lack of empathy on part of the Germans (1967, p. 37) by enacting guilty conscience as a defence.

Conclusion

Under the impression of a persisting general unwillingness after WWII to assess their Nazi past, the Mitscherlichs claimed that the Germans had avoided a process of mourning in order to escape their own devaluation in an outbreak of mass-melancholia (Mitscherlich & Mitscherlich, 1967, p. 27). According to the authors, the repression of the Nazi past was accomplished by a "turning away from inner concern for one's own conduct under the Third Reich"—a process that the authors saw as consisting of three successive phases: first, a "mechanism of derealisation", carried by "a striking rigidity of emotion"; second, an effortless shifting of identifications, allowing for a quickly fostered "identification with the victors" after the war, which facilitated the third phase, the "manic undoing"—in the case of post-war Germany, its gigantic rebuilding efforts.

In view of these aspects, or phases, the state of the ability to mourn on part of Germany's political media culture in 2011–2012 can be assessed. In the case of the 2011 findings of Nazi terrorism one can say that there was a fair amount of "derealisation" in the news media's coverage here too, albeit in a way significantly different from what the Mitscherlichs experienced. This "derealisation" was fostered by the absence of the victims on the one hand, as well as the intense focus on the terrorists and the highly abstract and symbolic sphere of political advocacy on the other. On the basis of this constellation, even some fetishist invitations to identify "with the victors", that is, the terrorists, could be detected (e.g., "The last photos of the killer-Nazis", see above), although these were individual cases of a typically sensationalistic news routine that remained insignificant for the overall process.

There was no trace of a "rigidity of emotions", yet the very non-rigid feelings of shock and urgency in the face of the "return of the repressed", which the findings were deemed to have triggered, would prove to have their own pitfalls. The appeal of the concept of the "return of the repressed" to a very narrow, exclusive definition of German ethnicity, specifically, that of the Germans at the end of WWII, sidelined the real, immediate victims of the terrorist attacks in the coverage. And while the actual deeds and their victims became less real, or at least: less important, over the course of the coverage, the notion of victimhood found a place closer to home. Gradually, the terrorist acts, which had first and foremost been directed at Germans with a migratory background, were reinterpreted as directed against the ethnic German mainstream. This time the "turning away from inner concern for one's own conduct", which the Mitscherlichs observed after WWII, was achieved through this redirection.

This time, then, one can say that mourning, or at least a process of working through, was not intentionally avoided but actively sought by the political media culture. Yet what was effectively reached was a state of melancholia, in which the shadow of the object did not fall onto the ego, as Freud famously described it (Freud, 1917e), but in which the political media culture actually sought out this shadow as a hiding place—a hiding place from genuine implications of guilt, as well as from genuine implications of horror.

Postscript

Returning to this chapter more than two years after having written it made for an uneasy experience. After all, I had conceived it while the reality of German right-wing extremist terrorism was still unfolding and new insights still frequently shifted the ground on which I was trying to build my argument. However, looking back on this argument from the distance of these two years, it does not seem to be weakened, and the tendency of a losing from sight and occupation of the victims' place by the German political media culture still seems to hold. In the months following the period of the initial findings after November 2011 that I researched, this tendency of making the victims disappear could be seen to be momentarily countered by the media coverage of the memorial service for the victims in Berlin in February 2012. Only weeks after, however, one could witness it fully reinstated in the planning and organisation of the court trial in Munich. The start of the trial, which had been scheduled for early 2013, had to be postponed because of its stunningly insensitive accreditation process. The court had turned down all requests from Turkish and Greek news media (i.e. media from the countries of origin of many of the NSU's victims) to be granted a permanent place in the courtroom. According to the representatives of one of the victims' families, Kerim and Semiya Simsek, the delayed start of the trial had been the result of a rigid attitude on part of the court "that ignored all critics and opposed all constructive attempts to solve the problem" (quoted in Diehl & Röbel, 2013). This problem directly relates to what I have discussed in the above chapter, specifically, the feeling held by the ethnic Germans of being confronted with the return of something that is inescapably, exclusively theirs—something that first and foremost needs to be treated as a family affair.

Fortunately, in the summer of 2014, the trial is well underway and it is mainly its content that now occupies the German news media. Especially the public service channels and broadsheet papers have made it their moral obligation to keep reporting. Coming back to the framing of the media coverage as a mourning process, one can thus say that there has been a definitive attempt on part of these media to work through the shocking insights gained in late 2011, even if the close focus on the trial makes the coverage now concentrate almost exclusively on the perpetrators and keeps the melancholic structure in place. Nevertheless, in this focus too there is much at stake. When Greg Forter (2003) observes that the Mitscherlichs (1967) had modified Freud's original ideas about mourning and melancholia in that they posited melancholia to be a necessary precondition for mourning after WWII (Forter, 2003, p. 135), the melancholia one experiences in the face of this trial might just prove a necessary step in the integration of Germany's past into its present and future.

In the trial against the perpetrators—against Beate Zschäpe, the only surviving alleged member of the core group of the National Socialist Underground, as well as various alleged helpers of this group— Germany as a constitutional democracy must prove that it is able and willing to open its eyes to violence and terror from the right. Whether this will succeed or not is still a question begging to be answered. By contrast, the terror attacks of the National Socialist Underground themselves seem to have been successful indeed, if measured by the standards of the extreme right. Their becoming public at the very moment of the death of their perpetrators rendered the deeds mythical and turned their doers into martyrs. According to a report by *tagesschau.de* (Gensing, 2014), there have been at least 220 right-wing extremist motivated crimes since the findings of November 2011 claimed to be directly inspired by the NSU and its deeds. Therefore, whereas SPD politician Sigmar Gabriel's calling the NSU's right-wing extremist crimes "attacks on the core of our society" (Gabriel, 2011) was surely populist and misguided, these attacks seem to have found another way of moving closer to this core: not as a threat, but as a possibility.

August 2014

Appendix

Focus of news media reporting on German neo-Nazi terrorism (11/11/2011—15/01/2012) in percentages*:

Spiegel(.de)	BILD(.de)	Tagesschau	RTL-Archive	
CRIME:	23.49 %	41.01 %	17.53 %	33.75 %
POLITICS:	21.69 %	8.55 %	28.57 %	15 %
INTEL:	16.87 %	12.82 %	11.69 %	8.75 %
NPD:	12.05 %	7.69 %	11.69 %	20 %
RIGHT-W:	10.24 %	10.68 %	9.74 %	8.75 %
PUB. OP:	7.83 %	5.55 %	9.74 %	5 %
VICT:	1.81 %	4.27 %	7.14 %	2.5 %
JUR:	3.61 %	1.28 %	1.30 %	5 %
MEDIA:	2.41 %	2.14 %	2.60 %	1.25 %

(CRIME = criminological focus; POLITICS = focus on the political sphere; INTELL = focus on intelligence services; NPD = focus on the right-extremist party NPD; RIGHT-W: focus on right-wing culture in general; PUB. OP = public-opinion focus; VICT. = focus on the victims; JUR. = focus on juridical aspects; MEDIA = media/self-reflective focus).

*calculations based on: *Spiegel/Spiegel Online:* 141 assessed articles/166 encodings; *Bild/Bild.de:* 207 assessed articles/234 encodings; *Tagesschau/Tagesthemen:* 89 features (often more than one within one show)/154 encodings; *RTL* news archive: 42 news items (23 of which were video clips [embedded in online articles], 10 of which were online articles without videos, 9 were short written reports)/80 encodings.

Notes

1. This and the murders are presented in the video in montage form, in which material from television news and photos that the murderers themselves apparently had taken of their victims at the crime scene are rendered into scenes from the cartoon series Pink Panther—to the astonishingly perfidious effect that the drastic sadism of the real deeds

is placed within a frame—the cartoon—that actively denies these deeds the weight and seriousness of the real.

2. Search results for the term "Rechtsextremismus" (right-wing extremism) for the period 11 November 2011 to 11 January 2012: taz, die tageszeitung—61; Spiegel—7; Spiegel Online—22; Welt am Sonntag—7; Welt—23; Hamburger Abendblatt—28; Berliner Morgenpost—26; Berliner Zeitung—23; Berliner Kurier—7; Tagesspiegel—26; ZEIT (inklusive ZEIT Magazin)—3; ZEIT-online—17. www.lexis.com/research/retrieve?_m=5 c52f3ae7fe846a51c395d845792eb24&csvc=fr&cform=searchForm&_ fmtstr=XCITE&docnum=1&_startdoc=1&wchp=dGLbVzS-zSkAl&_ md5=87e6bbff020df2e098fff80e6f404536 [last accessed 29 July 2016].

3. This circumstance becomes obvious in many of the news comments on the findings that actually use the term "repression". For example Ulrich Deppendorf, in a commentary on *Tagesthemen*, 16 November 2011: "We were big in repressing but small in investigating."

4. This statistic is based on a simple count of codified news items. There was no weighing of the news items along the lines of visibility, primacy, length, and so on; multiple encoding per news item (article or TV news clip) was permissible. The aim was a basic overview of what one could find the focus of the reporting to be placed upon per possible media contact during the two-month period (11 November 2011 to 15 January 2012) on a general basis. The low result for reports on the victims might have been slightly bettered by extending the research period so as to cover the central memorial service held in Berlin on 23 February 2012. The service was broadcast live on various TV and radio stations and functioned as a reminder for the news media to turn to the victims in order to come full circle.

References

3sat (2011). *Auf dem rechten Auge blind? Das braune Geschwür: Zwickau.* 30 November. www.3 sat.de/mediathek/?display=1&mode=play&obj= 28262 [last accessed 19 April 2012].

Akyün, H. (2011). Mein Glaube an den Staat ist erschüttert. *Tagesspiegel*, 9 November. www.tagesspiegel.de/berlin/kolumne-mein-berlin-mein-glaube-an-den-staat-ist-erschuettert/5867990.html [last accessed 18 April 2012].

Augstein, J. (2011). S.P.O.N.—Im Zweifel links: Wo bleiben die Anständigen? *Spiegel Online*, 24 November. www.spiegel.de/politik/deutschland/ 0,1518,799565,00.html [last accessed 17 April 2012].

Bild.de (2011a). *3 Stunden später sind sie tot—Die letzten Fotos der Killer-Nazis.* 16 November. www.bild.de/news/inland/nsu/die-letzten-fotos-der-killer-nazis-21058096.bild.html [last accessed 19 April 2012].

Bild.de (2011b). *Jetzt klagen die Kinder der Opfer an: "Warum hat niemand an Nazi-Morde gedacht"*, 14 November. www.bild.de/news/inland/opfer/warum-hat-niemand-an-nazi-morde-gedacht-21011508.bild.html [last accessed 19 April 2012].

Deiß, M., Müller, E., & Thüringer, A. K. (2011). *Acht Türken, ein Grieche und eine Polizistin* [Eight Turks, one Greek, and a police woman], 12 December. Documentary, first aired on *ARD*.

Diehl, J., & Röbel, S. (2013). Streit über Platzvergabe. Münchner Gericht verschiebt NSU-Prozess. *Spiegel Online*, 15 April. www.spiegel.de/panorama/justiz/nsu-prozess-oberlandesgericht-muenchen-a-894375.html [last accessed 3 August 2014].

Fiennes, S. (2006). *The Pervert's Guide to Cinema—Presented by Slavoj Žižek*. Documentary, released 17 June. P Guide Ltd.

Forter, G. (2003). Against melancholia. Contemporary mourning theory, Fitzgerald's The Great Gatsby, and the politics of unfinished grief. *Differences: A Journal of Feminist Cultural Studies, 14*(2): 134–170.

Freud, S. (1917e). Mourning and Melancholia. *S. E., 14*: 239. London: Hogarth.

Freud, S. (1919h). The "Uncanny". *S. E., 17*: 219. London: Hogarth.

Freud, S. (1927e). Fetishism. *S. E., 21*: 149. London: Hogarth.

Gabriel, S. (2011). On *RTL-Aktuell*, 17 November. Not retrievable online [19 April 2012].

Gensing, P. (2014). Der NSU-Terror als Vorbild. *tagesschau.de*, 21 July. www.tagesschau.de/inland/nsu-104.html [last accessed 3 August 2014].

Heitmeyer, W. (2011). Interview in *Tagesthemen*, ARD, 12 December. www.tagesschau.de/multimedia/sendung/tt3582.html [last accessed 19 April 2012].

Herding, K., & Stumpfhaus, B. (Eds.) (2004). *Pathos, Affekt, Gefühl. Die Emotionen in den Künsten*. Berlin: Walter de Gruyter.

Kiewel, M., Kurtz, M., Lemuth, C., Löhr, O., Reichelt, J., Schuler, R., & Sievering, S. (2011). Der kranke Hass der Nazi-Killer. *Bild.de*, 14 November. www.bild.de/news/inland/nsu/nationalsozialistische-terror-gruppe-20982014.bild.html [last accessed 19 April 2012].

Kuzmany, S. (2011a). Neonazi-Debatte bei Illner—Deutschlands braunes Menetekel. *Spiegel Online*, 25 November. www.spiegel.de/kultur/tv/0,1518,799846,00.html [last accessed 17 April 2012].

Kuzmany, S. (2011b). ARD-Doku über Neonazi-Opfer: Die Schande. *Spiegel Online*, 12 December. www.spiegel.de/kultur/tv/0,1518,803138,00.html [last accessed 19 April 2012].

Laplanche, J., & Pontalis, J.-B. (1972). *Das Vokabular der Psychoanalyse*. Frankfurt: Suhrkamp.

Lorenzer, A. (1986). Tiefenhermeneutische Kulturanalyse. In: A. Lorenzer (Ed.), *Kultur-Analysen: Psychoanalytische Studien zur Kultur* (pp. 11–98). Frankfurt: Fischer.

Mazik, A. A. (2011). On *Tagesthemen*. ARD, 12 November. www.tagesschau.
de/multimedia/sendung/tt3510.html [last accessed 19 April 2012].

Merkel, A. (2011). On *Tagesschau*. ARD, 14 November. www.tagesschau.de/
multimedia/sendung/ts30242.html [last accessed 19 April 2012).

Minkmar, N. (2011). Hauptsache, es macht peng! *Frankfurter Allgemeine
Sonntagszeitung*, 20 November, p. 49.

Mitscherlich, A., & Mitscherlich, M. (1967). *Die Unfähigkeit zu trauern* (20th
edn). Munich: Piper, 2007.

Pfetsch, B. (2007). Political communication culture. In: W. Donsbach (Ed.),
International Encyclopedia of Communications. Oxford: Blackwell. www.
communicationencyclopedia.com/subscriber/uid=1268/tocnode?
id=g9781405131995_chunk_g978140513199521_ss52–1 [last accessed
19 April 2012].

Santner, E. L. (1992). History beyond the pleasure principle. In:
S. Friedlander (Ed.), *Probing the Limits of Representation—Nazism and
the "Final Solution"* (pp. 143–154). Cambridge, MA: Harvard University Press.

Schneider, F. (2011). Mein Vater wurde Opfer der Döner-Killer. Die Polizei
nahm unseren Neonazi-Verdacht nicht ernst. *Bild.de*, 14 November.
www.bild.de/news/inland/nsu/tochter-eines-ermordeten-tuerken-
spricht-20991336.bild.html [last accessed 19 April 2012].

Staud, T. (2011). Nicht mehr blind?—Jetzt wird auch wieder diskutiert, wie
viele Menschen Opfer rechter Gewalt wurden. *Die Zeit*, 24 November,
48: 8.

Völkerling, J., Reichelt, J., & Ley, J. (2011). Ein rechter Aussteiger packt aus:
Die Nazi-Braut galt als heißer Feger.*Bild.de*, 16 November. www.bild.de/
news/inland/nsu/die-nazi-braut-galt-als-heisser-feger-21035460.bild.
html [last accessed 19 April 2012].

von Altenbockum, J. (2011). Schreckensbild—Ermittlungen gegen Rechtsextremismus. *Frankfurter Allgemeine Zeitung*, 14 November, 265: 1.

Weiland, S. (2011a). Republik im Schockzustand. *Spiegel Online*, 13 November.
www.spiegel.de/politik/deutschland/0,1518,797509,00.html [last accessed
17 April 2012].

Weiland, S. (2011b). Reaktion auf Neonazi-Terror: Koalition fürchtet um
Deutschlands Ansehen. *Spiegel Online*, 16 November. www.spiegel.de/
politik/deutschland/0,1518,798013,00.html [last accessed 19 April 2012].

CHAPTER SIX

Politicising trauma—a post-colonial and psychoanalytic conceptual intervention*

Margarita Palacios

Introduction

Psychoanalytically informed research on political violence has shown time and again that political violence involves social and cultural processes of othering and libidinal dynamics of desire and enjoyment, usually associated with processes of "feminisation" of those excluded others. This complex nature of political violence begs rethinking of the conceptual and political challenges that post-conflict societies face in their transitions to democracy. For what have been mobilised in the violent events are not only "the strategic interests" of determinate social groups in their struggle for power, but also a whole array of symbolic displacements (that justify exclusion according to dynamics of desire and aggressive jealousy) and, more disturbingly, the "acting out" of those fantasy scenarios and the enjoyment of the suffering of the other. This complex situation disqualifies traditional player-centred approaches that delineate a clear-cut dichotomy between victims and

---

*An extended version of this chapter has been published in my monograph *Radical Sociality: On Disobedience, Violence and Belonging* (Palgrave, 2013).

perpetrators, leaving bystanders—or civil society in general—out of the picture and bearing no responsibility whatsoever.

As violence stands in this paradoxical intersection between meaning and desire, its study requires not only the crossing of disciplinary and methodological boundaries, but also the careful and subtle reading of the different and complex layers that seem to characterise this experience. In order to bring to light at least some of them, I would like to differentiate within the realm of meaning two different moments, one structural and related to processes of identity formation and the limits of the symbolic order, and one contingent, extremely "political" and related to the historical specificities and the power relations that trigger/facilitate experiences of violence—as well as their later acknowledgement/remembrance by the wider public. Certainly, both dimensions are interconnected, as the limits of symbolic representation are covered with fantasies about others who seem to threaten symbolic integrity and the possibility of meaning altogether. Within the realm of desire, on the other hand, one could also distinguish what is called "phallic enjoyment" (desire that is mobilised by fantasy and is related to the enjoyment of excluded, feminised others) and "feminine *jouissance*" (a form of unconscious desire that takes place outside the symbolic order and is linked to the Lacanian "real").

This preliminary conceptual matrix already informs us that episodes of violence do not spring up *ex nihilo* or belong entirely to the sphere of "the eventful" (that is, to the unexpected). On the contrary, violence always has a pre-history, a social-cultural process of othering. Furthermore, this conceptual matrix also points to the fact that violence is structural, as the limits of symbolic representation and the play of fantasies about what destabilises meaning seem to imply a logic of permanent othering. Obviously hegemonic displacements take place, and societies tend to change their conceptions of "who" the other is. This is important to remark on here, at the start: post-conflict societies do not, strictly speaking, "get rid" of violence, but they tend to transform it, whereby different groups—either openly or not—become new targets of hatred and exclusion. Indeed, one could even say that every society is a post-conflict society, as either physical or symbolic violence has inaugurated (and perpetuated) the existing social order. Let me just add here that certain fantasies are much more deeply ingrained in social structures than others. As the experience of racism and homophobia show, "race" and sexuality keep informing exclusionary practices linked to forms of nationalism and masculinity.

When violence is theorised this way, any account of trauma (preliminarily defined here as experiences of being without language) requires a complex conceptual apparatus which, I would like to argue, benefits not only from conceptual sophistication, but mostly from finding ways out of otherwise existing discourses on victimhood and apolitical melancholia, of voyeuristic representation of violence and of naïve and patronising accounts of symbolic closure. I would like to suggest that these latter approaches towards trauma colonise, once again, the excluded other and reduce the ethical challenges of violence to the limits of existing power-ridden cultural practices.

In what follows, I will attempt to contribute to some of the existing debates on trauma and to the theorising of structural violence and the logic of meaning and desire that inform it. Particularly relevant for this endeavour is the contribution of Cathy Caruth to the field, not only because she defines trauma as exceeding the symbolic (that is, as linked to the Lacanian "real"), but also because she situates the possibility of thinking of ethics within the experience of trauma. It is Caruth's theorising of the inescapable imbrication of the self and other in their respective traumas, however, that makes her work a pivotal piece and an unavoidable starting point in my research.

Through a critical engagement with her work, I will try to show how, although being able to draw on the field of trauma studies in its very complexity, Caruth's theorising of trauma could still be pushed further in two ways: first, by incorporating the "sociological-political" layer involved in the social construction of otherness (in such a way that would also account for different experiences of trauma without running the risk of universalising notions of it); and second, by bringing in the notions of desire and enjoyment (that is, expanding her reading of the death drive as compulsion for repetition).

It seems that in her effort to differentiate trauma from any other similar experience of rupture, and to foreclose any possibility of historical "revisionism" (of the Holocaust), Caruth denies both the existence of any form of meaning formation (i.e., there can be no interpretation as the "thing" appears and remains uncovered) and any form of libidinal experience associated with trauma. The not minor consequence of this theoretical choice is that the involvement of the self in the pain of the other (and in its own pain) is defined "as passive, repetitive and blind", that is, as the product of the latency that characterises the traumatic experience.

Now, what is the nature of an experience that lacks a signifier to describe and interpret it? According to Caruth, one that can only be repeated in its literality, beyond the knowledge and the will of the (traumatised) subject. Although Caruth refers to the "act of surviving" as constitutive of trauma (i.e., there is action involved in trauma), still, as we will see in more detail shortly, according to her, the traumatised subject "is possessed" by the traumatic event and cannot process, signify, symbolise, or enjoy it. It is in this condition that the traumatised victim can only blindly and unknowingly "repeat" the trauma and thus become a perpetrator, as demonstrated by Caruth's use of Freud's examples of the murder of Moses and the double crime committed by Tancred against Clorinda (Freud, 1920g).

In what follows, I will explore ways in which ethical claims of mutual responsibility for each other's traumas can avoid being conceptually cancelled out by claims about blindness and compulsive repetition. Incorporating the sociological language of some of the most interesting critiques of "trauma studies" offered by post-colonial authors, and the psychoanalytic language of Lacanian Paul Verhaeghe's different interpretation of trauma (1998), I will bring in notions of meaning formation and enjoyment as ways of reconceptualising action and responsibility and therefore, offering a politicised the notion of trauma.

Limits of representation and the compulsion to repeat: passive victimhood and impossible/failed witnessing

Let us start by looking at Caruth's definition of trauma:

> While the precise definition of post-traumatic stress disorder is contested, most descriptions generally agree that there is a response, sometimes delayed, to an overwhelming event or events, which takes the form of repeated, intrusive hallucinations, dreams, thoughts or behaviours stemming from the event, along with numbing that may have begun during or after the experience, and possibly also increased arousal to (and avoidance of) stimuli recalling the event. This simple definition belies a very peculiar fact: the pathology cannot be defined either by the event itself—which may or not be catastrophic, and may not traumatize everyone equally— nor can it be defined in terms of a distortion of the event, achieving its haunting power as a result of *distorting* personal significances attached to it. The pathology consists, rather, solely in the *structure of its experience* or reception: the event is not assimilated or

experienced fully at the time, but only belatedly, in its repeated *possession* of the one who experiences it. To be traumatized is precisely to be possessed by an image or event. And thus the traumatic symptom cannot be interpreted, simply, as a distortion of reality, nor as the lending of unconscious meaning to a reality it wishes to ignore, nor as the repression of what was once wished. (Caruth, 1995, pp. 4–5)

In the same introduction of Caruth's edited volume *Trauma, Explorations in Memory* (1995), she radicalises what in the previous paragraph was presented more mildly: "Indeed, modern analysts as well have remarked on the surprising *literality* and nonsymbolic nature of traumatic dreams and flashbacks, which resists cure to the extent that they remain, precisely literal." (Caruth, 1995, p. 5) What is remarkable, argues Caruth, is that this literality (or truth of trauma) causes a crisis of knowledge:

For on the one hand, the dreams, hallucinations and thoughts are absolutely literal, unassimilable to associative chains of meaning. It is this literality as we have said that possesses the receiver and resists psychoanalytic interpretation and cure. Yet the fact that this scene or thought is not a possessed knowledge, but it itself possesses, at will, the one it inhabits, often produces a deep uncertainty to its very truth. [...] It is not, that is, having too little or indirect access to an experience that places its truth in question, in this case, but paradoxically enough, its very overwhelming immediacy, that produces its belated uncertainty. (Caruth, 1995, pp. 5–6)

Caruth's argument, although attempting to keep alive the non-reducibility of the "causes" of trauma to purely internal or external causes, still, in my view, clearly puts the accent on the external-event definition, while refusing to theorise the traumatised subject beyond the logic of "being possessed by the event". In this view, the psychosocial "history" of the subject vanishes or plays no role, and so do unconscious desires, metonymic symbolic displacements and fantasy. It is important to stress here that the subjective (internal) side in her account is defined precisely as non-action, or as the impossibility of action, and the hermeneutical stand from where the subject can interpret or assign meaning to the events is defined as being overridden by the structure of the reception of trauma. This, as we have seen, precisely means the incapacity to interpret or create meaning. "Psychoanalytic theory and trauma would indeed meet, in this perspective, on the grounds of this impossible saying." (Caruth, 1995, p. 10) In her account, what has not been symbolised and what possesses the traumatised victim, is "literally" acted out.

This emphasis on the event, rather than on the "structure of experience" (the definition she herself offers of trauma), could also be appreciated in her linking of trauma and history. Caruth argues that trauma is not a pathology of falsehood or displacement of meaning, but a symptom of history itself: "If PTSD must be understood as a pathological symptom, then it is not so much a symptom of the unconscious, as it is a symptom of history" (Caruth, 1995, p. 5).

Her study of the relation between history and trauma is presented in *Unclaimed Experience: Trauma, Narrative and History* (1996), particularly in the chapter "Unclaimed experience: trauma and the possibility of history". Caruth enters into Freud's *Moses and Monotheism* in order to make a case for deconstruction and post-structuralism, and her goal in this piece is to show how her reading of trauma can shed light onto ethical thinking inspired by these traditions of thought. The place of ethics, in her argument, will be the place of history, a history that, like trauma:

> is no longer straightforwardly referential (that is, no longer based
> on simple models of experience and reference). Through the notion
> of trauma, I will argue, we can understand that a rethinking of ref-
> erence is not aimed at eliminating history, but at resituating it in our
> understanding, that is, of precisely permitting *history* to arise where
> *immediate understanding* might not. (Caruth, 1996, p. 182)

According to Caruth, the pertinence of Freud's *Moses and Monotheism* in her analysis of history and trauma, is that "it might help to understand our own catastrophic era, as well as the difficulties of writing history from within it" (1996, p. 182).[1] Furthermore, Caruth states: "*Moses and Monotheism*'s most direct reference to and explanation of, its present historical context will consist in Freud's new understanding of the story of captivity, or exile, and return." (1996, p. 183) The experience of trauma, and in particular the fact of its "latency", refers not to the forgetting of something that once was known, but the inherent forgetting when it is first experienced. She argues:

> And it is this inherent latency of the event that paradoxically explains the peculiar, temporal structure, the belatedness, of the Jew's historical experience: since the murder [of Moses] is not experienced as it occurs, it is fully evident only in connection with another place, and in another time. If return is displaced by trauma, then, this is significant in so far as in leaving—the space of unconscious—is paradoxically what precisely preserves the event in its literality. For history to be a history of trauma means that it is refer-ential precisely to the extent that it is not fully perceived as it occurs; or to put it somewhat differently, that a history can be grasped only in the very inaccessibility of its occurrence. (1996, p. 187)

The ethical dimension springs from this fact: history—as trauma—always implicates the other; in this case, "Jewish history has also been the suffering of other's trauma" (1996, p. 188). "History, like trauma, is never simply one's own, that history is precisely the way in which we are implicated in each other's traumas" (1996, p. 192).

Mediating structural impossibility and meaning formation

Caruth's claim that trauma expresses the limits of language, resonates both with the structuralist claim of language as arbitrary system of signs and with the psychoanalytic notion of the unconscious. In my previous work, and rereading the "classics" of sociology, I have made parallels between the realms of the "sacred" and the "profane" in order to look at the logic of antagonism as different from the logic of differ-ence which spring from the limits of symbolic representation. I have argued that it is necessary to differentiate the "sacred as foundational" (the Durkheimian version of the sacred), from "sacred as quest for meaning" (the Weberian version of the sacred). The first one (sacred as foundational) expresses the original definition of the boundaries of the social, where the spaces for possible and prohibited actions are defined. This type of understanding of the sacred indeed leads to Freud's analy-sis of the relation between totemic religions and the existence of taboos. This Durkheimian/Freudian dimension allows us to see the radicalism of the social as the act of excluding the non-social. The understanding of the sacred as a quest for meaning, allows us to see the different ways in which different cultures address this dualism of inclusion/exclusion (Palacios, 2009). From a social-political perspective, this dualism between social and beyond-the-social is crucial to the understanding of antagonism: following the Durkheimian tradition and joining Castoriadis and Laclau in their assertions of social antagonism, I have argued that:

> society self-institutes itself but denies its own invention for the sake of its own stability. Unable to accept its contingent character, society creates a transcendental narrative about its own origin but since this narrative fails to conceal the existence of a prior pre-symbolic and meaningless pure being, society keeps experiencing a threat which this abyss presents to the constitution of society. (2009, p. 41)

In this context, social antagonism does not refer to the conflict within the symbolic sphere (that is, to the different and maybe opposing meanings—*à la* Weber), but to the expression of the conflict between the symbolic and non-symbolic dimensions of social life. Social antagonism, then, different from social disorganisation and episodic violence, is the act of exclusion of those who are considered to threaten the fragile/contingent symbolic integrity of society.

The question that emerges, and that Caruth's account does not seem to address clearly enough, is how does the structural impossibility of meaning acquire specific 'content'; that is, how is the logic of exclusion played out in our society?

This question becomes particularly relevant from a sociological point of view, such as the one endorsed by post-colonial authors who aim to understand the logic of racism and the particular type of trauma it inflicts. Not necessarily following my own argument, it seems that the post-colonial critique of Caruth's project lies precisely in the fact that her account does not seem to be able to provide either conceptual tools for the understanding of the socio-cultural hegemonies which are based on exclusion of others (such as racism), or political tools to bring about change in our society. Indeed, her positing of the existence of being "beyond the signifier" and the consequent definition of trauma precisely as what cannot be symbolised, can be read as universalising and apolitical if not theorised together with the social logic of meaning formation and othering which accompany it: first, and as I just mentioned, because there seems to be room for such a thing as a "universal trauma" (which a sociologically informed position would find most problematic); and second, because trauma appears as what cannot be known or represented and therefore as what cannot be acted upon (which is problematic from a political-emancipatory perspective). As some post-colonial authors have argued, this apparent universality of trauma seems to find its iconic event (or best example) in the Holocaust, leaving out of sight other sites of violence, such as slavery and contemporary forms of racism.

One interesting example of this type of critique is the work of Irene Visser (2011), who suggests that Caruth's "impossible saying" alienates trauma theory from post-colonial studies. According to Visser, post-colonial theorists might want to sign up to other approaches which keep an open space for narrative, empowerment and political action. The possibility of giving a voice to post-colonial trauma also defies this type of approach, which seems to unwillingly further victimise and pathologise the victim of violence by obscuring recuperation and psychic resilience. Caruth's argument may also give rise to forms of psychological reductionism: colonial trauma is a collective experience which, far from reducing the possibilities of the "working through" to the setting of the analysand and the analyst, is a trauma that demands economic, social and cultural changes. All this requires the acknowledgement of the social logic behind forms of racism which Caruth's definition of trauma is seen as incapable of providing.

The most poignant critique of a purely structural account of trauma consists, however, in the fact that conceptually it seems to open the door for the most problematic confusion between the victim and the perpetrator. In her provocative chapter "Who speaks? Who listens? The problem of address in two Nigerian trauma novels" (2008), Amy Novak argues that the problem with trauma theory is that "it is founded upon the erasure of the voice of the Colonial Other" (2008, p. 32). In *Beyond the Pleasure Principle*, Sigmund Freud refers to this moment in Tasso's *Jerusalem Delivered* as an example of the unconscious repetition of trauma. Tancred's unknowing killing of his beloved not just once, but twice illustrates for Freud a passive compulsion to repeat that makes up part of the dynamics of trauma" (2008, p. 16). In this sixteenth-century epic poem by Torcato Tasso (1822), Tancred, a Christian knight fighting a crusade against Muslims, unknowingly kills his beloved (Muslim) Clorinda, and then he slashes a crying tree where the soul of Clorinda was imprisoned. According to Novak, Caruth reads this scene as an illustration of the latency of trauma and the ethical address delivered through this belated knowing:

> The figure of Tancred addressed by the speaking wound constitutes,
> in other words, not only a parable of trauma and of its uncanny
> repetition, but more generally, a parable of psychoanalytic theory
> itself as it listens to a voice that it cannot fully know but to which it
> nonetheless bears witness. (2008, p. 31)

In Novak's view, this reading demonstrates that they "rewrite one
woman's bodily experience of trauma as the trauma of the male consciousness" (2008, p. 32); failing then both to see Clorinda as traumatised (and Tancred the perpetrator), and to "decipher" the voice of
the crying tree. As Novak states, "And the voice that cries out from
the wound is not a universal voice, nor is a generic female voice: it is the
female voice of black Africa" (2008, p. 32).

According to Novak, Caruth identifies trauma as an ethical discourse of the Other because it "opens up challenges as to a new kind
of listening, the witnessing, precisely, of impossibility" (2008, p. 10).
This formulation, however, erects a "barrier" to such understanding as
long as the Other remains as the spectre of impossibility. Novak states:
"Clorinda, already Westernised, now becomes an aporetic voice that
cries out but remains unsignified" (2008, p. 32).

Novak's essay is part of a special issue of *Studies in the Novel* (2008),
entitled "Post Colonial Trauma Novels". In the introduction, the editors
of this special issue remark on the fact that Caruth asserts that trauma
can bridge otherwise isolated individuals and cultures:

> Caruth insists on the ethical significance of this critical practice. She
> claims that "the language of trauma, and the silence of its mute rep-
> etition of suffering, profoundly and imperatively demand" a "new
> mode of reading and of listening" […] what would allow us to pass
> out of the isolation imposed on both individuals and cultures by
> traumatic experience. In a catastrophic age, such as ours, according
> to Caruth, trauma itself may provide the very link between cul-
> tures. (Craps & Beulens, 2008, pp. 9–11)

"With trauma forming a bridge between disparate historical experiences, so the argument goes, listening to the trauma of another can
contribute to cross-cultural solidarity and to the creation of new forms
of community." (Craps & Beulens, 2008, p. 2) Their view is that much
work needs to be done for the ethical impetus of trauma studies to reach

non-Westerners. In particular, they argue that "colonial" trauma has its own peculiarities. Understanding colonial traumas such as disposses-sion, forced migration, diaspora, slavery, segregation, racism, political violence and genocide, requires acknowledgement that, first and fore-most, this is not about an "event" that happened and that now can be looked back at, but that it constitutes the everyday life of vast numbers of people in our contemporary society. The challenge appears to be to politicise trauma by incorporating it within a hermeneutical tradition that acknowledges that trauma is related to social and cultural process of othering and that, therefore, far from being deprived of, is "full of meaning".

A different way to inquire about the suitability of a purely structural account of trauma departs from the question about whether what can-not be assimilated within language refers to the (external) realm of the traumatic event, or whether it is associated as well with the (internal) psychic life of the victim. If it only belongs to the "event", then the sub-ject is theorised as a passive victim of it (and indeed, under such prem-ise, there is conceptual room to theorise the victim as "possessed" by the event). From a sociological perspective, this definition of trauma is rather difficult to accept, as the traumatising event appears as "univer-sally traumatising" independently of the cultural and subjective dis-position of the victim. This type of argument has been put forward in the collection of essays edited by Jeffrey Alexander, *Cultural Trauma and Collective Identity*, where he argues that "trauma is a socially mediated attribution" (Alexander, 2004, p. 8) which responds to spirals of sig-nification that take place over time. Differentiating what he calls "lay theory" (an approach that takes a naturalistic stand regarding trauma) and his own "cultural trauma", he argues: "What is wrong with this lay trauma theory is that it is 'naturalistic', either in the naively moral or the naively psychological sense. Lay trauma theory fails to see that there is an interpretative grid through which all 'facts' about trauma are mediated, emotionally, cognitively, and morally" (2004, p. 201). Although Alexander is referring in his analysis to the process of social construction of trauma, and not to the individual experience of trauma, his sociological perspective still differs from a psychological one pre-cisely in his prioritising of the social hermeneutical context from which experiences (including trauma) are signified.

Now, the opposite statement seems to be the same problematic. If not the event but rather the psychic life of the victim is recognised as the origin of trauma, then the universalising claim of trauma is further depoliticised reducing it to individual psychology. Probably the leading critique of Caruth's work in this respect is Ruth Leys. In "The pathos of the literal", the last chapter of her *Trauma: A Genealogy* (2000), Leys scrutinises Caruth's reading of Freud and argues that her "ideological" approach leads her to foreclose the inherent tension between "mimesis" and "anti-mimesis" (identification and separation) that guides Freud's understanding of trauma, by entirely denying the subjective participation in the phenomenon of trauma. According to Leys:

> Caruth posits an absolute opposition between external trauma and victim in ways that have been associated historically with the repudiation of mimesis. But by imagining that trauma stands outside representation altogether, she also embraces a version—in fact is more like an inadvertent parody—of mimetic theory. Indeed, I demonstrate that although Caruth does not discuss the problem of hypnosis, historically central to the genealogy of trauma, the question of mimesis surfaces in her text in her insistence on the contagious effects of trauma. (Leys, 2000, p. 8)

In Leys's view, and based on Freud's various writings on trauma, trauma is related both to the "breaching of the protective field, or unbinding" and to mimetic identification "or binding" (2000, p. 33). This is because, according to Leys:

> in the economic terms associated with Freud's ideas, the traumatic experience involves a fragmentation or loss of unity of the ego resulting from the radical unbinding of the death drive, but it also entails a simultaneous binding (or rebinding) of cathexes: both unbinding and binding—hate and love—are constitutive of the traumatic reaction. (2000, p. 34)

Leys states:

> "Asocial and social". Doesn't that characterize the behaviour of the traumatized soldier as described by Kardiner and others? Paradoxically, the asocial traumatized soldier who is so antimimetically withdrawn from the world that he is completely numb to it is simultaneously so socially identified with it that the boundaries between himself and others are completely effaced. (2000, p. 35)

According to Leys, several problems arise from the dichotomy mimesis–antimimesis (which is replicated in versions of trauma as seated primarily inside or outside the traumatised subject), one of which is particularly important for my argument, namely that:

> the same dichotomy between internal and external reinforces an opposition between absolute aggressor and absolute victim in such a way as to render untheorizable the violence and ambivalence that, according to the mimetic hypothesis, is necessarily inherent in the victim of the traumatic scenario. The mimetic theory makes it possible to sympathetically acknowledge the hideous ways in which the victim can come to psychically collude in the scene of violence through fantasmatic identifications with the scene of aggression. Whereas the complete rejection of any idea of the mimetic renders the source of such identifications mysterious. (2000, p. 38)

Interestingly, Leys also pays attention to Caruth's problematic reading of *Jerusalem Delivered*. Not exactly agreeing with Novak, Leys still states that Caruth's use of the parable of the wound is misplaced. First, because Freud was not referring to the double crime of Tancred as an example of traumatic neurosis, but only as an example of how even normal people tend to repeat unpleasurable experiences, and hence an example of the compulsion to repeat or the death drive. She argues: "Just as Caruth converts the Israelites who murdered Moses into passive victims of the trauma of an accidental 'separation', so she converts Tancred into the victim of trauma as well." (2000, p. 294) Furthermore, she states: "It is not Tancred, but Clorinda who is the indisputable victim of a wounding." (2000, p. 294) With her reading, Leys asserts, Caruth also raises a question whether perpetrators are themselves victims too: "Caruth's logic would turn other perpetrators into victims too—for example, it would turn the executioners of the Jews into victims and the 'cries' of the Jews into testimony to the trauma suffered by the Nazis" (Leys, 2000, p. 297).

Summing up, compelling arguments have been offered in order to criticise Caruth's structural approach. In my view, however, it is not the structural approach *per se* that needs to be discarded; rather, it needs to be complemented and expanded. First, by bringing in theories of meaning formation which depict in its complexity the relation between "the sacred and profane", or the metonymic displacements that take place within and because of the limits of signification; and second, by a theory which expands on the 'affects' of the death drive, that is, anxiety and non-phallic enjoyment.

From traumatic event to fantasy and drive: back to the subject

A very different take on trauma is offered by Lacanian Paul Verhaeghe. In his *Trauma and Hysteria in Freud and Lacan* (1998), Verhaeghe carefully reads Freud's theorising, and attempts to show how trauma here becomes increasingly structural, that is, not related to any particular traumatic event, but to the (constitutive) experience of the death drive. The way he presents his argument is by going back to the classic distinction between a "hysteric" and a "traumatised neurotic", whereby the first one is supposed to be a fraud as opposed to the latter real patient that has actually undergone some traumatic experience. In an ironic gesture, Verhaeghe states that we live in an era where we tend to see less and less hysterics, and only victims and survivors. His point is precisely to show that there is no such thing as a "pure" victim:

> On the one hand, we find the hysterical patients with their merely fantasmatic aetiology, that is, an imaginary early infantile traumatic seduction [...] at the other end we find at last the real patients, which means, from this point of view, those who have been subjected to real traumatic situations and whose pathologies are direct consequence of these situations. The most remarkable thing about this binary categorization is that the first category tends to become smaller and smaller while the second keeps growing. Nowadays there are almost no patients left, there are only victims who are in no way whatsoever implied in their situation. (Verhaeghe, 1998, p. 88)

He then goes on to show how even those who advocate types of "victimhood" recognise that for therapeutic reasons the therapist should never 'take away' from the patient their own responsibility and choice (1998, p. 88). Verhaeghe states that this not only resonates with Freud's notion of *neurosenwahl*, but that ultimately this space of "responsibility or choice" is the only thing that gives certain hope in the recovery of a person; otherwise it is pure fatalism what remains, as the traumatic event has indeed taken place.

This first paragraph already shows us the distance between Caruth and Verhaeghe. For the latter, the structure of the reception of the event that characterises trauma does not *erase or possess* the subject, but as we will see in what follows, in complex ways it indeed interacts with the subject's structural trauma. According to Verhaeghe, trauma does involve mechanisms of displacement of meanings and forms of enjoyment.

Verhaeghe argues one can speak of two traumas, one "internal" and related to the drive, and another one "external" and related to a certain event. According to Freud: "Drive in itself, independently of any externally determined trauma has a potentially traumatising effect to which the psyche has to come up with an answer, that is, with a psychological elaboration. This elaboration takes place in and through the fantasy, which receives in this way, a very important function." (Verhaeghe, 1998, p. 96) In light of this, Verhaeghe argues that an "eventual" trauma will necessarily become in interaction with the "structural" trauma associated to the drive transforming hysteria into traumatic neurosis. According to him, the function of the fantasy remains the same, "namely, elaborating in the imaginary what could not find an adequate answer in the symbolic" (1998, p. 97). Now, it is important to note here how Verhaeghe does not claim that all trauma will be displaced into words: "In the case of accidental trauma, this (fantasy) elaboration will not be enough, the real aetiology of the traumatic neurosis would also cause symptoms in the real, psychosomatic phenomena and automutilation being the two most well known." (1998, p. 97) Indeed, the function of memory and remembering (or being able to symbolise) are quite different in the case of unconscious fantasies, and in the case of non-verbalised traumatic experiences. While the latter led Freud to formulate the necessity of remembering and "speaking-out" as routes to find cure, in the former case it is the notion of "working-through"—or, in Lacanian terms, "transversing the Fantasy"—that emerges as the analytic goal of the therapy. Certainly, at this point waters separate, and some would tend to think this *durch-arbeiten*, the working through, would allow some sort of symbolic closure. A Lacanian reading, however, is quite different: instead of symbolic closure, the traumatic kernel of the real is theorised as not finding resolution in the symbolic order; desire as never satisfied; and the experience of anxiety—as the experience of closeness to the real—as a permanent threat to the fragile symbolic integrity of any existing fantasy.

How, then, does this view differ from Caruth's? First, and more evidently, Verhaeghe stresses the fact that what will necessarily fail to find representation within language is the structural trauma, and not necessarily the eventual/historical trauma. But beyond this, and more significantly for this chapter, is the fact that for him this unrepresentability does not annul or come to possess the subject, as the subject will be able to build unconscious fantasies as forms of elaboration or protection, and also experience anxiety and forms of enjoyment. Although what will not be linguistically mediated will appear in forms of symptoms, this account differs from Caruth's notion of the literality of the acting out. But this is not all: Freud's analysis of the compulsion to repeat stimulated him to rethink the limits of the pleasure principle. In his studies of war trauma, Freud realised the peculiarity of how physical injuries worked in a "positive way", so to say, regarding trauma, as if the physical injury would work as a sort of "verbalisation" of what is not otherwise signified in words. But what is it that escapes signification? Lacan, as is well known, provides a structural reading of this. In Verhaeghe's words:

> Something stays beyond the symbolic order, beyond the pleasure principle, because it is different, even alien. One of its most bizarre characteristics besides this impossible verbalization resides in the fact that it produces a strange form of pleasure, strange because it differs from phallic pleasure provided by the pleasure principle and symbolic order. (Verhaeghe, 1998, p. 102)

In *Beyond the Pleasure Principle*, Freud (1920g) was precisely trying to understand the confusing dynamic of the drives (*eros* and *thanatos*), which, far from operating in separate modes, operated together in what he called "*Triebmischung*". According to Verhaeghe, the pleasure principle seems to operate closer to the symbolic realm, as it can indeed be verbalised; *thanatos*, on the other hand, operates beyond the signifier, and is mute. Verhaeghe goes on to suggest that:

> this is the most uncanny about trauma and probably also the most traumatizing aspect about trauma, namely the experience that something in the body enjoys the situation a kind of enjoyment from which the subject shrinks back in horror. (Verhaeghe, 1998, p. 104)

Final remarks: from blind repetition to unconscious performativity?

We have seen throughout this chapter that trauma in different ways points to that paradoxical and radical experience that takes place between meaning and non-meaning, that is, in Heideggerian terms, between "knowledge and truth". In particular, we have addressed how ethics of responsibility seem to be cancelled out when trauma is defined only structurally (as what exceeds signification and is acted out literally. Instead I have tried to present modes of expanding such definition in ways that enlarge and displace the identity—of trauma victim—in ways in which this "existential position" could claim *a priori* experiences of transparency, wholeness and passivity. Instead, trauma (and I would argue witnessing as well) seems to involve opacity, absence-partiality, and activity, in what could be called forms of conscious and unconscious performativity. The conceptual and political reach of these notions is yet to be explored, but it seems that a theoretical account which acknowledges activity and responsibility—derived from the participation in processes of meaning formation and enjoyment—is worth taking as a point of departure when thinking of violence and belonging in their always interconnected and paradoxical dimensions.

Note

1. In this highly speculative book, Freud hypothesises that Moses was not Jewish but Egyptian. Contradicting the biblical story, Freud claims that Moses was killed by the Jews and that years after this murder the rebels (out of guilt) formed a new concept of the Messiah in the hope of a return of Moses as the Saviour of the Israelites.

References

Alexander, J., Eyerman, R., Giesen, B., Smelser, N. J., & Sztompka, P. (2004). *Cultural Trauma and Collective Identity*. Berkeley, CA: University of California Press.

Caruth, C. (Ed.) (1995). *Trauma. Explorations in Memory*. Baltimore, MD: Johns Hopkins University Press.

Caruth, C. (1996). *Unclaimed Experience*. Baltimore, MD: Johns Hopkins University Press.

Craps, S., & Buelens, G. (2008). Post-colonial trauma novels. *Studies in the Novel, 40*(1–2): 1–12.

Freud, S. (1920g). *Beyond the Pleasure Principle. S. E., 18*: 7. London: Hogarth.

Leys, R. (2000). *Trauma: A Genealogy*. Chicago, IL: University of Chicago Press.

Novak, A. (2008). Who speaks? Who listens? The problem of address in two Nigerian trauma novels. *Studies in the Novel, 40*(1–2): 31–51.

Palacios, M. (2009). *Fantasy and Political Violence: The meaning of Anti-Communism in Chile*. Wiesbaden: Verlag für Sozialwissenschaften.

Palacios, M. (2013). *Radical Sociality: On Disobedience, Violence and Belonging*. London: Palgrave.

Tasso, T. (1822). *Tasso's Jerusalem delivered: an heroic poem; with notes and occasional illustrations*. Philadelphia, PA. https://archive.org/details/tassosjerusalemd01tass.

Verhaeghe, P. (1998). Trauma and hysteria in Freud and Lacan. *The Letter: Lacanian Perspectives on Psychoanalysis, 14*: 87–106.

Visser, I. (2011). Trauma theory and postcolonial literary studies. *Journal of Postcolonial Writing, 47*(3): 270–282.

CHAPTER SEVEN

Ongoing mourning as a way to go beyond endless grief—considerations on the Lebanese experience

Nayla Debs

There is no doubt that contemporary narratives have been largely dominated by the discourse on trauma that has influenced various academic fields ranging from psychoanalysis and psychiatry to philosophy and aesthetics, and determined movements of thought that aimed to reconsider the principles of politics and ethics in the light of the catastrophes that took place during the twentieth century. These extreme situations challenged the ability of traditional discourses to give an account of what happened and opened the way to new frames of narration that sought to deal with past atrocities and reflect on ways supposed to prevent their recurrence. One of the main changes was the relinquishment of a sort of master-narration in favour of a fragmented history (Lyotard, 1979), without giving up the claim to truth that remained imperative mainly in situations where the material traces were subject to effacement. This particularly characterised the works produced in the wake of the Holocaust, an "event at the limit of" (Friedlander, 1992, p. 3), which resisted representation but at the same time necessitated historical rendition, resulting in a multi-layered construction that called upon a plurality of discourses to address the complexity of the genocide. But this cultural rendition was also facilitated by the judicial work that helped establish a rupture with past events and handle their consequences. By recognising mass crimes and prosecuting those responsible for them, post-war trials did indeed contribute to reinstating democratic principles and ideals of justice on the basis of which new social and national bonds could be forged.

Different yet of crucial importance was the contribution of postcolonial literature that, by embracing emancipatory narratives, tried to restore the subjectivity of the "colonized" or the "subjugated". What is at stake here is a critical analysis of some dominant policies and epistemological discourses, with the aim of exposing the ideological soil they are rooted in, the contingent nature of the truth they claim, and the power relations they conceal and perpetuate. This was mainly theorised by scholars such as Edward Said and Gayatri Spivak whose work helped better understand how certain modes of "othering" are constructed, the violence they entail, and the types of subjects they produce, who in most cases either don't have the right to narrate (Said, 1984) or simply cannot speak (Spivak, 2010).

What underlies these narratives is the question of mourning that remains the counterpart of any work on trauma. If the concern about mourning is certainly not new, contemporary events have nevertheless imposed a reformulation of the terms through which mourning was articulated. It was indeed imperative to confront unprecedented experiences of destruction and loss, and find means to symbolise them. And this necessarily involves the work of mourning insofar as it implies an attempt to come to terms with these experiences; that is, the ability to go beyond them and at the same time to integrate and transform their effects through the work of remembering and forgetting (Ricœur, 2004).

In this chapter, I will consider the question of mourning within the particular context of the Lebanese experience. The recent history of Lebanon has been marked by a series of violent events whose repetitive character has rendered their elaboration as necessary as it is difficult. This chapter proposes to examine, from a psychoanalytic perspective, the specific modalities of mourning that accompanied these events. More specifically, it aims to shed light on the relations between mourning and repetition: the way repetition has hindered the work of mourning and vice versa; and how certain experiences of mourning have contributed to displace and modify repetition. The psychic processes involved in each case are discussed on a collective and individual level.

Based on Freud's early view on mourning (1917e), I will consider two modalities of mourning the past that mainly reflect the limit of mourning: one that is governed by the over-presence of the trace and the permanent attachment to the lost object; the other characterised by the absence of the trace that also strengthens, yet in a different way, the relation to what is lost. These two models, insofar as they fail to address loss, may be considered, in a normative perspective, as variants of "unresolved" mourning.

But there are also other forms of dealing with the past that merit attention. These forms consist mainly of acknowledging loss while preserving the relation to the lost object, questioning hence a strictly binary reading of the Freudian model and highlighting the complexity of the work of mourning as suggested in Freud's later texts. Drawing on these texts as well as other philosophical writings, and reflecting on them through an example taken from the realm of cultural production, I will put forward the idea of unfinished mourning as the condition of coming to terms with the past, a process that preserves the relation to the past while transforming the latter and opening it to future possibilities. It is this conception of mourning and its subjective implications that I try to account for in the last section of this chapter.

But first, it seems important to go over some of the events that marked the history of Lebanon during the last decades. This historical review helps better identify the problem of repetition and constitutes a situated framework without which the understanding the work of mourning in Lebanon, or some of its aspects, remains abstract if not spurious.

Lebanon's unfinished wars and the politics of amnesia

The Lebanese civil war officially ended in 1989 with the Taif Agreement, known also as the National Reconciliation Accord, which aimed to provide a return to political normalcy after fifteen years of armed clashes. However, the return to normalcy remained hypothetical or, at best, very partial. In fact, except the cessation of fighting, few significant changes occurred. The Syrian domination of the country, the Israeli occupation of the southern part, in addition to the laws and the amendments that were ratified resulted in a situation reminiscent in many respects of the past one and these conditions deterred any serious effort to reflect critically on the past. The amnesty law issued in the wake of the Taif Agreement (law 94/91) played a decisive role in this respect. By pardoning all those who engaged in war crimes, in other words by whitewashing the perpetrators who were to become political leaders, the amnesty law prevented from addressing responsibilities and blocked any legal process that would help deal with the legacies of the past. In a sense, it prepared the ground for a politics of forgetting.

Indeed, there was a deliberate attempt to impose silence regarding past events by avoiding public trials that could reveal the truth about what happened by giving voice to the victims to express their grievances and to the perpetrators (the fighters) to account for their acts. As complicated as it might be—since in a context of civil war the positions of the victim and the aggressor may be interchangeable—this process was the only way to reinstate the rule of law and ensure reconciliation in a society torn by fifteen years of fratricide wars. What happened is that not only was this work circumvented but also the amnesty law itself was misused so as to bring to court only opponents of the established regime, namely those who opposed the Syrian hegemony over the country, leading to a selective and arbitrary application of the law that has become a common practice in the post-war period.

This loophole was in fact part of a broader political and cultural system characterised by the desire to forget that has impregnated different realms of the Lebanese life. What best embodied this state of forgetfulness was the process of reconstruction of Beirut, mainly the downtown area, initiated in the aftermath of the war and conceived in a way as to leave no trace of the past. Indeed, all the elements, the ruins or the remains that could witness of the destruction that wilted the heart of the city, were systematically wiped out giving way to a "new city" that reflected the wish to break off the ties with the past and substitute it with new beginnings. Yet, the new beginning in the Lebanese sense meant mainly the return to the pre-war era, those two or three decades of social and economic prosperity that followed the independence (1943), usually described in historical narratives as a golden era that has resulted in forging a mythical image of the city (Kassir, 2010) that the reconstruction sought precisely to revive.

This search for new beginnings achieved through the reification of a previous state found its symbol in the myth of the phoenix that the Lebanese were inclined to adopt, probably encouraged by the etymology of the word evoking Phoenician origins they can identify with and by the facility of the narrative that allowed them to assign a meaning to their experience without having to delve into their history. The myth of the bird able to arise from its own ashes announcing a sort of triumph of life over death was used in a way as to mask the inability to come to grips with a war that was never appropriated by the Lebanese as theirs. Indeed, it was always considered as "The War of the Others" to cite the title of a book written by well-known Lebanese publicist, Ghassan Tueni, during the war, that soon became the motto adopted by the Lebanese to make sense of what happened. Although Tueni's book (1985) was initially a personal account witnessing the role of foreign forces in Lebanon's wars, it has fuelled a whole theory that, by framing the war as an event caused by outside powers, contributed to estrange the Lebanese from their history and enhanced the refusal to reckon with it.

In short, all the elements converged to create a vacuum in the collective consciousness regarding war events: the myth, the regional context, and the interests of local politicians who knew that remembering would lead to their defeat. This went hand in hand with active policies in favour of forgetting as attested by the total absence of memorials, museums, or monuments dedicated to the war or the victims. Even the work of the French sculptor Arman, created to commemorate the end of the war (consisting of an imposing column with tanks and war vehicles inserted in the concrete), couldn't find its way to the city centre and ended up in the suburb of Beirut (Young, 2010).

Only art and literature were able to create spaces where remembering was still possible. Indeed, various writers, artists, and filmmakers have placed memory issues at the centre of their work trying in some way to unearth what politics and urban renewal were razing. But these productions, as important as they were, couldn't bring public awareness to memory issues, nor were they able to transform them into a political question. Thus, these issues remained confined in the cultural interstices of the society, although these interstices were vital enough in a city like Beirut.

However, this politically organised amnesia couldn't succeed in eradicating all the traces of the war. The process of reconstruction itself reveals the impossibility of a total effacement since part of the city was rebuilt over the rubble resulting from the ruins and debris of destroyed buildings. In fact, there was a double process taking place, which sought to efface the visible traces of the past while inscribing them in the depth of the city. As the Lebanese writer Elias Khoury observed, reconstructing Beirut consisted of recycling the old city and this yielded to a paradoxical operation where emptiness was feeding a dump on which part of the new city was being built (Khoury, 1995, pp. 137–142). But this recycling process is necessarily incomplete. There were indeed materials that resist transformation like, for instance, the toxic wastes imported during the war and buried in the mountains surrounding Beirut, as Khoury recalls. In some way, these non-convertible materials that have conserved their potential toxicity resonate with this part of the past that even buried continues to haunt the present with its traumatic effects.

These dormant effects came to the fore in the wake of the current crisis that started in 2005. The series of political assassinations that rocked Lebanon (the assassination of former Prime Minister Rafic Hariri and other politicians and public figures), the Israeli war in 2006, and the change in the political configuration that followed proved that the memory of past conflicts remained very vivid and that these conflicts could be easily reactivated in the present. Indeed, in the midst of the rampant chaos that was taking over Lebanon, divisions and front lines emerged that recalled and reproduced scenes of the civil war. This has resulted in a general state of instability that turned out to be more threatening to the Lebanese entity than the war itself. Lebanon was indeed lurching toward a new civil war that was destroying what has remained of its political institutions and putting into question the very sustainability of Lebanon as a country.

Beyond the political and historical factors that trigger and sustain these unfinished wars, there is here a repetitive pattern that gains to be elucidated from a psychoanalytic standpoint. Referring to Freud's text on repetition (1914g)—and transposing it from an individual to a collective level—one might say that what was not elaborated by the Lebanese was being repeated and re-enacted. As Freud put it, the compulsion to repeat is a "way of remembering" (p. 150) when the traumatic load of the experience hinders its conscious elaboration. But the repetition is also an attempt to mediate the trauma and work it through, as Freud suggests later on when reformulating his views on drives. In *Beyond the Pleasure Principle* (1920g), repetition is conceptualised as the site of a hypothetical death drive but it is also a manner to gain control over a traumatic element. The *fort/da* game that the child resorts to enables him to master the distress resulting from the mother's absence (Freud, 1920g). Through the rhythm it establishes, the repetitive play contributes to create a space where a symbolising activity becomes possible, allowing the transformation of trauma and therefore the restoration of the pleasure principle. In this perspective, the vicissitude of repetition depends mainly on how it is linked to the pleasure and unpleasure principles and, more generally, to life and death instincts. What seems decisive in this process is the work of mourning that, by elaborating the dire consequences of trauma, helps disentangle what is locked in a repetition compulsion. But this also operates the other way around: repetition can temper the negativity of some feelings and memories and prepare for an encounter with them.

To return to the Lebanese context, some collective manifestations that emerged as reactions to violent events can be elucidated through this conceptual grid that tries to link together repetition and forms of mourning. The following section aims to explore this.

The becoming of loss, between the excess and lack of trace

The assassination in 2005 of former Prime Minister Rafic Hariri in a massive truck-bomb explosion marked a turning point in the very recent history of Lebanon and was to inaugurate a cycle of violence that brought about a large movement of revolt and counter-revolt. Within a short period of time, a series of political murders happened at whirlwind speed, targeting some of the country's most prominent politicians and journalists. This gave rise to a massive popular reaction that expressed the rejection of this state of affairs and refusal of violence as a way of settling political problems. Hariri's murder in particular provoked huge rallies in the streets of Beirut where people of different faiths (except Hezbollah, the powerful Shiite formation, and other pro-Syrian groups) came together to demand the withdrawal of the Syrian forces from Lebanon—a movement known as the Cedar Revolution that led to the ousting of the Syrian troops. As Michael Young put it, "indignation was their first impulse when Hariri was killed; from that indignation emerged an assumption that the absence of freedom and rule of law would only bring on more indignities" (Young, 2010, p. 5).

In fact, the series of assassinations that targeted leading figures who overtly challenged the Syrian domination was at the limit of what could be tolerated by the Lebanese in the sense that it exceeded the "ordinary" violence and compromises they were accustomed to. This bare violence constituted such a shock in the collective consciousness that it was impossible to carry on with the same processes of denial and resignation that predominated before. There are many reasons that could account for this outcry, not least among them the killing of Hariri himself. Given the role of the man and his political weight, his elimination bore significations that extended to the regional scene and left a deep impact locally leading to a considerable change in the perception of politics and the relation to the past. Concerning the last point, it's worth noting that the late Prime Minister played a major role in the process of forgetting by implementing liberal policies that were turned toward the future at the expense of the past. The controversial project of the reconstruction of Beirut, that he initiated and controlled, expressed at best the amnesic scope of his plans. Therefore, it appeared as a logical consequence that the assassination of Hariri would also reverse this tendency, bringing back all the questions that were eluded, mainly those pertaining to civil conflicts, justice, and accountability. But what was also shaken by his brutal death was the faith in the social contract, in the broadest sense of the term, and the value of life. Hariri indeed was associated with such an image of invulnerability that his killing resonated as a message signalling that the life of every citizen would be at risk were they to defy those who have got the upper hand in the country. In fact, the recourse to physical elimination, that was a common practice during the war—but didn't really stop after, posed a threat to this primary rule that forms the basis of social life: the prohibition of murder. The series of assassinations brought this harsh reality to the fore, stirring up feelings of indignation in large segments of the population. That's why one of the first reactions many Lebanese had was the demand for justice. This materialised in a specific claim that the rallies were repeating: an international investigation to shed truth about the killing, which resulted later in the establishment of the Special Tribunal for Lebanon (STL).

There is no doubt that Hariri's funeral as well as the funerals that followed were instituting public forms of mourning that allowed the Lebanese for the first time to express collectively their grief and sorrow. The popular processions that took place were in fact occasions to work through the death of all the people whose loss couldn't be mourned in the past. But they also constituted occasions to reaffirm the refusal of terror and the will to end the political-security system that has long ruled the country. And this has transformed mourning into an act of resistance, the site of an agency that carried a potentiality of change.

However, what started as a mourning process was soon to become a repetitive act, a ritual that was progressively being emptied of its meaning. The relentless pursuit of assassinations, the banalisation of violence, and the political divisions that (re)appeared have transformed these national ceremonials into partisan manifestations where rivalries and the struggle for power superseded all the rest, pushing each group to consolidate its position by reviving a sectarian discourse where the figure of the "martyr" occupies a central role. On the other hand, the slowness and shortcomings that characterised the work of the STL deferred prospects of accountability and justice, leaving the Lebanese—or part of them—in the grip of a violence they could neither avoid nor elaborate. This obviously complicated any attempt to come to terms with these events and led practically to the opposite extreme where mourning the dead became synonymous with the refusal to let go. Indeed, the martyrs were constantly convoked on the political scene; they induced discourses and cultural practices that mainly aimed to reify them. Their images and posters have filled the streets of Beirut and this obsessive presence was signing the difficulty of a city to deal with absence while realising the price it had to pay for not doing so.

The need to mourn got sharper in the aftermath of the Israeli war (2006) that bred damage and death mainly in the ranks of Hezbollah and the Shiite community. Here again the cult of martyrdom was pushed to the limits. Huge posters were hoisted in honour of the martyrs, ceremonials were regularly held where the victims were glorified and depicted as heroes or models to be imitated. Death was not deplored—at least in the official discourse—but rather perceived as a necessary sacrifice, a goal that gives meaning to life. In fact, the importance of sacrifice in the Shiite imagination, mainly among Hezbollah's militants, stems from two distinct elements: on one hand, the religious history of Shiite Islam that tends to be identified as a history of injustice and persecution with respect to the early divides that opposed Shiites to the dominant Sunnis; on the other, the social conditions, mainly the forms of wretchedness and marginalisation that characterised the Shiite community in Lebanon before the outburst of the civil war. Hezbollah, literary the Party of God, has accentuated and exploited these components to promote an ideology where the idea of suffering and sacrifice takes precedence over the value of life. The slogan "Each day is Karbala" (referring to the religious battle that has marked the Shiite imaginary and identity) that many people in South Lebanon share shows the extent to which ideas of sacrifice and fighting injustice have infused mentalities and illustrates the way Hezbollah conflates local grievances and religious narratives in order to push for its cause. Of course, sacrifice finds its most radical expression in martyrdom, a notion that plays a major role in Hezbollah's ideology revealing the preponderant place of death in its doctrine. In his work on suicide bombers, Farhad Khosrokhavar (2005) observes that martyrdom in this context doesn't mean bearing witness to the righteousness of a cause; death is not for the sake of a better life but in the service of a sacred cause. Of course, the double significance that the term "martyrdom" (*shahâda*) bears in Arabic facilitates the confusion since it can mean witnessing but also dying as a martyr. In the history of religion, these two meanings were sometimes associated; there were indeed situations whether in Christianity or in Buddhism where bearing witness could be at the point of death. But in Hezbollah's ideology, bearing witness to a right cause yields to a sort of quest for death, a fascination with it as attested in Hezbollah's narratives, whether in the discourse of its leaders or militants. Annihilation of the self and the other becomes the ultimate target as it allows the combatant to rise to the status of martyr. Of course, the question of self-sacrifice touches on the controversial notion of *jihad* and holy wars that it is not possible to discuss here. But one can say that this framing of death has deeply affected the significance of mourning that would involve less feelings of grief than of triumph and a lament less for the one who passed than for those who remained, who are incited to follow his path rather than to transform the conditions that led to his death.

Needless to say, the idealisation of the figure of the martyr and the overinvestment of the absent contrast with the model of mourning Freud laid out in *Mourning and Melancholia* (1917e), since the work of mourning primarily aims to withdraw the attachments to the lost object. If Freud admits that this process "arouses understandable opposition" (p. 244), he reaffirms nevertheless that the end of mourning coincides with the severance of all the ties to the loved object. In fact, Freud describes a two-phase process whereby the mourner tries first to prolong the psychic existence of the lost object, by bringing up and hypercathecting the memories and the expectations related to the latter, before withdrawing the libido in accordance with the reality principle that judged that the object not longer exists (pp. 244–245). In a way, the mourner is driven to cease the relation to the lost object in order to continue to live and it's only when this operation is completed that the subject is able to reinvest new objects.

If we compare this theoretical outline to the different rituals that took place in Lebanon (whether in the case of the assassinations or the Israeli war), one cannot say that these manifestations aim to prolong psychically the existence of the lost objects. What these features reflect is rather an attitude that tends to disavow the reality of loss itself. The images, the posters, and the various materials were not just symbolising or reminding of the lost objects; somehow, they became these objects effacing the distance that separates the sign from the original object or the trace from what marked it. And this evidently creates affinities with fetishism since what seems at stake is the particular way an object is used so as to stand in for what is lost just as the fetish, as Freud contends, is supposed to cover up the mother's castration. There is in fact a contradictory trait that characterises the Lebanese response to loss since the perception of loss co-existed with its denial, and this brings to mind the functioning Freud describes in *Fetishism*:

> It is not true that, after the child has made his observation of the woman, he has preserved unaltered his belief that women have a phallus. He has retained that belief, but he has also given it up. In the conflict between the weight of the unwelcome perception and the force of his counter-wish, a compromise has been reached, as is only possible under the dominance of the unconscious laws of thought—the primary processes. (Freud, 1927e, p. 154)

If this process indicates a psychic functioning under the primacy of the pleasure principle that precludes the possibility to elaborate lack or frustration, it also puts forward a narcissistic fragility that tends to reject any perception of lack which acceptance would shatter the imaginary unity of the social body. This concern for unity seems to determine a whole relational and social organisation based on a system of divisions that excludes all what is perceived as other—the unacceptable in the self that is localised in the outside—in order to preserve a putative homogeneous and pure identity (of a group, community, etc.). So what seems at stake in the work of mourning, in addition to the elaboration of loss and in relation to it, is also the recognition of alterity, in the absence of which the cycle of violence has all the chances to continue.

In addition to this model—if one can speak of a model per se—there is another way of dealing with loss that ought to be brought to light. It basically concerns the suffering of those who lost a friend or family member whose death couldn't be confirmed; what was known as the question of the "missing" or "forced disappearances", those thousands of persons (around 17,000) who disappeared during the civil war and whose fate remains unknown, with the possibility that they could have been killed or detained. If this subject constitutes a chronic problem, a wound that only gets sorer with time, it's mainly because of the refusal of the Lebanese authorities to recognise it and address it with the seriousness it requires. There was indeed an implacable censorship regarding this issue that remained almost a taboo in post-war Lebanon. The fact that the majority of today's political leaders took part in fighting explains partially this reaction. Why would they be interested in solving this matter if it would reveal their criminal deeds? But there's also another reason linked to the political situation that prevailed during the war and up until the Syrian withdrawal in 2005, particularly the close cooperation between the Lebanese and the Syrian authorities concerning security issues. This resulted, among other things, in the arrests of thousands of persons who were then sent to Syrian prisons without the possibility to enquire about their fate, since both successive Lebanese governments and the Syrian regime opposed all efforts that could serve this purpose. Indeed, while the Lebanese authorities have banned access to archives and refused to identify mass graves, the Syrian officials kept merely on denying any detention of the sort. Later, the situation didn't change significantly. If the last decade has surely witnessed an increased public and official interest regarding the fate of the missing, few concrete measures were nevertheless undertaken. For instance, in 2012, after a long struggle led by some associations of the civil society, the Ministry of Justice drafted a decree for the establishment of an independent national commission for the victims of enforced disappearance that, nonetheless, was not adopted.

This state of things has left many families suffering alone anguish of loss and uncertainty regarding the fate of their relatives. As it was mentioned, no public discourse helped name their fears and the official authorities denied the problem while only recognising one category of detainees: those held in Israeli prisons. That's why, in order to save the memory of their loved ones from oblivion, families had to make their grief and intimate pain public and this supposed a struggle against this principle that relates the recognition of the victim to the identity of the aggressor—as far as the victim confirms the enmity of the latter.

But this struggle for recognition constitutes also an attempt to counter melancholia that, in this particular configuration, seems inevitable. The fact that these persons disappeared without leaving a trace has transformed their absence into a spectral presence that continues to haunt family members, complicating significantly the work of mourning. It is indeed impossible to mourn those whose death is not even confirmed. Any effort to let go would only prompt guilt and remorse that would strengthen the relation to the absent. But it's a relation based essentially on identification that helps perpetuate the existence of the lost person, as Freud argued in his work on melancholia; and this supposes the vanishing of the limit between the self and the other. In the absence of the corpse or any material sign that gives form to absence, the disappeared is indeed incorporated, encrypted within the self (Abraham & Torok, 1972). For these reasons, the effort to shed light on the fate of the disappeared was a matter of life or death for the families themselves; it was the only way to make these losses grievable through the restoration of the trace that would help mourners accept to separate from their loved ones.

Mourning as an ongoing work

However, and beyond melancholic relations, one might ask if a complete separation from the lost other is possible, if one can repudiate all ties to the lost object as Freud seems to suggest in his view on mourning (1917e). In this regard, it is important to point out that this binary model based on a clear-cut distinction between a mourning that succeeds, that relinquishes all ties to the object, and a mourning that fails, or melancholia, cannot be read separately from what Freud put forward in his work *On Narcissism* (1914c), namely the idea of a primary narcissism that precedes and governs object-relations. Indeed, in this text Freud postulates the existence of an initial relation of the ego to itself, a sort of libidinal investment of the ego designated as primary narcissism from which derives object-libido and to which it remains related: "we form the idea of there being an original cathexis of the ego, from which some is later giving off to objects, but which fundamentally persists and is related to the object-cathexes much as the body of amoeba is related to the pseudopodia which it puts out" (p. 75). While Freud conceives the relation between these two types of libidinal investment on an antithetical mode, he emphasises the importance of a balance between them that seeks to maintain ego-libido at a certain level so as to prevent its overconcentration in the ego. The function of object-libido is precisely to redirect the excess of ego-libido that, if left as such, would inevitably lead to a pathological reaction. In this respect, Freud writes: "A strong egoism is a protection against falling ill, but in the last resort we must begin to love in order not to fall ill, and we are bound to fall ill if, in consequence of frustration, we are unable to love" (p. 85).

We have here a conception of subjectivity where object-relations fall under the primacy of a narcissistic economy that seeks in the first place the wellbeing of the subject by providing a balanced distribution of libido. Accordingly, one might say that the object is not important in its own right but only to the extent that it contributes to this economy, by contracting the excess of libido that threatens the ego. Without taking this model into consideration, it would be difficult to understand the work of mourning Freud put forward in *Mourning and Melancholia*. Indeed, when the presence of the object is so contingent in the economy of the subject, it becomes possible to abandon the object without the risk of dissolving the self. The work of mourning refers precisely to the process through which a sovereign and autonomous subject recovers the libido that was once invested in a particular object in order to reorient it toward a new one.

However, it is this idea of an autonomous subject not affected by the loss of the other that Freud put into question in his later works. In *The Ego and the Id* (1923b), he considers the other as constitutive of the ego that not just keeps the traces of lost objects but is formed by these traces. Freud affirms in fact that there is no relinquishing of bonds without the alteration of the ego: "when it happens that a person has to give up a sexual object, there quite often ensues an alteration of his ego which can only be described as a setting-up of the object inside the ego, as it occurs in melancholia". And he adds that these alterations form the character of the ego: "It may be that this identification is the sole condition under which the id can give up its objects … it makes it possible to suppose that the character of the ego is a precipitate of abandoned object-cathexes and that it contains the history of those object-choices" (p. 29).

By claiming this, Freud operates a radical change: what was considered as a pathological mourning becomes the condition that renders separation possible. But it is here a paradoxical separation since the object is not really abandoned but rather interiorised or incorporated. It is upon this particular point that Judith Butler lays stress when elaborating the idea of ungrievable loss and its relation to the gendered character of the ego (Butler, 1997). As Butler points out, if the loss of the object is accepted, it is only because the object has been interiorised. This melancholic identification "provides a way to preserve the object as part of the ego and, hence, to avert the loss as a complete loss" (p. 134). In other words, what is lost in reality continues to live internally, is taken into the structure of the ego, and becomes coextensive of it. What is at stake here is a contradictory process whereby loss is at the same time accepted and refused, or it is accepted because it is being refused as Butler argues: "Internalisation preserves loss in the psyche; more precisely, the internalisation of loss is part of the mechanism of its refusal" (p. 134). Accordingly, one can say that there is no such thing as a complete abandonment of the object and this of course questions the whole model described in *Mourning and Melancholia*. Indeed, what comes out of these later reformulations is the idea of a mourning that necessarily fails because of what remains of the relation to the other, a rest that cannot be entirely assimilated.

Even if Freud, in the same text (1923b), seems to challenge his own assertions moving on to affirm the primacy of oedipal identifications, he then questions again this assumption by admitting the role of infantile bisexuality that makes it difficult to obtain a clear view regarding object-choices and identification (p. 33). With these remarks, he surely makes room for a less hetero-normative model of object-choices and more importantly draws attention to the importance of ambivalence in early object-relations. By doing so, he brings to the foreground the question of melancholic identifications by relating mourning to the vicissitudes of ambivalence—an ambivalence that precedes Oedipal rivalry and seems to result from the early separation with the object (the mother). This early ambivalence signals that the internalisation of the other is always incomplete and that the work of mourning entails an inevitable incorporation of the other.

Indeed, there is something of the object that exceeds all forms of appropriation and can be only incorporated by the self, enfolded as a foreign body within its structure or that is interiorised "only by exceeding, fracturing, wounding, injuring, traumatising that interiority that it inhabits", to use Jacques Derrida's terms (Derrida, 1996, p. 188). In this sense, introjecting the other implies an encryption of the other as Derrida argues, contradicting the traditional view on mourning. In his *Memoires for Paul de Man* (1989), Derrida unsettles the distinction between introjection and incorporation as established by Abraham and Torok (1972), blurring jointly the very opposition between successful and failed mourning. In fact, what matters for Derrida is not how to relinquish ties but rather how to be faithful to the other. It is from this ethical perspective that he addresses the question of mourning that he formulates as follows:

> What is an impossible mourning? ... Is the most distressing, or even the most deadly infidelity that of a possible mourning which would interiorise within us the image, idol, or ideal of the other who is dead and lives only in us? Or is it that of the impossible mourning, which leaving the other his alterity, respecting thus his infinite remove, either refuses to take or is incapable of taking the other within oneself, as in the tomb or the vault of some narcissism? (Derrida, 1989, p. 6)

It is this impossible mourning that Derrida underlines, impossible because of the otherness of the other that resists total assimilation and, by doing so, assigns to mourning a necessary irresolution. Hence, mourning becomes an unfinished work that goes in parallel with a renunciation to the idea of a sovereign and self-centred subject: "we can get over our mourning of him only by getting over our mourning, by getting over, by ourselves, the mourning of ourselves, I mean mourning of our autonomy, of everything that would make us the measure of ourselves" (Derrida, 1996, p. 189). In final analysis, it is possible to say that the experience of mourning, by revealing this essential interdependency that constitutes the subject, transforms the lack that results from the loss of the other into a site where the mourner can welcome "hospitality, love and friendship" (Derrida, 1996, p. 188). In this way, mourning lays the ground for a politics of the social.

In regard to the Lebanese experience, it is possible to illustrate this conception through an example taken from the realm of film production. *One Man Village* (2008) is a documentary that depicts the life of Semaan al-Habre, a middle-aged man who lives almost alone in his home village in the Lebanese mountain. By following Semaan in his daily activities varying between working the land, milking the cows, or selling the dairy products, the documentary brings to light a dark aspect of the history of the mountain often omitted in official narratives. As the conversation with Semaan and other ex-villagers unfolds, the viewer learns that the village has been levelled by a sectarian war that demolished almost everything and emptied the village of its population. Indeed, the ruins scattered all over the place and the state of desolation that predominates witness of the ferocious battles that opposed

Druses and Christians after the Israeli withdrawal in 1983 and that resulted in displacing the majority of the Christian population of the mountain. Whereas many other villages were rebuilt in the wake of the official "reconciliation" that took place after the end of the civil war, Ain al Halazon, the village in question, remained almost deserted and its vestigial landscapes reflect negatively the life that once existed there. However, after the reconciliation, the inhabitants began to re-visit the village mainly to cultivate their lands during the day and leave again at sunset. Only Semaan returned for good. In fact, after the war, he decided to leave the northern suburb of Beirut where he used to work and settle again in Ain al Halazon, realising his "dream", as he says, of leading a peasant life in the village.

What characterises Semaan in particular is the relation he builds with the places and sites that surround him and, indirectly, with all the people who are not there anymore but who continue to mark the place with an invisible presence. Unlike the other villagers whose perception of the village remains completely absorbed by past traumas and who seem unable to move beyond what happened (this probably explains the reason why they didn't move back), Semaan inhabits a world and a time that belong to both past and present. There is indeed an undecidable temporality that the documentary makes visible; a sort of memory that attests of the continual presence of past things and at the same time assumes their pastness. Semaan's mode of life embodies this double movement: he lives with memories—one can even say that his mode of life is an act of remembering—but at the same time, he doesn't seek to resurrect the past. Somehow, he assumes that a world has been lost and co-lives with this loss in the present. This seems particularly true when he evokes his parents, whose deaths profoundly affected his life, as he confesses. In fact, the death of the parents that occurred in the midst of the war (the circumstances surrounding the father's death are not elucidated but Semaan witnessed the death of the mother who was shot in the village and died before reaching the nearest hospital in Beirut) seems here to be the nodal point that articulates together the general and personal history, past and present.

Indeed, this traumatic event inaugurates a memorial temporality where past and present intermingle without conflating. The parents are at the same time present (through remembrance and imagination) and absent (the graveyard that occupies a central place in Semaan's spatial environment is the material sign of this absence). One might say that

Semaan remembers through the prism of the present or, more precisely, while taking fully into account the distance that separates past and present. And this distance, insofar as it allows him to slightly disidentify with the past, liberates memory from the weight of ambivalence and resentment and opens it to an unknown future that is not a mere reiteration of the past. What this mode of reminiscence reflects is also a form of mourning that goes beyond melancholic attachments insofar as it tries to maintain a loving relation to those who are not there without foreclosing the reality of loss. This integration of loss, the loss of the other and the indelible mark it leaves in the subject, prevents from forging an image of the subject as a unified and undivided subject, that is, against the mirage of narcissistic completeness. In this sense, mourning refers to this ongoing process through which a subject is formed out of the ruins of narcissism.

It's clear that this example of mourning remains an individual case that doesn't express a general tendency. But this doesn't undermine its pertinence nor does it limit its scope. On the contrary, mediated by the work of culture that projects it in the public realm, it acquires a signification and a life of its own that go beyond the private sphere. In fact, the important thing about it is that it puts forward the relations and the porosity that exist between personal experiences and the broader idea of a regime of memory that doesn't merge with the past but is informed by it and, as such, is able to sketch new future possibilities; what could also be called a "horizon of expectation" (Koselleck, 2004). This of course doesn't replace a national and collective memory work that goes in parallel with political and legal measures that have been lacking in Lebanon. It's only this kind of work that can oppose and resist the current politics that were rooted in the violence of forgetting and resulted in producing more violence.

References

Abraham, N., & Torok, M. (1972). Mourning or melancholia: introjection versus incorporation. In: N. T. Rand (Ed.), *The Shell and the Kernel* (pp. 125–137). Chicago, IL: University of Chicago Press, 1994.

Butler, J. (1997). *The Psychic Life of Power: Theories in Subjection*. Stanford, CA: Stanford University Press.

Derrida, J. (1989). *Memoires: For Paul de Man*. New York: Columbia University Press.

Derrida, J. (1996). By force of mourning. *Critical Inquiry, 22*(2): 171–192.

Freud, S. (1914c). On Narcissism: an Introduction. *S. E., 14*: 69. London: Hogarth.

Freud, S. (1914g). Remembering, Repeating and Working-Through (Further Recommendations on the Technique of Psycho-Analysis, II). *S. E., 12*: 147. London: Hogarth.

Freud, S. (1917e). Mourning and Melancholia. *S. E., 14*: 239. London: Hogarth.

Freud, S. (1920g). *Beyond the Pleasure Principle. S. E., 18:* 7. London: Hogarth.

Freud, S. (1923b). *The Ego and the Id. S. E., 19*: 3. London: Hogarth.

Freud, S. (1927e). Fetishism. *S. E., 21*: 149. London: Hogarth.

Friedlander, S. (1992). Introduction. In: *Probing the Limits of Representation* (pp. 1–21). Harvard, MA: Harvard University Press.

Kassir, S. (2010). *Beirut.* Berkeley, CA: University of California Press.

Khosrokhavar, F. (2005). *Suicide Bombers: Allah's New Martyrs.* Ann Arbour, MI: Pluto Press.

Khoury, E. (1995). The memory of the City. *Grand Street, 54*: 137–142.

Ricœur, P. (2004). *Memory, history, forgetting.* Chicago, IL: University of Chicago Press.

Said, E. (1984). Permission to narrate. *Journal of Palestine Studies, 13*(3): 27–48.

Spivak, G. (2010). Can the Subaltern speak? In: R. C. Morris (Ed.), *Can the Subaltern Speak? Reflections on the History of an Idea* (pp. 21–78). New York: Columbia University Press.

Tueni, G. (1985). *Une guerre pour les autres.* Paris: Lattès.

Young, M. (2010). *The Ghosts of Martyrs Square: An Eyewitness Account of Lebanon's Life Struggle.* New York: Simon & Schuster.

CHAPTER EIGHT

When the "comfort women" speak—shareability and recognition of traumatic memory

Jenyu Peng

Introduction

Survivors of collective violence often need to traverse a long journey before their voices can be heard. The former "comfort women"—as the sex slaves of the Japanese Imperial Army during the Second Sino-Japanese War and World War II were known—did not reveal their stories until half a century later. The latency between the event and its recognition reflects the extreme difficulties for survivors to narrate the horrible real, and for listeners to receive those narratives. In this chapter, I will discuss the psychosocial conditions in which the comfort women's narratives are formulated, as well as their interactions with other traumatic narratives also searching for justice.

For many Asian observers, the "comfort system" is an emblematic case of war crimes committed by the Japanese Imperial Army that have not been properly faced. The unsolved legacy of the war continues to afflict the victims and creates geopolitical tensions in East Asia. Although historians have been debating the total number of comfort women, most agree on the estimate of 200,000. The majority were young Korean and Chinese women and girls. But there were also Japanese, Indonesian, Filipino, Dutch, and Taiwanese women, either transported as "military supplies" to the war zones, or forcibly drafted on the spot (Yoshimi, 2000). The Taiwanese comfort women are commonly known as "Ah-ma", or grandmas, a term of affection used by most of their Asian proponents based on the survivors' advanced age. (Indeed, this quasi-kinship designation exists in every Asian country where feminist activists work for the recognition of comfort women.) In this chapter, I will focus on the traumatic narratives of the Ah-ma, the conditions for their emergence, and the social impact of their public sharing.

In Taiwan, historians have estimated that around two to three thousand young Han (usually including the Hoklo and the Hakka) women, mostly from poor socioeconomic backgrounds, were abducted to be "comfort women" (Zhu, 2009). They were deceived into accepting fake offers of high paying jobs overseas, instead winding up in "comfort stations" on different Southeast Asian islands, where they became "Emperor's gifts" (Nishino, 1992, p. 44) or even "public toilets" (Kako, 1996, p. 36) servicing the Japanese soldiers' sexual needs. Only about ten per cent of them managed to stay alive and return home at the end of the war. Later investigation shows that young Taiwanese aboriginal women had also been victims of a less organised sexual slavery in military barracks in remote mountain areas of Taiwan (TWRF, 1999). Feelings of shame and guilt compelled all of them to remain silent.

Scholars disagree on the necessity of disclosing buried trauma. Some emphasise its benefits (Agosin, 2007), while others warn of possible retraumatising effects from revisiting the unbearable (Haaken, 1998; Rosenblum, 2009). As Sandor Ferenczi (1932) indicated, in the case of sexual assaults committed on children, the denial of the abuser or other adult is as traumatising as the initial traumatic event itself. This implies that it is not so much the disclosure itself that is beneficial or retraumatising, as the reactions of immediate circles that are decisive in the organisation of psychotrauma in its aftermath. Hence, in the process of publicising comfort women's traumatic narratives, several questions catch our attention. How can one encourage these elderly women to disclose a sexual trauma kept secret for decades, while protecting them from unpredictable reactions? Is the recognition obtained from the international movement, a somewhat abstract achievement for them, sufficient for their recovery? Does the traumatic memory have to be shared by each member of society to allow victims to go through the work of mourning?

In order to explore the psychosocial conditions allowing the construction of the comfort women narrative, I undertook clinical anthropological fieldwork, from 2007 to 2009, alongside the Taipei Women's Rescue Foundation (TWRF, 2009). The TWRF is a Taiwanese feminist non-governmental organisation (NGO), which collaborates with Korean and Japanese NGO networks to appeal for international recognition of sexual war crimes, and to urge the Japanese government to issue an official apology and reparations. It also provides social and psychological care for Taiwanese comfort women.

By analysing how the "Ah-ma comfort women" narrative is told and received, I will extract some elements to answer questions often raised in regard to collective violence about the possibility of sharing traumatic experiences, especially when personal trauma narratives interact with the construction of collective identities and different versions of nationalism (Claverie, 2010; Eyerman, 2001; Giesen, 2004; LaCapra, 2001). This problem is even more accentuated in a state where different ethnic or political groups have experienced collective violence exerted by different oppressors over the course of history. In that situation, it would not be possible to construct a collective narrative without listening to each other's suffering. I will argue that the "shareability" of collective trauma narratives resides in an inquiry into the narrator's singularity. In other words, the Other is to be conceived as a face (*visage*) in a Lévinasian sense, an ultimate other that transcends any kind of ethnic or political belongingness. As Figlio (2011) argues, if singularity is to be an exponent of universality, collective identities and narratives need to be less collective in order to be more "successful" (p. 161).

Bearing witness to a repressed past

Forty-seven years after the end of World War II, the buried, haunting past resurfaced. In 1992, three former "comfort women" made their first public appearance in a press conference held by lawyers and social workers of the TWRF. A big black curtain covered the three Ah-ma from the top of their heads to their knees. They spoke behind the curtain to a tiny public, mostly journalists, to reveal the "shameful" stories of their youth still felt by them to be a burning dishonour.

Figure 1. Black curtain. Courtesy of the TWRF.

One of the old women who was supposed to speak on this occasion eventually shied away from the task. Years later, a dozen Taiwanese Ah-ma, emboldened by the mobilisation of international supporting groups and the courage of their Korean homologues to demand justice, went abroad to reveal their secret in the public sphere of different countries. Yet, the majority are still not willing to share their stories with others, not in the relatively private therapeutic workshops, and even less in front of cameras or in court. Many comfort women died without ever letting their families know what had happened to them in their youth (Peng, 2012).

It is worth noting that, in the first place, the former comfort women neither view their traumatic experience to be part of the collective memory, nor did they link their trauma to any national suffering. Most of them attributed it to personal bad fortune, or serious miscalculations during the chaos of wartime. Fifty years later, feminist activists provided human/women's rights discourses to these survivors, redefining the shame of their past as a major violence to humanity, and transforming their self-blame into legitimate anger. In this sense, the comfort women's traumatic narrative is a co-construction of subaltern local knowledge and representative elite knowledge.

Despite ongoing international support, testimonies of the former comfort women have been confronted by a strong revisionist current within Japanese society. In 1993, Chief Cabinet Secretary Kono Yohei apologised to the victims and admitted the military's culpability, but Kono's statement has never been endorsed by the Japanese parliament. A private compensation fund, set up by the government in 1995, was largely rejected by the victims for its condescending nature and evasion of official responsibility. Indeed, right-wing Japanese politicians and historians, including the present Prime Minister Abe Shinzo, have repeatedly denied the active role of the Japanese Imperial army in the organisation of the comfort station system. They claim that these women, instead of being coerced into sexual service, either "volunteered" for military prostitution or were sold into it by their own impoverished families. In March 2014, however, Abe declared that—despite indications to the contrary—the Kono statement would not be revised.

From a positivist point of view, it is difficult to controvert this version for at least two reasons. For one thing, almost every document that could prove the direct implication of the Imperial army was destroyed at the end of the war. Also, the trajectories by which the victims found themselves trapped in the comfort stations were quite diverse and often involved private brokers. In spite of these difficulties, Yoshiaki Yoshimi, a professor of history, has uncovered confidential telegrams showing that high-ranking officers had ordered the colonial governments in Korea and Taiwan to send "indigenous comfort women" to the fronts in China and Southeast Asia. Still, without the archival evidence to prove the coercive nature of the comfort system, the survivors' testimony is the last resort for confronting right-wing negationism.

It is clear that without the help of NGO activists to co-construct "comfort women" narratives, the voices of Taiwanese survivors, nearly all illiterate, would never have been heard. In a deconstructive concern, there is much to be discussed about how official feminist narratives, in their efforts to mobilise public opinion, tend to be too normative to display individual differences, and so eager to stress the victims' innocence as to downplay any uncomfortable departures from the official historical "truth" (Soh, 2008). However, one cannot deny that the reification of the comfort women's traumatic real is a necessary step for its historicisation, and the stereotyping effect is consequential to, and reinforced by, the repeated denial from officials of the former perpetrators' country.

Ethnic politics, gender politics, geopolitics

Apart from the psychological burden, the difficulties for Taiwanese "comfort women" to testify arose mainly for sociocultural and political reasons, which exacerbated the victims' feelings of shame and guilt. First, the traditional patriarchal ideology that praised virginity and chastity as an indispensable virtue for women was still extremely influential. Second, in the immediate postwar period, those who had been close to the Japanese for any reason were considered traitors. More recently, the complex geopolitical tie between Taiwan and Japan has rendered it even more difficult to recall this "disturbing" past.

These Ah-ma were born in the 1920s and 1930s, when the socio-cultural context in Taiwan was still permeated by an extremely conservative patriarchal ideology. When women were raped, they were considered—and considered themselves—to be "sullied". They would be encouraged, explicitly or implicitly, either to be wed to their rapists (Luo, 2000), or to commit suicide to prove their innocence (Zhuo, 1993, p. 144). This notorious tradition has been challenged by the feminist movement that arose in Taiwan in the mid-1970s. Essentially influenced by the North American current, this movement has contributed greatly to criminalising rape and raising public awareness about sexual assault, an evolution that has rendered the comfort women's narratives audible to the public. Yet things are not that easy for the Ah-ma themselves. After years of feminist activists' endeavours to "empower" these women, approximately only one out of six Ah-ma who came into contact with the TWRF is willing to speak openly. The majority of them could admit the past only in murmurs, expressing their pain more so through artwork than in group therapy; and some would never be able to speak of those experiences.

For a better understanding of the political issues at work, a brief historical reminder will be necessary. Since the seventeenth century, Taiwan has experienced multiple colonisations and waves of immigration. At the end of the first Sino-Japanese war in 1895, the vanquished Qing Dynasty ceded Taiwan to Japan, ushering in a half-century of Japanese rule. Following World War II and his defeat on the mainland to the Chinese Communists, Chiang Kai-shek arrived to take over the island, bringing with him over a million soldiers and civilians; thus began a forty-year dictatorship. During the "white terror" period of martial law (1947–1987), Chiang's Chinese Nationalist Party or Kuomingtang (KMT) massacred tens of thousands of dissidents and ordinary people. For many Taiwanese, especially the severely oppressed intellectual elite, this regime represents a colonisation even worse than the Japanese one (Lin & Keating, 2000).

The Japanese colonial government, while imposing a far more brutal rule in Korea, had allowed the emergence of an intellectual class in Taiwan, with relative freedom of thought, and even democratic participation at the local level. Hence, for the older generations of Taiwanese, the Japanese colonial experience was a mixture of discrimination, oppression, and enlightenment. This explains why some Taiwanese opinion leaders reacted ambivalently to the first public unveiling of the comfort women's narrative.

Since political ideologies have centred on ethnic differences and obscured problems of class and gender, the post-Chiang period provided an ideal nursery for radical nationalism. Chinese nationalism, still eager to rebuild a great China, seems to pursue a mental war with the Japanese, seizing any opportunity to demonstrate that cruelty is deeply rooted in the Japanese "national character". Taiwanese nationalism, originally a counteraction against Chinese nationalism's oppression and the threat of unification with China, has tended to overvalue the "good old days" under Japanese colonisation and has even sought alliance with right-wing Japanese politicians, who can be considered the descendants of the colonial imperialists. The consequence is that, when the comfort women issue first burst out, it was easily subjected to political recuperation to fuel the already burning conflicts between the two.

The narrative refiguration of history, or Nachträglichkeit of collective trauma

The infiltration of the comfort women's traumatic narratives into the public sphere not only shakes up Taiwanese representations of their own history, but also reactivates other repressed memories of collective violence in which the roles of the antagonists in one event might be reversed in another. The various reactions of members from different groups reflect their divergent sociopolitical experiences and, consequently, their conflicting versions of history.

In a climate of politicised ethnic tension, the juxtaposition of different traumatic narratives, instead of inducing empathic "resonance" between survivors, tends to strengthen the "psychosocial enclave" (Figlio, 2011) of each victim group by rejecting any antagonistic narratives. Figlio suggests that collective memory can function as a psychosocial enclave, "an internal world of psyche, shared and bound into a social psyche" (p. 162), which allows the idealisation of the group to which one belongs, as well as the projection of negativity (or "bad objects" in a Kleinian sense) onto any adversary group(s). However, when the external reality changes, the once well-functioning collective memory, along with the self-identity, could be threatened with collapse.

In this perspective, the revelation of the comfort women's traumatic memory presents a force that modifies or challenges existing versions of historical narratives, the basis for the self-image-building of different political groups. This can eventually reshuffle socio-political configurations. This "refiguration" of time through narration (Ricœur, 1985) sheds new light on the Freudian notion of *Nachträglichkeit*, underlining the nonlinear and retrospective nature of traumatic temporality.

At the individual level, the differed effect of early trauma is due to a meaning (re)construction triggered by a second scene, which appears trivial but contains an associative potency. The traumatogenic meaning is mostly related to the superego's accusation shaming the self. In the comfort women case, when they finally returned home, the rejection by their families was almost as traumatising as the slavery itself. "Coconut Ah-ma", a ninety-two-year-old woman who still earns her living by selling coconuts, described her own homecoming in the documentary "Song of the Reed" (TWRF & Wu, 2013): having finally managed to make it home after three and a half years, she stood before her family's house, trembling with exhaustion and emotion, when her uncle saw her and greeted her with "Go away, we don't want a bitch in our family!" The disdaining gaze bestowed on the traumatised subject petrifies them into an "ab-ject" (Kristeva, 1980) onto which negative sentiments are projected so as to exclude it from the orderly life-world. Hence the sense of shame comes from the constructed belief that one should be exiled to protect the community's integrity.

At the collective level, the deferred effect of trauma, or the refiguration of traumatic narrative and self-image, becomes more complex. Each subject identifies herself more or less with a specific political group and appropriates the version of collective narrative accordingly. The heterogeneity within a group can be grasped in the dialectical interaction between this version and one's personal encounters. The prototype of a specific nationalistic narrative, which I would call "proto-myth", can be considered the product of transmission and reinvention. It supports the ego in quest of identity but can also confine its horizon. Given the imaginary dimension of the collective, there exists an intrinsic disconnect between proto-myth and individual belief. I suggest that openness in encountering otherness depends on the ways the ego deals with the perturbing disconnect. The ego could ignore it and fully merge herself with the imaginary collective to the point that divergent voices become unbearable. Or it could constitute its identity with some aspects of the prototypal narrative fabric, while refusing its domination. While refiguring the proto-myth, the re-emerging trauma can drive the unsettled spirits to extreme positions.

Politicisation of the trauma

In Chinese nationalistic proto-myth, the unearthed comfort women's trauma resonates with its own unsolved war traumas, first imposed by the imperialist Japanese and then by the Chinese communists. When Chinese nationalists integrate the Taiwanese comfort women trauma into what is experienced as a humiliating past, they find a legitimate outlet to express their suppressed resentment. In Taiwanese nationalistic proto-myth, its habitual position of victimisation vis-à-vis the KMT's dictatorial regime is undermined by its alliance with the "wicked" Japanese. Taiwanese nationalists, geopolitically dependent on Japanese nationalist politicians, feel that their already traumatised subjectivity suffers another injustice by being wrongly put in a culpable position. Some Taiwanese nationalist leaders, mobilising the defence mechanism, indeed go so far as to repeat the self-acquitting discourse made by the Japanese government.

Paradoxically, most of the Ah-ma assume a Taiwanese identity at the ethnic level while accepting the KMT's rule at the socioeconomic level, but they do not assimilate themselves into the greater Chinese nationalism. This political affiliation reflects the "pragmatic" stance of the majority of Taiwanese, whose primary concern is personal social striving rather than political ideologies. Adopting the economic priority—the focus of which is strictly on the present and the future—has, to a certain point, anesthetised the experienced trauma. Interestingly, that trauma indirectly acted to eclipse the political oppression felt during the White Terror period.

Here, the theory of collective identity formation based on "cultural trauma" or "national trauma" (Eyerman, 2001, p. 3) meets its limit in comprehending the complex interaction of traumatic memories in a multicultural society, as well as the transcultural aspect of gender-specific traumas. In the case of the Taiwanese comfort women, the exclusive cultural identity fantasy tends to foster hatred and eliminate otherness, instead of providing the foundation for subjectal emancipation. However, from a psychoanalytic point of view, subjectification understood as assuming one's singularity in a multi-layered interrelational collective is crucial for the work of mourning and healing. Traumatised subjects need to regain the power of interpretation over their own experience, which was taken away by the perpetrator. One of the signs of subjectification is the ability to contain the Other without being paralysed by the threat it could represent.

It is true that the denial of Taiwanese fundamentalists engenders a secondary trauma. But when Chinese nationalism equates the comfort women trauma with its "national trauma" for the benefit of the constitution of a greater China, the manipulation process itself is traumatising. As Chinese nationalists discredit Taiwanese nationalists as Japanese henchmen, they position themselves as pure victims and avoid reflecting on their own wrongdoing.

The case of comfort women reveals that remembering a forgotten traumatic past is always entangled in a complex history of multiple oppressions. Theoretically speaking, if the mourning process is really to begin in a society, the remembering should not be partial. Every historical trauma that each ethnic, class, religious, or gender group has suffered needs to be unearthed and re-examined; no one of them should be singled out to be the emblem of all human rights violations. In reality, however, the imbalanced power structure tends to favour some and obliterate others. This can encourage indulgence in one's own traumatic melancholia, instead of working through the trauma. As Paul Ricœur (2004) indicates, different ethno-political groups need to actuate a "mutual recognition". This implies recognising the other as a speaking subject with a singular history.

Limits of human rights discourse

In the last decade of the twentieth century, defending human rights had become a universal discourse for victims of collective trauma to claim justice (Schaffer & Sidonie, 2004). Supporting the comfort women's cause became an easy stance. But as we have observed, certain ethnopolitical groups embraced the cause more easily than others. And it was not an easy task to free the humanistic campaign from other political interests.

Thanks to the global diffusion of comfort women narratives, the cause had gained considerable international recognition by the end of 2008. However, if the comfort women narrative is to be examined solely through the lens of human rights—while it can certainly facilitate temporary social and political mobilisation—the victims' figures are not necessarily transformed into faces (Lévinas, 1971). For Lévinas, the face is the starting point of the ethical, which imperatively calls for taking responsibility for the Other. The Japanese government, on the contrary, bypasses its responsibility by setting up a private organism, the Asian Women's Fund, to provide seemingly humanitarian aid. Using the same human rights discourse as the comfort women advocates do, it in effect effaces the victims. Thus there are no more perpetrators, but only victims and philanthropists.

When the human rights discourse and the charitable act can be utilised to silence and humiliate the victims once again, we should raise the question, paraphrasing Spivak and Morris (2010), "Can the 'comfort women' speak?" Does elevating the oppressed to the international scene necessarily give them a voice? Spivak asserts that in the Indian postcolonial context, the subaltern subjectivity could be muted by the intellectuals' invoking a Eurocentric subject. From the psychoanalytic perspective, the subjectification or emancipation implies a self-authorisation to interpret one's own lived experience. That also includes inventing a singular way to confront the power structure engaging intra-psychic and interpersonal conflicts, institutional constraint, and state domination.

The shareability of trauma: from the singular to the universal

Practitioners treating trauma from extreme human violence are aware of the ineffability of traumatic experience, owing to the fragmentation of the sensorial impressions and an extreme sense of humiliation. Remembering a traumatic event is often entangled with a profound feeling of shame and guilt, thus inevitably evoking a negative self-image. The importance of anamneses cannot be emphasised enough in view of recognising the historical reality, so as to allow the reconstruction of meaning. However, we should keep in mind that the historical reality affects the psychic reality and the transferential relationship of the here and now. Freud's claim—that hysterics suffer from reminiscence—implies that if the memory traces fail to find their way to symbolisation, they will maintain the symptom-inducing (pathogenic) power and compel the victim to re-enact the traumatic scene in compulsive repetition. Symbolisation is a step further towards mourning and probably healing.

However, the testimonial act comprises a risk of psychic collapse when evoking the horror. It therefore requires certain conditions, both subjective and objective. The symbolising journey needs to be accompanied by listeners capable of containing the unbearable stories. As in psychoanalytic situations, the quality of listening preconditions the speaking. The fundamental rule of "neutrality", or suspending moral judgment of a person, aims to guarantee that quality. But it is comprehensible that when the listener's psychic space is busy metabolising its own traumatic memory, neutrality gives way to self-defence. This unavailability is to be found not only among opponents, but also among supporters. For one's political affiliation does not guarantee a capacity for containing, just as political disagreement does not necessarily block the way to empathy.

The question of the shareability of traumatic experiences through narration relies on the capacity to confront the Other in the epiphany of the face-to-face, prior to any ethnic or political classification. As our earlier discussion shows, it proves to be difficult for the listeners to suspend their own political tendencies, as it is for the advocates. But if the human voice of trauma is to be heard, both the narrator and the listener need to transcend partisanship so as to meet each other in the universal. I will demonstrate how the universal can only be heard in its singularity, before being absorbed in any ready-to-hand political discourses.

Narration, or subjectification through singing

The few women who had the courage to speak publicly about their trauma were more or less compelled to repeat their stories on multiple occasions, progressively becoming the "icons" of Taiwanese comfort women. Here I would like to describe the experience of one of these icons: Iwar Tanah. Ms. Tanah is an elderly Truku (one of Taiwan's sixteen officially recognised aboriginal tribes, with some 30,000 members). When she was sixteen, she was abducted by a Japanese policeman to a military base near her village and for years was gang-raped repeatedly in a storage cave for munitions.

I have selected three scenes of narration from Iwar Tanah's engagement in the international "comfort women" supporting movement:

her appearance in a documentary film, her testimony in court, and her participation in a therapeutic workshop.

1. Speaking to the camera

Iwar Tanah appeared in the first documentary film on Taiwanese comfort women, "The Secrets of Grandma" (1998). In the film, we see her guiding Ms. Wang, then president of the TWRF, into a cave. Iwar Tanah seems haunted by painful images while telling how she was taken there every evening after having worked all day. Years after the Japanese army left, she still avoids taking the path past this cave, unable to bear the sight of it. Now she forces herself to come back to testify before the camera.

When the film came out, some villagers heard about it and spread the news among Iwar Tanah's family members. Her son, an elected local representative of the county, blamed her for participating in the film and staining his reputation. Some neighbours accused her of aggravating the stigma of the Truku people, calling her "coming out" a disgraceful act. Apparently, in this tiny aboriginal village, where virginity is still a required virtue, victims of rape continue to be blamed. When the perpetrators are outsiders, the dishonour lived by one is experienced as the defilement of all. Since revenge is no longer possible, the

Figure 2. During the Pacific war, two Truku Ah-ma, both teenagers at the time, were repeatedly taken to this military supply storage cave after their daily duties to provide sexual "service" to Japanese soldiers. Courtesy of the TWRF.

victims are urged to bury the past, to act as if nothing had happened. This resistance to the resurgence of traumatic memory seems to be related to anxiety over the possible dissolution of the positive collective identity—an identity gained laboriously after years of struggle by the aboriginal movement for autonomy, cultural rights, and retrocession of traditional territories. One cannot simply conclude, therefore, that the aboriginals are more conservative than the "westernised" Han, or that the aboriginal comfort women suffered more gender oppression than other ethnic groups. Han comfort women were, and some still are, confronting the same sexual discrimination. There are numerous examples showing that when collective identity (including family and clan identity) is at stake, the demand for sacrifice can be found in every culture.

2. Testifying in court

In 1999, following the example of the Korean "Halmoni" ("grandma" in Korean) and assisted by Japanese volunteer lawyers, nine Taiwanese Ah-ma filed a lawsuit against the Japanese government to obtain an official apology and financial reparation. During a three-year inquiry, five Ah-ma were convened before the local court of Tokyo; Iwar Tanah was one of them. It was her first time going abroad. An anecdote shows to what extent it was a frightening experience for this seventy-year-old woman. While approaching the security check line in the airport, she was seized by a great panic, and suddenly turned around, refusing to go further. When asked by the translator, she explained that the policemen in blue uniforms looked exactly like the Japanese soldiers during the war. It took her companions a long time to calm her and persuade her to finally pass through the security check. This episode clearly illustrates the long-term impact of her trauma. The uniform and checkpoint atmosphere triggered her sensorial and affective memory, sparking the panic attack.

Iwar Tanah managed to attend the court as expected. The process was lengthy. Since it was difficult to find a Truku-Japanese translator, the translation was done from Truku to Mandarin Chinese, then from Mandarin to Japanese. Hence, when Iwar delivered the story of her victimisation, she observed that the judges paid little attention to her testimony. After giving all the facts required by the court, she began to sing in Truku. Everyone in the audience was overwhelmed by her croaky, moving voice. The court policeman wanted to stop her inappropriate behaviour, but a judge held him back and allowed her to finish the song.

Iwar's unexpected act challenged the positivist logic of the court in gathering evidence, and in measuring the damage caused by the traumatic past; more broadly, it contested the judicial, objectifying approach to a victim's narrative. She tried to show the judges that she did not come just to provide evidence, but also to express her long-suppressed story and unbearable sorrow. One social worker recognised the melody. It was a church hymn that Iwar sang at the end of the documentary, but she did not know its significance.

In 2011, thirteen years after the film was released, I had the opportunity to visit Iwar Tanah in her mountain village. She was very ill, and her daughter was taking care of her. I invited her daughter to watch the film with me, and asked her to translate the lyrics. She agreed, having never watched it before. When she saw the part where her mother was testifying in the cave, her face became agitated. As soon as she heard her mother singing, she began to weep and translate immediately for me. The translation was as follows: "*I suffered much injustice and squalor, but Jesus purified me with his precious blood. If I survived all this, it's because I put my entire faith in Jesus. I wish to go back soon to my heaven's home, into the arms of my Lord.*" I wondered how she knew the lyrics beforehand. She replied, "When I was a little girl, my mother always took me with her to work on the hill. She used to sing this hymn while working. She would change the words a bit, but always used the same tune." She added a few moments later: "My mother was so brave, I don't know if I could endure it if I were her…".

The hymn transmitted a mute heritage beneath the Christian faith. Iwar Tanah transformed her sorrow into a cathartic praise of God. Beyond the self-comforting effect, the lyrics also suggest an eagerness to depart the mortal world having been unable to encounter an other who could bestow true recognition. With the hymn, she found an oblique way to formulate an expression that, while not against the normative narrative, created another register somewhere between speaking and listening. My visit as a supportive third party from the outside world has perhaps kindled the beginning of a mourning process for Iwar Tanah and her daughter.

3. Disclosure in a therapeutic setting

Most of the former comfort women live in poverty and isolation. In 1995, the TWRF started a psychotherapeutic workshop to provide a meeting space for these women, hoping that they could develop a kind of sisterhood. About a dozen Ah-ma participated in the beginning, but their number declined over time. Since 2008, I have twice been allowed to participate in the workshop and noticed that the assistants outnumbered the grandmas.

Different therapeutic settings have been introduced, for instance: group talk therapy, yoga and relaxation, artistic activities (painting, photography, etc.), and psychodrama therapy. The group leaders were mostly experienced psychotherapists with solid reputations. However, the NGO social workers had trouble explaining to these elderly women with scarcely any education what psychotherapy was about, so they decided to present the therapists as teachers, who would guide them in dealing with their suffering.

The sessions were conducted mostly in Hoklo (Taiwanese), which could also be understood by the Hakka grandmas present, but not by the aboriginal ones. Iwar Tanah, for example, spoke only Truku and a little Japanese. Sometimes, a daughter of another deceased Truku Ah-ma helped with the translation. Still, Iwar Tanah spoke very little. Yet, quietly and devotedly, she made paintings, pictures, did manual arts and so on, like a well-behaved schoolgirl. Here the double impact of Japanese colonisation and Chiang's dictatorship on obeisant behaviours is still palpable.

Once, she made a paper-tearing picture. It was a heavenly garden with a church surrounded by flowers and food. She said to me that this was for the Ah-ma who had lately passed away, so that they could get comfort and nourishment from God's love. I felt the affective weight in these words. Her invincible faith coexisted with an omnipresent melancholy.

Compared to their public testimony, the workshop has been a safe place for disclosure. For Iwar Tanah and most of the other Ah-ma, this semi-private space probably served more for creating a sense of togetherness than receiving psychotherapy in a strict sense. Different media used in the workshops—drawing, collage, photography, yoga, drama, and so on—provided a time and space allowing relations to be woven, with or without words. Here, the Ah-ma could suspend their "comfort women" identity without concealing it.

Conclusion: collective memory beyond nations

The trauma that comfort women suffered originates from the combination of militarist imperialism, colonialism, and sexist patriarchy. In

Figure 3. During a workshop session, the psychotherapist asked the Ah-ma to paint masks to wear for a picture, to represent their psychological state before unveiling their long-hidden secret. Courtesy of the TWRF. Photographer: Zi-ming Huang.

this sense, it should be qualified as historical collective trauma, rather than individual misfortune. Nonetheless, it must not be categorised as "national trauma", to prevent expropriation by the dominant class to justify its governance. The sharing of a trauma narrative that calls for the listener's responsibility does not imply that the latter should vicariously transform the trauma and its corollary emotions into her own. It resides rather in the inscription of the event into collective memory, and not in the production of a shared resentment to fuel patriotic nationalism, which, in effect, results in the usurpation of the narrator's position as subject.

The collectiveness in the sharing of traumatic memory requires further clarification. There are multiple ways and motivations to integrate or not a collective trauma into one's identity construction. However, one should caution that the tendency to purify and sacralise the image of victims of collective trauma is often rooted in the need to maintain the Ideal-I. That same need can also lead to denial and negation. As discussed earlier, when the collective memory serves as psychosocial enclave, it consolidates the idealised collective identity, but it can also expel those who are not conceived as one of "us". The capacity for the collective memory to bear heterogeneity proves to be crucial when the "collective" is to be construed without the violence of exclusion.

To what extent is the comfort women's traumatic memory "collective"? The international feminist network has succeeded in raising the visibility of the comfort women issue worldwide. If examined by the three categories of recognition proposed by Axel Honneth (1992), victims of the "comfort system" have gained some social and legal recognition, but subjective recognition has proven to be more delicate. Based on my observations, there is a big gap between local recognition and global recognition, and this gap raises the question of transgenerational transmission. The official inscription of historical events does not seem to exercise a direct impact on its inscription at family and local levels.

In contrast to the significant international recognition, there has never been any important local mobilisation in Taiwan. It seems that not long after the forgotten past has been exhumed, Taiwanese society hurries to leave it behind. In addition, many family members, relatives, and neighbours are still reluctant to accept that there is a "comfort woman Ah-ma" in family or local history. Paradoxically, it is often easier for the comfort women to share their traumatic memory with total strangers than with their own relatives. One possible hypothesis for this resistance is that, on the international level, these women are considered by feminist activists as the oldest women's rights fighters, heroic figures, and thus their narrative can be reframed into a postcolonial human/women's rights discourse. However, at the local level, the stigma related to sexual aggression is still deeply rooted in the cultural imagination; the comfort women's history resides, for many, in a narrative of shame.

Iwar Tanah's example shows that the victim's search for recognition is an incessant dialectical movement between the act of narration and that of unpredictable listening. Her subjectivity is revealed less in her heroism as a human rights fighter, as feminists praised her, than in her improvised singing which disarmed dubitative ears. Each of

Figure 4. A synthetic portrait composed of thousands of pictures of "comfort women", Ah-ma, illustrating the common suffering behind each singular history. Courtesy of the TWRF. Photographer: Zi-ming Huang.

the singular traumatic experiences of each Ah-ma participating in the campaign forms a universal image of humanity suffering from human violence.

In Taiwan, there are only four Ah-ma left at the time of publication. Soon, there will be no more Ah-ma to speak publicly to confront the Japanese government's revisionism. And most of their children prefer to stay in the dark. Until the younger generations find their own ways to connect to the memories of the Ah-ma, the TWRF is creating a virtual museum project about the former comfort women to ensure the transmission of that collective memory (www.womandpeace.org.tw/). But just like other collective trauma born of state violence, the real mourning process is still waiting to be accomplished.

References

Agosin, M. (2007). *Tapestries of Hope, Threads of Love: The Arpillera Movement in Chile* (2nd edn). Lanham, MD: Rowman & Littlefield.

Claverie, E. (2010). War memory—the case of Yugoslavia. In: G. Mink & P. Bonnard (Eds.), *The Past in the Present: Memorial Deposits And Historicising Actions in Central and Eastern Europe* (pp. 105–129). Paris: Houdiard.

Eyerman, R. (2001). *Cultural Trauma: Slavery and the Formation of African American Identity.* Cambridge: Cambridge University Press.

Ferenczi, S. (1932). Confusion of tongues between adults and the child. In: *Final Contributions To The Problems And Methods Of Psychoanalysis* (pp. 156–167). London: Maresfield, 1955.

Figlio, K. (2011). A psychoanalytic reflection on collective memory as a psychosocial enclave: Jews, German national identity, and splitting in the German psyche. *International Social Science Journal, 62*(203–204): 161–177.

Giesen, B. (2004). The trauma of perpetrators: the holocaust as the traumatic reference of German national identity. In: J. C. Alexander (Ed.), *Cultural Trauma and Collective Identity* (pp. 112–154). Berkeley, CA: University of California Press.

Haaken, J. (1998). *Pillar of Salt: Gender, Memory, and the Perils of Looking Back.* Newark, NJ: Rutgers University Press.

Kako, S. (1996). *Comfort Women.* Y. Huang (Trans.). Taipei: Chuan.

Kristeva, J. (1980). *Pouvoirs de l'horreur: essai sur l'abjection.* Paris: Seuil.

LaCapra, D. (2001). *Writing History, Writing Trauma.* Baltimore, MD: Johns Hopkins University Press.

Lévinas, E. (1971). *Totality and Infinity: An Essay on Exteriority.* Paris: Livre de Poche, 2003.

Lin, C. J., & Keating, J. F. (2000). *Island in the Stream: A quick case study of Taiwan's complex history.* Taipei: SMC.

Luo, T. (2000). "Marrying my rapist?!" The cultural trauma among Chinese rape survivors. *Gender & Society, 14*(4): 581–597.

Nishino, R. (1992). *Comfort Women: Testimony of Former Soldiers.* Tokyo: Akashi Shoten [translated for this edition].

Peng, J. (2012). Secret trauma going public: testimonial narratives of Taiwanese "comfort women" as healing scenes. *Router: Journal of Cultural Studies, 14*: 139–196 [in Chinese].

Ricœur, P. (1985). *Time and Narrative. Volume III.* Paris: Le Seuil.

Ricœur, P. (2004). *The Course of Recognition.* Paris: Stock.

Rosenblum, R. (2009). Postponing trauma: the dangers of telling. *International Journal of Psychoanalysis, 90*: 1319–1349.

Schaffer, K., & Sidonie S. (2004). *Human Rights and Narrated Lives: The Ethics of Recognition.* New York: Palgrave Macmillan.

Soh, C. S. (2008). *The Comfort Women: Sexual Violence and Postcolonial Memory in Korea and Japan.* Chicago: University of Chicago Press.

Spivak, G. C., & Morris, R. C. (2010). *Can The Subaltern Speak? Reflections on the History of an Idea.* New York: Columbia University Press.

Taipei Women's Rescue Foundation (Producer) (1998). *The Secrets of Grandma* [Documentary].

Taipei Women's Rescue Foundation (2009). *Report on Taiwanese Comfort Women.* Taipei: Taiwan Commercial Press [translated for this edition].

Taipei Women's Rescue Foundation (Producer), & Jing, W. X. (Director) (2013). *Song of the Reed* [Documentary].

Yoshimi, Y. (2000). *Comfort Women: Sexual Slavery in the Japanese Military during World War II.* S. O'Brien (Trans.). New York: Columbia University Press.

Zhu, D. (2009). *Taiwan Comfort Women.* Taipei: Wu-Nan [translated for this edition].

Zhuo, Y. (1993). *Lives of Taiwanese Women in Qing Dynasty.* Taipei: Independence Evening Post [translated for this edition].

CHAPTER NINE

A relational approach to trauma, memory, mourning, and recognition through *Death and the Maiden* by Ariel Dorfman

Jean-François Jacques

Introduction

I intend to discuss in this chapter shared trauma and loss in the context of the devastating effects of political violence and terror, more precisely in relation to the Chilean dictatorship that followed the overthrow of the Allende government in 1973 and came to an end in 1990. I will do this by reflecting from a play, *Death and the Maiden*, by the Argentinean-born playwright Ariel Dorfman. The play will offer an opportunity to explore key aspects of trauma resulting from exposure to political violence. In this instance, this will be done from the singular perspective of the fictional characters themselves. It is my intention to explore the play from within (as opposed to approaching it from the motivations of the author or the spectator/critic) and to extract from it themes that can deepen our understanding of processes contributing to a traumatic reaction and possible ways of coming to terms with it. This also encompasses questions about the relationship between the arts and the world and how one is constantly the mirror of the other, throwing light and revealing hidden or disavowed truth that could not be tolerated in any other way.

I will adopt a psychoanalytic relational perspective on trauma and will explore the play by discussing and referring to the views developed by the American psychoanalyst Doris Brothers who defines trauma as the destruction of relational systems and of the certainties that shape psychological life. This resonates quite closely with the work of Michael Balint and his views on trauma in adult life, which, according to him, destroys the trust of individuals in their environment (Balint, 1969). I will develop my argument by considering the work of Judith Herman on remembrance and mourning following traumatic events, and the implications of these processes at a collective and individual level. *Death and the Maiden* by Ariel Dorfman depicts characters torn by internal conflicts and dilemmas in a way that reflects the shattered certainties of the society they lived in. The author raises essential questions about the conditions for individuals and society to mourn their past and restore trust in the future. I will illustrate my argument with a number of vignettes from the play.

Death and the Maiden: *betrayal, destruction and exile*

The play takes place at a time of transition in a country (not named but that the author refers as being "probably Chile") that "has given itself a democratic government after a long period of dictatorship" (Dorfman, 1990, stage direction). The three characters are Paulina Salas (a woman in her forties), Gerardo Escobar (her husband, a lawyer), and Roberto Miranda (a doctor). Gerardo is a lawyer who has been appointed as member of a national commission investigating human rights violations under the previous regime and that ended in death or presumption of death.

The play is a close encounter between the three characters. It takes place in *huis clos* (to refer to a play by Sartre) or *in camera*, behind closed doors with no intrusion from the external world (the physical world, anyway) but with a violent intrusion of the past in a physical shape and presence similar to an act of rape. This encounter will gradually take the characters onto a descending spiral of masochistic and perverse violence where, as in Sartre's play (Sartre, 1982), they will torment and torture each other. In that way, the play seems to capture the paralysis of the characters (paralysing each other as well as their own internal paralysis), unable to move away from the psychic torments of surviving a traumatic past.

On one evening, Gerardo Escobar is rescued by Roberto Miranda who helps him to get back to his beach house after he got a flat tyre driving back from town. Gerardo invites him to stay overnight at the house. Paulina recognises the voice of Dr. Miranda as being the voice of the person who tortured and raped her fifteen years before under the previous regime. She had then been abducted to provide information about her husband although she never confessed under torture. The doctor used to play *Death and the Maiden* by Schubert whilst torturing and raping his victims who remained blindfolded. Paulina decides to take Dr. Miranda captive and to get him to confess his crimes by putting him on a makeshift trial. Gerardo is torn between his role of lawyer committed to a fair trial and his emotional bond and commitment to his wife. They eventually reach an agreement that Paulina will set him free if Dr. Miranda confesses his crimes in writing. As the doctor continues to deny his role of perpetrator, Gerardo deceives Paulina by first convincing her to tell the story of her abuses and then by getting Dr. Miranda to confess his story by retelling the words of Paulina. Dr. Miranda signs his confession but Paulina knows that Gerardo attempted to mislead her. She confronts Dr. Miranda's lack of remorse and threatens to kill him, as this seems to be the only way for her to find peace.

The play rests on two uncertainties. First, it is never established whether Dr. Miranda is guilty of what he is accused of, whether he is the actual perpetrator and rapist, or whether he is the product of Paulina's fantasies and her desperate efforts to restore self-integrity. This uncertainty makes the play quite uncomfortable to watch as we are left in a no-man's-land where neither trust nor justice can be restored. Secondly, it is also unclear what happens to Dr. Miranda at the end and whether Paulina carries out her murderous act. What we know for sure is that the figure (or shadow) of Dr. Miranda reappears in the background of the final scene like a haunting and obsessive presence.

By leaving the audience in a heightened state of tension where moral judgement becomes impossible to hold and is as such suspended, Dorfman makes us directly experience the unbearable living experience of the traumatised individual for whom all certainties have receded. In the case of Paulina, the events that led to her trauma plunged her into a world where the familiar became unfamiliar, where comprehension becomes replaced by incomprehension, and where the ability to create meaning was deemed impossible. Doris Brothers regards trauma as the destruction of certainty (Brothers, 2008, p. 47). Even though Brothers identifies existential uncertainty as an ontological condition whose experience contributes to psychic development through a process of regulation and attuning within relational systems, it is very different from the uncertainty resulting from a traumatic experience whose violence, writes Brothers, "threatens us with annihilation" (ibid., p. 45).

The world of Paulina Salas collapsed on the day of the 6 April 1975 when she was taken to a detention and torture centre in Santiago:

> Paulina: I met Dr. Miranda for the first time three days later when … That's when I met Dr. Miranda. [...] At first, I thought he would save me. He was so soft, so—nice, after what the others had done to me. And then, all of a sudden, I heard the Schubert. There is no way of describing what it means to hear that wonderful music in the darkness, when you haven't eaten for three days, when your body is falling apart, when … . (Dorfman, 1990, p. 46)

In the language of relational theory, human development is continually shaped by one's psychological experiences with others (Brothers, 1995, p. 30). The nature and quality of relationship with others ultimately determine the way the individual develops and the views she constructs of herself as well as others. Self-experience is therefore the product of a relational process; and self-structure, an operational system (social in essence) of organising principles that will orientate the ways individuals navigate through the uncertainties of their own life. Brothers calls "systemically emergent certainties" (Brothers, 2008, p. 37) the way the self through a process of development within relational systems builds for her own survival a comprehensive edifice of convictions and beliefs associated with emotional states. The construction of systemically emergent certainties will occur in the context of self-object relations that Brothers defines as the experience of another person as "providing self-sustaining experiences" (ibid., p. 49). The systemically emergent certainties seem to have two main properties. The first one is to provide a sense of self-safety in a way that counterbalances the inherent vulnerability of the human subject, as Judith Butler would probably put it (Butler, 2003). The other property is to provide a sense of what to expect and whether the conditions are met for self-sustainment. Psychic integration could be seen in this context as being a collection of certainties that provide stability, safety, and meaning to our lives (Brothers, 2008, p. 46).

Political terror and political violence constitute a purposeful effort to annihilate and destroy the most fundamental foundations of self-structure and self-experience. The shattering effects of political violence on the self refers to a process of disintegration or dismemberment where the ability to construct meaning, to maintain selfhood and a sense of connection with others, is lost. A physiological understanding of trauma helps see how acts of violence are absorbed and remembered by the body beyond visible scars (Rothschild, 2003). A body that is remembered is also a body whose dissociated parts have been re-formed or reintegrated into some kind of whole inevitably different from its initial structure.

In Paulina's experience, we are left with not knowing much about her formative experiences of self-object relations that contributed to the development of her systemically emergent certainties. But what could be suggested from the extract above is that the process of self-development also includes cultural and social self-object relations. The meaning attached to cultural productions and social roles also contribute to the process of self-validation and to a sense of self-safety. In the case of Paulina, the restorative quality of music and the caring attitude of the medical profession are two systemically emergent certainties that we are aware of. For one moment, Paulina expects that the music of Schubert and the presence of a doctor as cultural and social self-object experiences will save her and put an end to the violence and the abuse, like a desperate attempt to hold on to the belief that the familiar will one more time deliver. But what has now become unfamiliar will rapidly plunge her into a deeper state of psychic decomposition.

Alongside the destruction of certainties and beliefs in self and others, Paulina also lost the trust that she had put in others:

PAULINA: Did you expect me to keep on talking with that bitch there? That bitch came out of your bedroom half naked asking why you were taking so long, and you expected me to—

GERARDO: She wasn't a bitch.

PAULINA: Did she know where I was? Of course she did. A bitch.

GERARDO: We're not going to start all this again, Paulina.

PAULINA: You're the one who started.

GERARDO: How many times do I have to …?—I'd spent two months trying to find you. Then she came by, she said she could help. We had a couple of drinks. My God, I'm also human.

PAULINE: While I defended your life, while your name stayed inside
me and never left my mouth,—ask him, ask Miranda if I ever
so much as whispered your name, while you …

GERARDO: You already forgave me, you forgave me, how many times
will we have to go over this? We'll die from so much past,
we'll suffocate. Let's finish this. Let's close this book once
and for all and never speak about it, ever again. (Dorfman,
1990, pp. 42–43)

Trusting others is an integral part of our interpersonal world that gets
activated from the very moment we come into being throughout the
whole life. Trust will develop in the inner world of the infant as he
gradually realises that the adult is capable of offering a containing hold
(Zinkin, 1989) and of attuning to affects and needs. Basic trust, writes
Judith Herman, is "acquired in earliest life in the relationship with the
first caretaker" (Herman, 1992, p. 51). It is the condition for a sustaining sense of self, capable of responding and adapting to the unexpected
turmoil of a shared reality. But trust seems also to be an inescapable
position for the infant giving that he has no choice but to surrender to
the power of the adult for its survival. Trust can therefore be conceived
as an expression of our total dependence on others for satisfying self-
object experiences. In that sense, trust is the expression of a blind investment when necessity dictates it. It reminds us again of our ontological
insecurity and vulnerability that can be exacerbated at times of intense
stress and how easily it can be betrayed.

Doris Brothers writes, "psychic trauma can only be fully understood
as the betrayal of trust in the self-object relationships on which selfhood
depends" (Brothers, 1995, p. 55). She defines self-trust as "the hope or
wishful expectation of obtaining and providing the self-object experiences necessary for the development, maintenance and restoration
of cohesive selfhood" (ibid., p. 33). Paulina experienced an accumulation of betrayals that undermined her "secure sense of connection"
(Herman, 1992, p. 52) and that constituted a violent rupture of the bonds
that attached her inner self to others and the outside world. A succes-
sion of "traumatising betrayals" (Brothers, 2008, p. 62) forced her into
a world of exile dissociated from what constituted once the bedrock of
her self-experience. Doris Brothers describes how traumatised individuals find themselves expelled from their "relational homeland" (ibid.,
p. 48). She also suggests that it is not so much the event itself that causes

trauma but rather the unconscious meaning of the event for the victim (Brothers, 1995). The extract above illustrates how Paulina's self-object fantasies projected onto Gerardo became betrayed when she found him with another woman. He represented for her the ideal of justice that she herself remained desperately faithful to even under torture. The first extract illustrated how her internal representation of medicine had been previously betrayed. Even though both events are hardly comparable, they both in conjunction represent intolerable violations of her worldviews that leaves her now to face the void of the arbitrary.

Rage and compensation

GERARDO: What are you trying to do?

PAULINA: I already told you—put him on trial.

GERARDO: Put him on trial, what does that mean, put him on trial? We can't use their methods. We're different. To seek vengeance in this fashion is not—

PAULINA: This is not vengeance. I'm giving him all the guarantees he never gave me. Not one, him and his—colleagues (Dorfman, 1990, p. 28).

PAULINA: I want him to confess. I want him to sit in front of the cassette-recorder and to tell me what he did—not just to me, everything, to everybody—and then have him write it out in his own handwriting and sign it and I would keep a copy forever—with all the information, the names and data, all the details. That's what I want. (Dorfman, 1990, p. 35)

Trauma "inevitably brings loss", writes Judith Herman (Herman, 1992, p. 188). She describes the physical and psychological losses that appear very relevant to Paulina's situation. The repeated rapes attacked her body integrity to an unbearable point. But what she also lost is the "internal psychological structures of a self attached to others" (ibid., p. 188). I have to some extent already illustrated the loss of trust, the loss of certainty, the loss of connection, the loss of meaning, and an ensuing loss of identity. I will examine loss and mourning in relation to the play later on, but it might be useful to stop a moment on what constitutes the "disguises" (ibid., p. 189), which prevent the expression of grief.

Paulina denies that she is seeking vengeance. But whichever way she is describing her intentions, she clearly makes her own the methods of her captors (i.e. deprivation, humiliation, and intimidation) to extract a confession from Roberto Miranda. Let's not forget that the ambiguity remains as to whether he is the right man or not. Her rage takes her into a place where she believes that justice can be restored in the here-and-now of her private house. Rage, says Doris Brothers, is an intense affect associated with the betrayal of self-trust (Brothers, 1995). She writes that "rage is likely to predominate when others prove untrustworthy in providing self-object experiences" (ibid., p. 57). This is consistent with Paulina's sense of betrayal in the hand of her captors and her expectations and beliefs associated with the medical profession.

Judith Herman identifies revenge and compensation as fantasies of "magical resolution" for the traumatised individual (Herman, 1992, p. 189). She writes, "the revenge fantasy is often a mirror image of the traumatic memory, in which the roles of perpetrator and victims are reversed" (ibid., p. 189). The fantasy that Paulina entertains results in her being locked in the role of the victim which results paradoxically, when facing her alleged perpetrator, in a merging of roles where they both become joined in a sameness of perverse violence. This is further explained by Herman when she writes about the compensation fantasy that "ties the patient's fate to that of the perpetrator and holds her recovery hostage to his whims" (ibid., p. 190). The relationship dynamic between Paulina and Roberto illustrates how they keep each other hostage of their own fantasies and deceits.

Memory

GERARDO: I think I understand Paulina's need. It coincides with a need of the whole country. The need to put into words what happened to us (Dorfman, 1990, p. 39).

PAULINA: (…) If you could listen to me for a change, my love. I'm not trying to harm your career and I most certainly don't want to jeopardise the Commission. But you see the Commission only deals with the dead, with those who can't speak. And I can speak—it's been so long since I as much as whispered a word, even a breath of what I'm thinking, years living in terror of my own … but I'm not dead, I thought I was but I'm not and I can speak,—so for God's sake let me have my

say and you go ahead with your Commission and believe
me when I tell you that none of this will be made public.
(Dorfman, 1990, p. 31)

Paulina desperately seeks to break a silence—the silence of the victims
of the violations of human rights under the dictatorship whose stories
yearn to be heard. In an effort towards self-restoration and self-healing,
Paulina wants to bring into the consciousness of her own self the atrocities of the past. This effort doesn't seem to be an expression of the part
of her that seeks vengeance, but rather the expression of another part
that seeks peace and whose pain needs to be acknowledged and recognised by others in order for it to be integrated in her own life. The act
of narration of experience needs a witness to be fully validated and to
bring Paulina back from a world of exile. Concomitantly, her efforts to
break the silence of the trauma also seem to be an attempt to bring the
truth of the past into the collective consciousness. As Judith Herman
suggests, the act of truth telling aims at restoring connections between
the public and the private worlds (Herman, 1992).

Doris Brothers writes that experience is continually transformed by
means of regulatory processes (Brothers, 2008). Within these processes,
she identifies the creation of narratives and memory. She argues that the
construction of narratives which depends on the ability to remember,
functions as a key mode of organising human experience (ibid., p. 32)
and of creating meaning for oneself. Paulina's capacity to reconstruct
a "self-narrative" (Gergen & Gergen, 2001) seems an important part of
her healing process of reconnecting with the dissociated aspects of her
self-experience (Brothers, 1995)—provided that it is not being denied,
as it would then result in the collapse of her attempt for self-regulation.
Gerardo understands that "putting into words what happened" is not
just a need for Paulina but also an aspect of collective healing and the
capacity of a society to work through the horrors of the past.

Collective healing corresponds to a psychosocial and political process of integration of shared trauma into collective memory. The creation of the National Commission for Truth and Reconciliation in Chile
in 1990 was aimed at facilitating this process at a time of transition
between dictatorship and democracy. Ariel Dorfman writes in the after-
word to the play that "it was an important step towards healing a sick
country: the truth of the terror unleashed upon us that we had always
known in a private and fragmented fashion would finally receive
public recognition, established forever as official history, recreating a

community fractured by divisions and hatred that we wished to leave behind" (Dorfman, 1990, p. 58). I will return to the notion of recognition later on in this chapter.

Gerardo provides Paulina with an opportunity to testify about the extent of her sufferings, similarly to what his role would be in the investigating commission. Judith Herman suggests that in the act of telling, the "trauma story becomes a testimony" with personal and collective implications (Herman, 1992, p. 181). She also refers to the "testimony method" as a therapeutic technique that interestingly was developed by psychologists in Chile to help the survivors of political torture (ibid., p. 182). But Gerardo's motivation is not aimed at individual healing in a therapeutic sense. It is primarily motivated by his commitment to save Roberto Miranda. There is a moment in the play when the story of Paulina becomes merged with the confession of Roberto Miranda and where he takes over the narration from her. This is not an instance of collaborative narration (Rawlinson, 2006) leading to potential reconciliation and forgiveness. This is an instance of further alienation where Paulina's self-narrative is taken hostage with the view of being used as a means of redemption not for her but for her alleged perpetrator.

Loss and mourning

PAULINA: I was horrified at myself. That I should have such hatred in me, that I should want to do something like that to a defenceless human being, no matter how vile—but it was the only way to fall asleep at night (…) (Dorfman, 1990, p. 34).

ROBERTO: I need to know what it is I did, you've got to understand that I don't know what I have to confess. If I were that man, I'd know every—detail, but I don't know anything. If I make a mistake, she'll think I'm—I'll need your help (ibid., p. 41).

GERARDO: Forgive, yes, forget, no. But forgive so we can start again. There's so much to live for, my … (ibid., p. 43)

The shattering of self-experience through traumatic events results in irreplaceable losses and a life that will never be the same as before. The ability to mourn traumatic losses is considered by Judith Herman as the most necessary but also the most dreaded task of the recovery process (Herman, 1992). In the case of Paulina, her desperate attempt to establish justice and to seek the truth is akin to what Freud called "obsessive neurosis" (Freud, 1917e)—a compulsive search for what appears to have been irremediably lost in the dreadful events that followed her abduction. This doesn't mean that justice cannot be restored through the process of healing but rather that Paulina seems to have substituted her inner sense of hope (initially provided by the love object of her country and the promises represented by the Allende's government) by a false hope, expression of the persistent identification with the lost love-object and of a melancholic self. Gerardo seems to capture this when he suggests to Paulina that "people can also die from an excessive dose of truth" (Dorfman, 1990, p. 44), since truth appears to be the reflection of her false sense of hope.

Doris Brothers writes, "all traumas are to some extent shared" (Brothers, 2008, p. 51). She expresses how, through a process of interconnectedness, the pain felt by one is endured by all and ripples across the whole social structure. The traumatic history of Chile between 1973 and 1990 is epitomised in the character of Paulina Salas who carries the ambivalence associated with the subsequent period of transition for the country. Her reaction to loss is also indicative of the efforts of a whole country to mourn its past. I have previously illustrated how the difficulty of mourning can be profoundly defended against. The three characters in the play seem to represent in their own right three different reactions to loss. The three extracts above can be seen as reflecting three of the five stages of the grieving process identified by Elisabeth Kubler-Ross: denial, anger, and acceptance/forgiveness (Kubler-Ross, 1969). Despite the fact that these three positions are mutually relevant in the context of shared trauma, they are not able in any way to relate to one another in the play. They are rather being played out in isolation from one another, making it quite impossible to envisage them as part of one single process where they would all represent concomitant steps towards some form of integration. It is that difficulty of finding and accepting a common and shared narrative that I will now turn to.

Recognition and reconciliation

ROBERTO: So we go on and on with violence, always more violence. Yesterday they did terrible things to you and now you do terrible things to me and tomorrow the same cycle will begin all over again. Isn't it time we stopped?

PAULINA: Why is it always people like me who have to sacrifice, who have to concede when concessions are needed, biting my tongue, why? Well, not this time. If only to do justice in one case, just one. What do we lose? What do we lose by killing one of you? What do we lose?

They freeze in their position as the lights begin to go down slowly. We begin to hear music from the last movement of Mozart's Dissonant Quartet. Paulina and Roberto are covered from view by a giant mirror which descends, forcing the audience to look at themselves. For a few minutes, the Mozart quartet is heard, while the spectators watch themselves in the mirror. (Dorfman, 1990, p. 53)

Traumatic events in the history of a nation will eventually require it to face a delicate and painful exercise of repairing and healing the ruptures and conflicts that have divided it, and of creating the conditions for this to be achieved. That collective responsibility raises essential questions about the ability to live alongside, engage, and co-exist with an Other who might have been on the receiving or inflicting end of the suffering.

The efforts towards reconciliation in Chile resulted in the creation of the National Commission for Truth and Reconciliation (also named the Retig Commission) by the newly democratically elected president Patricio Aylwin in 1990. It had a mandate of investigating death and disappearance under the military regime. The commission was limited to an investigating role and not a prosecuting role that would have resulted in bringing the perpetrators to justice. Beside, a rule of amnesty was still protecting the militaries following the self-amnesty decree of 1978. The commission had also no mandate to investigate the human rights abuses that were non-fatal. As we know, the play takes place at the time when the Commission was formed. Paulina is one of the victims whose voice is not to be heard, acknowledged, or recognised since she is still alive. Her silent trauma is at the interface between reconciliation and recognition.

Nancy Potter suggests that reconciliation is a moral concept that establishes the "inseparability of self-other relations" (Potter, 2006, p. 7). The concept became a political imperative for societies divided by internal conflicts and working on restoring social ties between parts of the population or between ethnic groups such as in South Africa after the fall of the apartheid regime. Reconciliation appears to primarily translate a socio-political concern for re-engagement with the other as a desired outcome and a resolution of past divisions. It maybe overlooks deeper dynamics for the actors involved in the process (Zachar, 2006). This is where the concept of recognition becomes helpful.

At the end of the play, the music of Mozart replaces the music of Schubert. The musical dissonance illustrates the dissonance in the relationship dynamic between Paulina and Roberto and their mutual failure of acknowledging one another (Benjamin, 2009). They fail to recognise their mutual dependence or, as Judith Butler would say, they fail to "take stock of their interdependence" (Butler, 2003, p. 17) which seems to be the condition for them to overcome the nightmares of the past. The communication between the two appears irremediably damaged and beyond reparation. They don't only fail to recognise each other as individual subjects invested with consciousness, they also fail to recognise the presence of the other within themselves. This illustrates a process of what I suggest be called distorted intersubjective mirroring, where they project onto one another their own violence and deny each other's vulnerability.

Recognition, writes Judith Butler, is "a process that is engaged when subject and Other understand themselves to be reflected in one another, but where this reflection does not result in a collapse of the one into the Other or a projection that annihilates the alterity of the Other" (Butler, 2000, p. 272). It is a process that enables the "capacity to appreciate the other as a centre of consciousness separate from the subject but also in relation to it" (Frosh, 2011, pp. 228–229). Recognition therefore seems to refer to a shared space of mutual encounter, a space of intersubjective relationship, or what Jessica Benjamin calls the "shared third" (Benjamin, 2009). The shared third is invested with qualities that derive from the abilities of those involved to engage in a process of "collaborative narration" where the story told is neither yours or mine but rather ours (Rawlinson, 2006). It is a relational space where recognition is simultaneously the condition for it and the expression of it. The relationships between Paulina, Gerardo, and Roberto movingly illustrate the difficulties of restoring a "shared third" in the context of shared trauma where the different voices of the past and the present can transcend their dissonance.

Conclusion

I have endeavoured in this chapter to discuss aspects of shared trauma and loss resulting from political violence as it happened under the dictatorship in Chile through the lens of a play, and the actions and behaviours of the characters within it. I haven't spent as much time considering the role of the arts in the efforts towards reconciliation and healing following a shared trauma. Yet, this seems to be an important aspect of the approach of the author to reveal through arts the complexity of a shared reality and to reach beyond a dualistic perspective. In that sense, the arts can be considered as transitional phenomena in their ability to integrate a range of narratives and discourses. But this must be left for now as a possible subject for another reflection.

References

Balint, M. (1969). Trauma and object relationship. *International Journal of Psychoanalysis, 50*: 429–435.

Benjamin, J. (2009). Psychoanalytic controversies: a relational psychoanalysis perspective on the necessity of acknowledging failure in order to restore the facilitating and containing features of the intersubjective relationship (the shared third). *International Journal of Psychoanalysis, 90*: 441–450.

Brothers, D. (1995). *Falling Backwards: An Exploration of Trust and Self Experience*. New York: Norton.

Brothers, D. (2008). *Towards a Psychology of Uncertainty: Trauma-Centred Psychoanalysis*. New York: Analytic.

Butler, J. (2000). Longing for recognition: commentary on the work of Jessica Benjamin. *Studies in Gender and Sexuality, 1*: 271–290.

Butler, J. (2003). Violence, mourning, politics. *Studies in Gender and Sexuality, 4*: 9–37.

Dorfman, A. (1990). *Death and the Maiden*. London: Nick Hern.

Dorfman, A. (2011). *Feeding on Dreams: Confessions of an Unrepentant Exile*. Boston, MA: Houghton Mifflin Harcourt.

Freud, S. (1917e). Mourning and Melancholia. *S. E., 14*: 239. London: Hogarth.

Frosh, S. (2011). The relational ethics of conflict and identity. *Psychoanalysis, Culture and Society, 16*(3): 225–243.

Gergen, K. J., & Gergen, M. M. (2001). Narratives of the self. In: L. P. Hinchman & S. K. Hinchman (Eds.), *Memory, Identity, Community* (pp. 161–184). Albany, NY: State University of New York Press.

Herman, J. (1992). *Trauma and Recovery*. New York: Basic.

Kubler-Ross, E. (1969). *Death and Dying*. London: Tavistock.

Potter, N. N. (2006). Introduction. In: N. N. Potter (Ed.), *Trauma, Truth and Reconciliation* (pp. 1–13). Oxford: Oxford University Press.

Rawlinson, M. C. (2006). Beyond virtue and the law: on the moral significance of the act of forgiveness in Hegel's *Phenomenology of spirit*. In: N. N. Potter (Ed.), *Trauma, Truth and Reconciliation* (pp. 139–169). Oxford: Oxford University Press.

Rothschild, B. (2003). *The Body Remembers: Casebook—Unifying Methods and Models in the Treatment of Trauma and PTSD*. New York: Norton.

Sartre, J.-P. (1982). *Huis Clos and Other Plays*. London: Penguin.

Zachar, P. (2006). Reconciliation as compromise and the management of rage. In: N. N. Potter (Ed.), *Trauma, Truth and Reconciliation* (pp. 67–81). Oxford: Oxford University Press.

Zinkin, L. (1989). The group as container and contained. *Group Analysis*, 22: 227–234.

Victory and defeat—from Beveridge to Thatcher without tears

Jane Frances

The 1979 general election that brought Margaret Thatcher's government to power, with policies of individualisation and privatisation, came just thirty-four years after the 1945 landslide Labour victory that had ushered in the Welfare State and the National Health Service. How can a society change so much across just one generation?

Unlike the 1979 electorate, the 1945 electorate, who voted overwhelmingly Labour immediately after the 1939–1945 war, would have included many people born before the Great War of 1914–1918. This exploration focuses on the impact of these two world wars, and draws upon attachment research to argue that a terrible mismatch between private loss and public mourning shaped a generation, leading to reduced social concern.

Britain was hugely involved from beginning to end in both world wars. In each war, in spite of terrible losses, Great Britain was on the side that won, was never invaded, never occupied. In wartime Britain, British people did not become refugees. The 1914–1918 war was fought over there in mainland Europe, with uniformed combatants taking trains from Victoria Station to the coast and the boat to France, followed by a regular supply of letters and parcels delivered to the front by the Royal Mail (Fussell, 1975). During the 1939–1945 war, although invasion was felt to be imminent, it never happened. British cities were massively bombed, destroying hundreds of thousands of homes as well as factories and docks. Sometimes mortuaries overflowed but there were no mass graves. Municipal and voluntary organisations processed people's applications for practical help following the loss of everything through bombing. Individuals and families were re-housed and received clothing and other necessities, along with cash to tide them over. Food rationing was sometimes sparse but there was always just about enough. BBC radio never went off air, broadcasting regular programmes, concerts of music, and comedy shows, as well as news bulletins and occasional steadfast speeches by Mr. Churchill or King George VI. The maintenance of civilian morale on the "home front" was considered vital.

Across Britain, on or near 11 November each year, the ultimate sacrifice of the vast numbers of servicemen who gave their lives is honoured in formal Remembrance ceremonies and church services. VE Day (Victory in Europe) is also marked on 7 May; VJ Day (Victory in Japan) on 15 August, perhaps less so. In English lessons at school, children encounter war poetry from "the trenches". Dunkirk Spirit has come to indicate an uncomplaining determination in the face of great difficulty, which we believe to be especially British. The bad things that happened to people in the process are somehow minimised. This is the "problem" I set out to address: how has this played out in British society since 1945?

The damaging transmission of unprocessed loss and trauma across generations and the impact of these silenced, internalised distresses upon each new generation is well understood (Coles, 2011; Hesse & Main, 1999; Zuluetta, 2006;). A seemingly safe and stable family situation can nevertheless foster disorganised attachments with very particular consequences for children as they grow up. What is the impact of these early childhood experiences on the subsequent adult's social or societal perspective? The relative ages of the different generations at the times of key events across the twentieth century are shown on the timelines diagram in Figure 1.

Let us explore what this timeline means, psychoanalytically and socially, culturally and politically, for each new generation of parents and children.

World Wars	First			Second				
Governments					Atlee		Thatcher	
Key 20th century people ... ... and their ages across the decades...								
Chamberlain 1869–1940	46 yrs	56 yrs	66 yrs (d:71 yrs)					
Churchill 1874–1965	41 yrs	51 yrs	61 yrs	71 yrs	81 yrs	d.90 yrs		
Beveridge 1879–1963	36 yrs	46 yrs	56 yrs	66 yrs	76 yrs (d.84 yrs)			
Atlee 1893–1967	22 yrs	32 yrs	42 yrs	52 yrs	62 yrs	72 yrs (d.74 yrs)		
Thatcher 1925–2013			10 yrs	20 yrs	30 yrs	40 yrs	50 yrs	60 yrs
John Major 1943–				0 yrs	10 yrs	20 yrs	30 yrs	40 yrs
Evacuated child			1 yrs	11 yrs	21 yrs	31 yrs	41 yrs	51 yrs
Years	1915	1925	1935	1945	1955	1965	1975	1985

Figure 1. Twentieth-century Britain: timelines for the generations.

A very brief history of Britain from 1914 to 1945

The 1914–1918 war

In 1914 Britain's population has been estimated at 46 million and its army was smaller than Belgium's. By January 1916, in response to a vigorous recruitment campaign rousing great patriotic fervour, more than 2.6 million men had volunteered for the British Army. Military leaders insisted that yet more men were needed so in 1916 Parliament initiated conscription.

> The statistics defy comprehension. On 1 July 1916 British troops were sent into battle at Somme. On that first day there were 57,470 casualties, including 19,240 deaths—the bloodiest day in the history of the British Army. 'Pals' Battalions, comprising men from the same town who had enlisted together, suffered catastrophic losses and local newspapers back at home were, for days and weeks, filled with lists of dead, wounded and missing. (BBC, 2006; BBC, 2013a)

Of all British men who in 1911 were aged between nineteen and twenty-nine, by the end of this war, one third were dead (Bragg, 2012). Shell shock was first described in print in 1915 by Dr. Charles Myers of the British Psychological Society. By 1918 the army was dealing with 80,000 cases of men who were unable to cope (BBC, 2013b). With fathers, sons, brothers, uncles, and cousins away at the war, families all over Britain were at constant risk of receiving a letter or telegram informing them that a relative had been killed, wounded, or was missing (BBC, 2006). More than 800,000 British dead left behind 248,000 widows and 381,000 fatherless children (Zulueta, 2006). Countless other families managed as best they could when their mentally or physically disabled ex-servicemen came home.

For Britain, from almost the start of the war, the decision was made not to repatriate the bodies of the dead. For women especially, personal and familial mourning had accompanied their tasks of arranging the funeral and of washing and laying out the body, which remained in the home for several days while family and friends visited to pay their respects and say goodbye (Gorer, 1965; Roper, 2009). "In what appears to be a socially induced form of psychological defence, patriotic stoicism was encouraged, with the result that pre-war funeral and mourning customs were abandoned" (Zulueta, 2006, p. 56). The disappearance of mourning traditions and rituals led grieving mothers to create "symbolic markers" (Roper, 2009, p. 219). "In 1927, almost a decade on from the war's end, many women ... were still dressed in deep mourning" (Roper, p. 219). With no physical location for her son's body, a mother used his photograph, his war medals and pressed poppies to create a memorial for him in her front room "where it remained until she died ..." (Roper, p. 219).

After 1918, over there, close to where the trenches had been dug and the battles fought, 2,500 British military cemeteries were established to be managed in perpetuity by the Imperial (now Commonwealth) War Graves Commission. Rudyard Kipling, who had himself lost a son in the war, devised enduring epitaphs such as "Their bodies are buried in peace; but their name liveth for evermore". Displaying impossibly large numbers of neat white crosses, the cemeteries are "pretty and bizarre, fertile with roses, projecting an almost unendurably ironic peacefulness" (Fussell, 1975, p. 70).

At home, memorials proliferated. Among lawns and orchards in a Hampshire village, for example, Sandham Memorial Chapel houses a series of huge paintings by Stanley Spencer who used his experiences as a medical orderly in Macedonia to inspire his scenes of ordinary army life. The whole is dominated by the "Resurrection of the Soldiers" in which, from the foreground and into the far distance, huge numbers of British soldiers (and war horses too) are seen, as if re-emerged from the ground, among hundreds of white crosses. The chapel was built and Spencer's paintings commissioned for it by Mary and Louis Behrend as a memorial to Mary's brother, Lieutenant Henry Willoughby Sandham, who had died near the end of the war.

Throughout the 1920s, war memorials were built in every city, town, and village, and in factories, municipal buildings, railway stations, schools, and university colleges. Each bears the long list of names of local men, employees, former pupils, or students, who died. Town and village war memorials often list several or all of some families' sons. Ever since, each year, as Armistice Day approaches, red poppies are widely worn to remember "the fallen" (Fussell, 1975, p. 22). Remembrance services and ceremonies are held, during which wreaths of red poppies are laid at the base of these sombre war memorials, with a two-minute silence at 11 am.

The war (and the global flu pandemic which followed it) took a terrible toll across Europe, leaving millions of bereft mothers, widows, and orphans, and millions more families struggling with physically disabled and psychologically damaged ex-soldiers. My contention here is that all this, in the particular context of Empire and victory that characterised the British experience, gave rise to social and cultural developments in Britain, which both inhibited mourning and forbade forgetting (The even greater numbers of people killed by the flu epidemic of 1918–1919, having died at home or in local hospitals, were buried by their own families in their own local cemeteries and churchyards, and not memorialised as "the fallen").

The inter-war years—nihilism

The war changed everything. In Britain the confidence and imperial supremacy of the Victorian era and the Edwardian belle epoch gave way to a darker, more complex mood such that anything in a positive key was apt to be heard as mindless jingoism, empty frippery, or as if from across a vast wilderness of shell craters. T. S. Eliot's *The Waste Land* (1922) asserts that April (formerly the bringer of spring) is now the cruellest month. An American, Eliot perfectly engaged the eternal British preoccupation with the weather and the English love of gardens. But now you cannot push your border fork into the earth without turning up a body part. In lines 370–376, evoking cities and mountains, Eliot offers what seems like a dark antidote to "Jerusalem"—the much loved "rousing" alternative national anthem of mainstream England. Elsewhere (lines 379–384) baby-faced bats, a blackened wall, tolling bells, a "downward" and two "down"s, an empty and an exhausted surely hammer home the desolation. *The Waste Land* was a bestseller.

In 1925 came Virginia Wolf's *Mrs Dalloway* in which, alongside Mrs Dalloway's party preparations, the struggles and anguish of shell-shocked Septimus Smith, and his distraught wife's hopeless search for help for him, culminate in Septimus's suicide.

In D. H. Lawrence's *Lady Chatterley's Lover* (1928), the aristocratic, war injured, and emotionally remote husband, Clifford Chatterley, cannot make his young wife happy. She is drawn across a formerly inviolable class boundary to the gamekeeper, Oliver Mellors, with whom she can feel fully alive.

The soldiers' experience of trench warfare and the shadow that the war cast across British society, have been linked, especially by Paul Fussell (1975), to the development of a particular cultural condition, a kind of nihilism, in which irony is used to undermine or dismantle everything we thought we knew or cared about. Fussell fought as a US infantryman in Europe in the Second World War and dedicates his book "To the memory of Technical Sergeant Edward Keith Hudson ... killed beside me in France, March 15, 1945". He analyses extensively, mostly English or British, published and unpublished personal diaries, and other wide-ranging wartime writings, including poetry and literature, journalism, and propaganda, to show how the literature and literary conventions which grew out of "The Great War" were an expression of the indescribable and insupportable experience of the mass of officers and soldiers. Drawing upon Northrop Frye's (1957) ideas concerning the relationship between reader and literary hero, particularly regarding their relative scopes for action, Fussell shows how literary heroes who, before The Great War, had been greater than us, subsequently became smaller than us, occupying scenes of "bondage, frustration or absurdity" (p. 312). The special character of these wartime writings, argues Fussell, derives not from their telling of unspeakable occurrences but from their grip on "the knife-edge" (p. 312) separating ordinary life and the bloody absurd.

Turning from books to mountains, Wade Davis (2011) considers the impact of the war on the well-to-do British hobby of mountaineering. Virginia Woolf's father, Sir Leslie Stephen (1832–1904), who wrote extensively on philosophical, religious, and literary topics, was first an accomplished mountaineer, and president of the Alpine Club (1865–1868); in 1871, he wrote the recently reprinted mountaineering classic, *The Playground of Europe*.

After the Great War, *Playground* no longer applies. Davis (2011) argues that the British mountaineers who became obsessed with the most difficult and deadly climbs were responding to their war experiences. Six of the fourteen mountaineers who tackled Everest had been seriously wounded, a seventh, shell-shocked. Three former army doctors had dealt daily with the dying and the appallingly wounded. Two had nearly died of disease and another two had lost their brothers. The war had consumed their generation. Survivor guilt drew these mountaineers to the hardest mountain ascents, to silence, and closeness to death.

The 1939–1945 war

Evacuation

As war loomed, in anticipation of air raids, the government planned to "empty the cities" of children and mothers. On 3 September 1939, war was declared and the mass evacuation began. Some 800,000 children were sent away, mostly without their mothers. Some returned home after a few weeks. Others stayed in the countryside for the rest of the war.

The relatively prompt return home of many evacuees may seem to reassure that this evacuation was not so very traumatic for the young children involved. However, James and Joyce Robertson's (1971, 1989) seminal research at the Tavistock Clinic on short separations revealed how even a few days' separation involving no obvious unkindness, can seriously affect children's capacity to form, maintain, and mourn attachments.

Dunkirk

In May 1940, the Third Reich's rapidly advancing army had forced the British Expeditionary Force into retreat. Nearly 400,000 men, including French and Belgian troops, became trapped in a small area along the French coast. Operation Dynamo aimed to bring up to 30,000 of them back to the UK. But the Royal Navy's 220 light war ships were joined by 39 Dutch coasters that had just escaped the occupation of the Netherlands. Then, following a BBC wireless request for small self-propelled boats,

> Everyone who had a boat of any kind, steam or sail, put out for Dunkirk and the preparations, fortunately begun a week earlier, were now aided by the brilliant improvisation of volunteers on an amazing scale. (Churchill, 1949, p. 89)

Over several days, under constant enemy bombardment, and with the French valiantly delaying the enemy advance, some 650 small civilian boats pressed close to the beaches to collect and ferry thousands of exhausted soldiers out to the bigger ships. They also made hundreds of journeys, under fire, to and from the English coast. It took ten days to evacuate 338,000 stranded troops, mostly British but also French and Belgian (BBC, 1940a). The wounded were stretchered to waiting hospital trains, the rest walked, exhausted, to ordinary trains. "All the way along the [railway] line, the people of England stood at the level crossings and in the back gardens to wave to them. And so the BEF came home" (BBC, 1940b).

Dunkirk combines a number of great British tropes: the underdog, the amateur, messing about in boats, the sea (representing freedom of movement and spiritual liberty (Bradshaw, 2009, p. 101, citing Bourke, 1954)), our island home, and also, it has to be said, waiting your turn in a queue. In the re-telling, even gardens and home gain special emphasis (BBC, 1940b). But above all, there are these little boats. In Kenneth Graham's (1908) *Wind in the Willows*, "messing about in boats" (p. 11) establishes Rat's fine, easy-going, and quintessentially *English* character. Until more recent decades this was one of the most widely read children's stories in Britain, and has never been out of print. In 1930 *Wind in the Willows* was joined by Arthur Ransome's *Swallows and Amazons* about children spending an adventure-filled summer sailing and rowing about in small boats—another immensely popular book.

"On the last morning, Major-General Harold Alexander inspected the shores of Dunkirk from a motorboat to make sure no one was left behind, before boarding the last ship back to Britain" (BBC, 1940a). Surely Kenneth Graham could have written this sentence about Rat clearing up after another of Mr. Toad's misadventures? Somewhere in the back of our minds, something actually terrible is re-forming as a rather fine rescue. The Dunkirk evacuation was immediately followed by what is perhaps Prime Minister Churchill's most famous broadcast wartime speech, in which this "miracle of deliverance" is followed by the promise that we will fight for and never surrender our beaches, fields, streets, and hills (BBC, 1940a).

Operation Dynamo, the Dunkirk evacuation, seemingly now led by an *ad hoc* but doughty civilian fleet of pleasure cruisers, yachts, and dinghies (in fact partly crewed by naval reservists), became like something from Homer, or from a childhood storybook. "Another English epic ... snatching glory out of defeat ... our little holiday steamers made an excursion to hell and came back glorious" (BBC, 1940c).

The original BBC radio reportage included this sentence, quoting one of the survivors brought home: "There were bodies floating in the water and we were under constant attack from machine-gun fire, bombing, explosions sending shrapnel in every direction" (BBC, 1940a). Sixty-eight thousand men of the British Expeditionary Force were "lost" along with all the allies' heavy weapons. Of 693 British vessels whose involvement in the evacuation was recorded, 226 were sunk. Of the 311 vessels in the category "other small craft" (excluding lifeboats and some small, privately owned craft) 170 were sunk (Churchill, 1949, p. 102). The French troops who had enabled the evacuation by holding the perimeter were killed or captured.

In the transformational process from bloody evacuation under fire, to national fable, the bodies in the water have become ever fainter and the achievement ever more complete, a kind of air-brushing of the British mind. The ships and boats set sail bravely across the Channel. They sailed right in close to the beaches. The soldiers climbed aboard and they all came home. A miraculous deliverance.

In Britain, from *The Snow Goose* and *Mrs Miniver* in 1941, to *Atonement* (book, 2001; film, 2007), and with new additions each year (e.g. the rescue at the end of *The Boat That Rocked*, 2009, where fans come in little boats; the Thames Jubilee Pageant on 3 June 2012 in which 670 assorted boats sailed together down the Thames for the Queen's Diamond Jubilee), Dunkirk appears and reappears as theme or backdrop, named or nameless but always resonant, in a huge and ever-growing number of films, novels, TV dramas, re-enactments, and TV documentaries.

The Dunkirk evacuation was a courageous rescue against all the odds, which restored the manpower and secured the determination to resist the expected invasion. It was also a truly terrible ten days: not knowing if or when you would ever get away, with little to eat and nowhere to rest or sleep, queuing on the one remaining, bombed pier to board the larger ships, or waiting for days and nights on the beach, under constant fire, and then wading into the bloody sea to scramble into a small boat. But all this is curiously either very faint or absent from the mythologised version.

Balint (1969) located the establishment of a child's trauma in the parent's playing down of the hurt and shock that the child really experienced, by subsequently behaving towards the child as if nothing untoward had occurred. Here, I argue that a combination of official governmental and loyal journalistic management of civilian and military morale, a chance resonance, much exploited, with children's boating stories, and perhaps also the stiff upper lip in which we British are apt to take pride, facilitated some airbrushing of the Dunkirk evacuation. Setting aside for a moment the imperatives, how did the new Homeric myth affect the soldiers who waded among the dead bodies of their comrades to get to the "little ships", and the mourning process for families whose loved ones did not make it home?

D-Day

On 6 June 1944 Operation Overlord began. Some 5,000 vessels transported 150,000 men and 30,000 vehicles across the English Channel while six parachute regiments of 13,000 men were transported in more than 800 planes.

At this point, I turn to my own father, now ninety years old, who was twenty in 1944. Having failed his call-up medical due to deafness, he remained a civilian and spent the war working by day and firewatching by night. Portsmouth is a city with a large naval dockyard, on the south coast, just across from France.

Twice in my lifetime, my father has mentioned watching thousands of troops march down through the town to the rafts moored in the harbour. He watched them towed off to France. A few hours later, he watched a ship returning incredibly fast. (Having watched ships at sea all his young life he knew incredibly fast when he saw it). On the quayside, orderlies were waiting to unload. Over the ensuing days and weeks thousands of wounded men were transferred into scores of waiting hospital trains, which then steamed off at full speed to hospitals all over Britain.

Throughout Operation Overlord, the evacuation of large numbers of casualties

> was carried out at OMAHA Beach essentially as planned. With the exception of a few hours on D-day, there was little delay in evacuating casualties. The changing normal back-drift of casualties and route of casualty flow was met by the elasticity and mobility of evacuation station organization ... By D plus 17 days ... the casualty-evacuation system had become well regulated. (Bureau of Medicine and Surgery, 1941–1945, p. 723)

D-Day was a success: the beach head was established, the liberation of Europe was underway at last. During this first stage, from 6 June till 20 June, 40,513 Allied servicemen were lost.

As for the Dunkirk evacuation, so for the D-Day landings: in their different ways, Operation Dynamo and Operation Overlord were truly remarkable, courageous achievements which, for reasons of maintaining both military and civilian morale were and still are presented with their huge costs minimised and their positive outcomes maximised. With the liberation of Europe came newsreel of concentration camps and the catastrophe that had befallen six million Jews. British losses bore no comparison and the names of the 403,000 British military dead were quietly added to the lists of names on the already existing Great War memorials. They are remembered and honoured every year on 11 November.

Trauma and victory

The established metapsychological model of trauma envisages a quantitative overload in which trauma derives either from outside with no warning, like being hit by a train, or from inside, like a nightmare or neurosis, generated by unbearably conflicted id, ego and super-ego. By contrast Balint (1969) describes a three-phase model for childhood trauma. First a phase of sufficiently mutually appreciative relating between the child and the adult establishes trust. Second, a new event (which could include the adult's huge need for comfort, say) generates excitement and misunderstanding between the child and trusted adult. The trauma is only completed in the third phase, when the adult behaves towards the child "as if he does not know anything about the previous excitement or rejection; in fact, he acts as if nothing had happened" (pp. 432–433).

This model is used by Auestad (2012) to examine the impact of national or cultural histories or versions of events upon those minorities whose personal experiences are not contained or reflected therein. Therefore, I argue here that a process of this kind was inevitable and even necessary, while Britain was in the grip of ongoing war, arising from the mismatch between the "air-brushed" newsreel emphasis on doughty perseverance, deliverance, achievement, and victory on the one hand, and on the other the personal experience of loss affecting hundreds of thousands of bereaved individuals and families, whose grief is overshadowed by the demands of an ongoing national emergency.

In both wars, beginning with a sense of national belonging and trust, and recognition of powerful enemy threat and therefore of national need, many or most individuals, families, lovers, and spouses more or less accepted the idea that a war must be fought. Hundreds of thousands of fit, young conscripted men and volunteers go forward according to careful military plans, which planning, as we have seen for the D-Day landings, includes managing the "normal back-drift" of the thousands who will be wounded, and the collection and burial of the bodies of the thousands more who are to be killed. Death in battle is suffused with ideas of courage, glory, and sacrifice. Individual memories and attachments, loss and mourning are not so obviously addressed in the rituals of perpetual national remembrance. Any personal memory that contradicts the cleansed public version becomes dislocated or delocated, alienating, incommunicable, irresolvable: subjectivity is replaced by absence (Auestad, 2012).

To the extent that a person's constellation of traumatogenic objects or "educators" (Balint, 1969, p. 432) includes their nation or their national leaders, and the key traumatising role of the "third phase" when myriad highly charged personal events are differently retold or air-brushed out of different nations' national stories, we can see how each nation involved in war may be differently affected in terms of subsequent trauma in the population. My contention here is that in victory, British people's experiences were homogenised into a unified national war story which, following the 1914–1918 war, outlawed triumphalism in favour of a never-ending national sorrow, and for the 1939–1945 war, emphasises refusal to surrender and the Dunkirk spirit on the home front, while ordinary chaps were sent all over Europe and Asia to defeat enemies of unparalleled wickedness. The extent of match or mismatch between the national war story and individuals' personal experiences—including their need and scope for private mourning—will be a key factor, I suggest, in the degree of trauma across the population. Suffering and death in particular pose a problem: whether overshadowed by a necessarily positive, morale-boosting war story, or orchestrated with ceremonial public mourning, or shrouded in the quasi-religious rhetoric of deliverance or sacrifice, the victorious "national war story" always risks coming between individual people—both civilians and fighters—and their varying degrees of personal and familial loss and aloneness.

Unresolved loss and insecure attachment

Attachment theory reaches back into "the evolutionary origins or the adaptive function of the child's tie to its mother" (Hesse & Main, 1999, p. 481). A vital survival prerequisite for infants and small children, attachment concerns paramount safety (rather than, say, food and comfort). "[S]imple insensitivity to infant signals … is unlikely in itself to be alarming" (Hesse & Main, 1999, p. 498). But from as young as eleven months, infants have been found to be "highly alert to frightened expressions on the part of the parent which indicate danger" (p. 515). When the adult's frightened or frightening behaviour is a response to a danger that is external to the adult and therefore accessible to the infant's perception, the attached infant can go to their attachment figure for safety. Even when the parent accidentally does something that frightens the infant, "they are likely to immediately provide comfort, contact, or (in clinical terms) 'repair' …" (p. 515).

By contrast, where a mother manifests lapses in reasoning, or abrupt changes in speaking style, which are typical of unresolved loss internal to the mother and invisible to her attached infant, the infant becomes frightened by or of its own mother. Repeated experiences in which the infant is frightened by something that the parent does are likely to have what Hesse and Main describe as confusing, disorganising, and disorienting effects for attached infants (ibid., p. 483). Even if only one parent has an unresolved issue regarding loss, there is a very high probability that they will unwittingly frighten their children. They are their infant's biologically channelled haven of safety, but they also render their children alarmed or fearful (Hesse & Main, 1999, p. 495).

Psychoanalytic and attachment theory and research show how "unremembered" losses and traumas carry across from one generation to the next into the present where, unless and until they are worked through, they are apt to manifest as some kind of unexplained current distress or difficulty (Hesse & Main, 1999; de Zulueta, 2006; Coles, 2011). The impact of separation anxiety and loss upon children's attachments has been specifically linked to the effects upon families of the huge losses of the 1914–1918 war (Newcombe & Lerner, 1982). A link is also indicated by Hesse and Main's (1999) research, which draws upon Ainsworth and Eichberg's (1991) observations of mothers with unresolved loss, to highlight the kind of lapses of reasoning that are particularly damaging to secure attachment.

For example, a mother recalls the death of an elderly man who had worked briefly for her parents when she was eight years old. Jokingly, he had asked her to marry him when she grew up, and she had replied, "No, you'd be dead." Not long after this exchange, he had died unexpectedly of a brain haemorrhage. Crying, this mother told the interviewer that it was she who had killed him—"with one sentence" (Ainsworth & Eichberg, 1991, p. 175). "[A]s expected [her own] infant's strange situation behaviour was highly disorganized" (Hesse & Main, 1999, p. 507). This conforms to Freud's assertion that, in the unconscious, "a man who has died a natural death is a murdered man: evil wishes have killed him" (Freud, 1912–1913, p. 62). The 1918–1919 flu pandemic which killed more people than even the 1914–1918 war, may have added potency to unconscious ideas of having killed a loved one with one's words: "such a death naturally tends to make the soul revengeful and ill-tempered. It is envious of the living and is longing for the company of its old friends; no wonder, then, that it sends them diseases to cause their death" (Freud, 1912–1913, p. 59).

Other examples of mothers' behaviours, disturbed by unresolved loss, include: suddenly in mid-conversation switching to a speaking style more suited to delivering a eulogy at a funeral—"She was young, she was lovely, and she was torn from us by that most dreaded of diseases, tuberculosis"; speaking of the deceased as if they are both dead and alive; placing the time of a death at several widely separated periods; and speaking of being both absent, and a moment later, present at a death (Hesse & Main, 1999, p. 509).

All these confused and anguished failures of reality testing are suggestive of the way the lost object, instead of being finally let go through the work of mourning, is (in melancholia) drawn back into the ego in order that the love escape extinction. (Freud, 1917e, p. 256)

Every family is different, of course, and children are differently equipped to test reality, to reason, and to problem-solve. Nevertheless, with thousands upon thousands of soldiers dying at the front between 1914 and 1918, and mourning rituals curtailed at home, it is not difficult to imagine, in nurseries and playrooms, in kitchen corners and grubby streets across the land, many a child thinking or speaking a cross thought, as children do, only to hear or over-hear, a little while later, that the object of their cross thought or cross words was dead—seemingly killed "with one sentence". In the years following the end of this war, where the "modern" mood was personal, particular, and hopeless (Fussell, p. 70), it is hard to see how the annual Remembrance Day ceremonies and the post-war culture of irony and nihilism would assist grieving individuals resolve all this loss through personal mourning.

Thus, I contend, the seeds were sown for the next generation of parents to be at much greater risk of manifesting, unwittingly and unintentionally, behaviours that would alarm their children—born in the late 1920s and the 1930s—and thereby lead to attachment difficulties.

To this cohort of children, born in the 1920s and 1930s, liable to a high incidence of attachment difficulties, we must add many of the 800,000 children born in the 1930s who were evacuated away from the bombing danger in the cities in 1939. Thus, through the unfortunate sequence of events which befell children safe at home during the first war, later, during the interwar years, and, when war came again 1939, which uprooted yet more children, even if only briefly, Britain acquired two or more consecutive cohorts of youngsters more at risk than previously of attachment difficulties.

Felicity de Zulueta (2006) emphasises the "internalisation [of our] different types of attachment relationships" (p. 6) in the development of the self. She says that, in spite of our fundamental "physical and psychological need for the 'other' throughout our development" (p. 6), a depleted self will disregard the other in favour of defence of the self.

Even if this is a tendency rather than a rule, the numbers are such, I contend, that a different social ethos will be likely to take root across British society—more concerned with the defence of the self and more disregarding of the other.

We can formulate this in terms of object relations: the increased propensity for fear and reduced access to safety will tend to increase children's paranoid-schizoid preoccupations and make the depressive position more elusive, so that concern for others will be a harder state of mind to achieve or maintain.

Post-war 1. 1945: social concern

The cohorts of children whose parents were children during the 1914–1918 war, and whose attachment vulnerabilities have just been outlined, were mostly under twenty-one years old—too young to vote—in the 1945 general election (see timeline at Figure 1). In spite of Britain being virtually bankrupt following the hugely costly war, and needing to borrow vastly from the USA (Brown, 1998, p. 331), the government elected in 1945 successfully enacted a programme of fundamental reforms to create, at home, the welfare state and the National Health Service, and, overseas, to begin the long, painful decolonisation of the vast British Empire (Louis, 1995, p. 331). Not every social problem was resolved, and there were mistakes and flaws aplenty, but the welfare state and National Health Service projects represent a very particular expression of social concern among government and people.

According to my analysis, this government was drawn from and elected by a population who had known two world wars, including many who had themselves participated directly as soldiers, sailors, ambulance drivers, and in various medical roles, and many more who had grieved for lost family members. However, they had been children, for the most part, before the vast killing, the depletion of mourning, and the eternal memorialisation of the 1914–1918 war. So, I argue, there would have been, in this electorate, a less frequent incidence of attachment difficulties than was the case a few years later when the next generation came of age and went to vote.

Post-war 2. 1979: social disregard

Finally we come to Mrs Thatcher (1925–2013) who came to power in 1979, just thirty-four years after that Labour landslide. This prime minister is particularly remembered for saying that there is no such thing as society. I contend that by now a significant proportion of the electorate had been born to parents among whom there would have been a greater incidence of inadequately mourned childhood loss. Whereas the preceding generation was likely to be more capable of sustaining a more concerned, less self-seeking response to other people's needs, these later cohorts were more at risk of the attachment difficulties that, as de Zulueta (2006) has shown, lead to prioritising defence of the self over concern for others. Thus, hostility towards the other takes precedence, even though the NHS and the welfare state clearly benefit our own self as well as others, and their destruction clearly harms our own self as well as others.

> [People] are casting their problems on society and who is society? There is no such thing! There are individual men and women and there are families and no government can do anything except through people and people look to themselves first. (Thatcher, 1987)

Policies and rhetoric now emphasised self-reliance, nationalised industries were privatised, and long-established mutual societies were turned over to shareholders, as were the utilities such as electricity and water. Not only did the Thatcher government attack the welfare state's support for people who had fallen on hard times, but it also represented a substantial break with previous Conservative governments through its more dogmatic, ideological style (Gilmour & Garnett, 1997) and its strong commitment to the market, free trade, self-help, and laissez-faire. Conservative party values had previously emphasised community, protection, paternalism, and intervention (Gamble, 1983). Mrs Thatcher was re-elected in 1983 and again in 1987. Her Conservative privatising, free-market policies were carried forward by her successor, John Major, until 1997 (and some would argue, subsequently by Prime Minister Tony Blair, "New Labour" having espoused a very different politics from Prime Minster Atlee's Labour Party in 1945). The personal and political psychodynamics of this kind of self-harming identification with the aggressor, with its origins in earlier trauma, such that poor people whom the state supports nevertheless choose right-wing governments who dismantle the state to help only corporate giants, has been very interestingly explored by Jay Frankel (2015).

This analysis suggests that Margaret Thatcher's policies were successful because, by 1979, the attachment profile of the electorate had fundamentally changed. Social concern waned and defence of self at the expense of the other came to the fore only when a significant proportion of the electorate had experienced attachment difficulties due to their parents' experiences, as infants and children, of unresolved loss.

Conclusion

Undoubtedly myriad personal and social, micro- and macro-factors shape every nation's governing ideology at any one time. Here I have identified just a few possibilities particularly associated with silent loss and with unhelpful public and inadequate private mourning.

The official British treatment of death in war and remembrance, the cultural climate of irony and nihilism which all followed the Great War, and the "airbrushing" of bad news into something more positive for reasons of maintaining vital national morale, can all be seen to augment or embed people's experience of loss and of trauma. The personal experiences of loss when terrible war events (Dunkirk, D-Day, etc.) are also in a real sense positive events ("deliverance", "successful start to the liberation of Europe") and where this is allowed (again for reasons of national morale) to outshine the more painful realities of the bigger, more mixed picture, may turn pain and loss, as shown by Balint (1969), into trauma.

Drawing upon attachment theory and research to account for a huge socio-political change, across just one generation, this analysis contends that the political and social "will of the people" is at least partly shaped by people's experiences of war, trauma, and loss, the failure of public and private mourning, and the transmission of the emotional consequences of these experiences to subsequent generations.

The electorate who gave Clement Atlee's Labour Government a landslide victory to create a welfare state and build a million new homes, had largely been born late in the nineteenth century, and early enough in the twentieth century to have stood a better chance of secure attachment. Whereas the generation that followed, born to parents who had been children at the time of the Great War, were much more likely to have become burdened with experiences of unresolved loss following the irresolvable losses of that war.

I have used Hesse and Main's attachment research to show the relationship between parental experience of unresolved loss and infant experience of disorganised attachment; Freud's illumination of the way dying means killing in the unconscious illuminate an underlying dynamic at work; and then de Zulueta's research to linking attachment difficulties to a reduced concern for others and an increased concern for self alone. I have used Balint's three-phase model of the way a difficult, emotionally charged experience can become a trauma further to illuminate the profound change in social attitudes in Britain from the social concern of the 1940s to the social disregard of the late 1970s. I have suggested that this process of unresolved loss leading across the generations to increased infant and childhood attachment difficulties, helped to shape the outlook of Margaret Thatcher's Conservative electorate from 1979–1997, with their programme of radical privatisation and for whom there was no such thing as society.

We have achieved a Britain where private property matters and social inter-connectedness does not, where social disregard far outweighs social concern, where anyone who struggles to cope with the demands of life is apt to be seen as a feckless waster who needs to try harder, and where tax avoidance and the accumulation of vast personal wealth are largely condoned.

Acknowledgements

I am grateful to Susannah Burn, attachment-based psychoanalytic psychotherapist, for her advice and suggestions regarding attachment theory, which helped me to develop this chapter.

References

Auestad, L. (2012). Subjectivity and absence: prejudice as a psycho-social theme. In: L. Auestad (Ed.), *Psychoanalysis and Politics: Exclusion and the Politics of Representation* (pp. 29–43). London: Karnac.

Balint, M. (1969). Trauma and object relationship. *International Journal of Psychoanalysis, 50*: 429–435.

BBC (1940a). *Dunkirk rescue is over—Churchill defiant.* http://news.bbc.co.uk/onthisday/hi/dates/stories/june/4/newsid_3500000/3500865.stm [last accessed 5 August 2016].

BBC (1940b). *Bernard Stubbs reports on the returning troops.* www.bbc.co.uk/archive/dunkirk/14311.shtml [last accessed 5 August 2016].

BBC (1940c). *J. B. Priestley pays homage to the small boats of Dunkirk.* www.bbc.co.uk/archive/dunkirk/14310.shtml [last accessed 5 August 2016].

BBC (2006). *The Somme: its place in British history.* http://news.bbc.co.uk/1/hi/5083196.stm [last accessed 5 August 2016].

BBC (2013a). *The Battle of the Somme: 141 days of horror.* www.bbc.co.uk/history/worldwars/wwone/battle_somme.shtml [last accessed 5 August 2016].

BBC (2013b). *Shot at Dawn: Cowards, Traitors or Victims?* www.bbc.co.uk/history/british/britain_wwone/shot_at_dawn_01.shtml [last accessed 5 August 2016].

Bradshaw, D. (2009). The purest ecstasy—Virginia Woolf and the sea. In: L. Feigel & A. Harris (Eds.), *Modernism on Sea—Art and Culture at the British Seaside* (pp. 101–115). Oxford: Peter Lang.

Bragg, M. (2012). *Melvin Bragg on Class and Culture.* Television documentary, BBC Two, 24 February.

Bureau of Medicine and Surgery (1941–1945). *The United States Navy Medical Department at War, 1941–1945.* http://www.ibiblio.org/hyperwar/USN/Admin-Hist/068B-Med/068-Med-17.html [last accessed 5 August 2016].

Churchill, W. (1949). *The Second World War Volume II: Their Finest Hour.* London: Penguin, 1985. http://en.wikipedia.org/wiki/OCLC.

Coles, P. (2011). *The Uninvited Guest from the Unremembered Past.* London: Karnac.

Davis, W. (2011). *Into the Silence: The Great War, Mallory and the Conquest of Everest.* New York: Vintage.

Eliot, T. S. (1922). *The Waste Land.* www.poetryfoundation.org/poem/176735 [last accessed 5 August 2016].

Frankel, J. (2015). The traumatic basis for the resurgence of right-wing politics among working Americans. *Psychoanalysis, Culture & Society, 20*(4): 359–378.

Freud, S. (1912–1913). *Totem and Taboo. S. E., 13*: 1. London: Hogarth.

Freud, S. (1917e). Mourning and Melancholia. *S. E., 14*: 239. London: Hogarth.

Fussell, P. (1975). *The Great War and Modern Memory.* Oxford: Oxford University Press, 2000.

Gamble, A. M. (1983). *Thatcherism and Conservative Politics.* London: Lawrence & Wishart.

Gilmour, I., & Garnett, M. (1997). *Whatever happened to the Tories: The Conservative Party since 1945.* London: Fourth Estate.

Gorer, G. (1965). *Death, Grief, and Mourning in Contemporary Britain.* London: Routledge.

Graham, K. (1908). *The Wind in the Willows.* London: Penguin, 1994.

Hesse, E., & Main, M. (1999). Second-generation effects of unresolved trauma in non-maltreating parents: dissociated, frightened, and threatening parental behavior. *Psychoanalytic Inquiry, 19*: 481–540.

Lawrence, D. H. (1928). *Lady Chatterley's Lover*. London: Penguin, 2006.

Louis, W. R. (1995). The dissolution of the British Empire. In: J. Brown (Ed.), *The Twentieth Century, The Oxford History of the British Empire Volume IV* (pp. 329–356). Oxford: Oxford University Press, 1999.

Newcombe, N., & Lerner, J. C. (1982). Britain between the wars: the historical context of Bowlby's theory of attachment. *Psychiatry, 45*(1): 1–12.

Robertson, J., & Robertson, J. (1971). Young children in brief separation— a fresh look. *Psychoanalytic Study of the Child, 26*: 264–315.

Robertson, J., & Robertson, J. (1989). *Separation and the Very Young*. London: Free Association.

Roper, M. (2009). *The Secret Battle—Emotional Survival in the Great War*. Manchester: Manchester University Press.

Stephen, L. (1871). *The Playground of Europe*. London: Archivum, 2007.

Thatcher, M. (1987). Interview for *Woman's Own* ("No such thing as society"). www.margaretthatcher.org/document/106689 [last accessed 5 August 2016].

Woolf, V. (1925). *Mrs Dalloway*. London: Penguin, 2002.

Zulueta, F. de (2006). *From Pain to Violence: the traumatic roots of destructiveness*. Chichester: John Wiley.

INDEX

Keating, J. F., 135
Kfir, R., 52, 58
Khosrokhavar, F., 113
Khoury, E., 99–100, 113
Kiewel, M., 65, 75
killing, xxvi, 27, 60, 101–102, 148, 168, 171
Kindertransport, 21
Kipling, R., 156
Kjär, R., 15
Klein, H., 50, 58
Klein, M., xvii, xxx, 15, 30, 47, 122
Knight, C., 3, 13
knowledge, 33–34, 50, 62, 66, 80–81
    representative elite, 118
    unconscious, 58
Korea, 119, 121, 135
Krell, R., 50, 58
Kristeva, J., 122, 134
Kubler-Ross, E., 147, 151
Kuomingtang, 120
Kurtz, M., 75
Kuzmany, S., 61, 67, 75
Kuzmany, Stefan, 67

labour, xxviii, 38, 153
labour landslide, 168
Lacan, J., 78–92, 94
LaCapra, D., xxi, xxx, 117, 134
Laclau, E., 84
laissez-faire, 169
Lammert, N., 68
language, 36, 43, 45, 62, 79, 83, 86–87, 91, 140
    sociological, 80
Lanzmann, C., 21
Laplanche, J., xxvii, xxx, 75
latency, 79, 82, 85, 115
law, 37, 97–98, 101, 151
    amnesty, 97–98
    canonical Jewish, 44
    martial, 120

unconscious, 105
Lawrence, D. H., 158
Leader, D., xvii–xviii, xxx, 21, 28–30, 104
Lebanon, 97, 100–101, 103–104, 112
Lemuth, C., 75
Lerner, J. C., 173
Levi, P., 37–38, 47
Lévinas, E., 117, 125, 134
Lewinska, P., 47
Leys, R., xxii, xxx, 65, 76, 88–89, 93
liberation, 163, 170
libido, xvi, xxix, 32, 104, 107–108
Lichtman, H., 50, 58
Lin, C. J., 120
link, xxiii, 33, 47, 86, 101, 118, 166
listeners, 115, 126
literality, 80–81, 83, 92
literary conventions, 158
    hero, 158
    topics, 159
logic, xxvi, 37, 78–79, 81, 83–84
    acts defy, 46
    of destruction of Auschwitz, 32, 45
    positivist, 129
    resist Auschwitz's, 44
    social, 84–85
Löhr, O., 75
London Liverpool Street, 21
longing, 6, 13, 58, 150, 166
Lorenzer, A., 63, 75
loss
    catastrophic, 155
    familial, 165
    irreplaceable, 146
    irresolvable, 170
    psychological, 143
    ungrievable, 108
    unprocessed, 154
    unremembered, 166
    unresolved, 165–166, 170–171